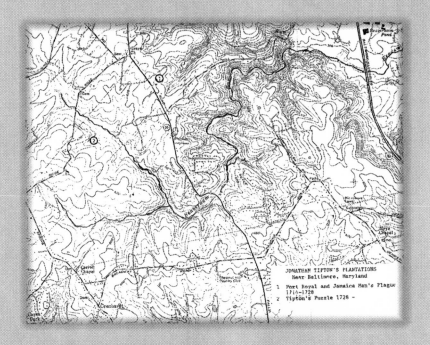

JONATHAN TIPTON'S PLANTATIONS
Near Baltimore, Maryland

1 Port Royal and Jamaica Man's Plague
   1714-1728
2 Tipton's Puzzle 1728 -

Courtesy of David L. Wilson - Albuquerque, NM

The Legacy
of a
Country Boy

Written by

F. James "Jimmy" Fox

Edited by Mary Martin Fox

Fox Meadow Publishing
Falcon, Colorado

Cover photo of my older brother and me was provided by my cousin, Mrs. Betty Lindsey Young.

Fox Meadow Publishing, LLC
Falcon, CO 80831
www.foxmeadowpublishing.com
Copyright © 2007 by F. James Fox
All Rights Reserved.

Library of Congress Control Number: TXu1-319-053

ISBN 0-9777818-5-2

First Edition

Cover Design by Chris Volberding, Tiffani & Associates, Ltd., Colorado Springs, CO

Book Format, layout and web design by David Fox, Point & Click, Inc., Phoenix, AZ

Graphic Design by Linda Tousley Snyder, Special Effects Design, Monument, CO

Printed in the United States of America.

Table of Contents

A Note from the Author

This book took root as the twentieth century was coming to a close and a new millennium had embarked with fresh beginnings. For some, it is an exciting time and for others, it brings a bit of nostalgia. Not yet being of the walking-cane age, I clearly remember the horse-and-buggy days. I distinctly recall riding a mule to school on visitor's day at Otterdale's one-room schoolhouse to see my older brother and sister. The past becomes deeper and deeper until it is finally buried and if left alone, it will die. This book is trying to keep part of it alive. Life-loving characters provided the fodder that fed the stories that made the book.

Only the reader of the future will know of a writer's need for today. I do not apologize for the truth and honesty or the country ways and terms of a twentieth-century country boy. This is a down-home book and was written with that era in mind.

Writing these stories was a battle with the English language all the way. I was like the salmon fighting to get upstream, leaping in and out of a pool of punctuation and grammar. Spawning a complete English sentence with some clarity was comparable to driving a nail into a brick wall. If the letters in a word weren't reversed, then it was a spat with a sentence. I struggled with my thoughts in a paragraph that was doing an about-face. I was at war with words and their sounds, but I was determined that my grandchildren were going to know something of my past.

Like most dyslexics, I have a short attention span. I would work a little; then stop, but I never gave up. I have always found writing to be a troublesome task; nevertheless, my fondness for the former ways of life has motivated me. Feeling more closely associated with the past than with the present, my desire is to preserve part of my heritage so it can be passed on. Sometimes in the middle of the night I would awake with a thought, so I got up and went to work. I tell people I didn't write this book, "God wrote it."

Jimmy Fox

Preface

When Jimmy Fox asked me to read <u>The Legacy of a Country Boy</u>, his memoirs of growing up in a tenant farming family in Maryland in the 40s and 50s, I was dubious. I've read dozens of farming and homesteading memoirs.

Read one and you've read most of them. They blend into a blur of sameness: the grueling work, the long hours, numbing cold in the winter, suffocating heat in the summer, crops destroyed by weather or locusts, accidents and sickness, and above all, never enough money. All recalled with that peculiar cheerfulness with which so many of us remember the not-so-cheerful events of many years ago. And too often tinged with an annoying "holier-than-thou-ness," as if all that suffering, struggle, and poverty made one a better person. So much for "the good old days."

And I was busy with a new career far removed from the days of studying frontier and homesteading families. Now I was teaching Brain Gym®. But a little voice said, "Well, probably won't amount to much but oh, why not." And with that inauspicious beginning, I began my association with Jimmy Fox. I found <u>The Legacy of a Country Boy</u> enchanting, and he was equally intrigued with Brain Gym®.

A few chapters into Jimmy's book and I was hooked. I kept reading. What would happen next to Jimmy, his family and friends? Not to mention all those wonderful, quirky animals: Harley, the horse, and Madeline, the goose, and the ever-patient mules, Kit and Kate.

<u>The Legacy of a Country Boy</u> brings to mind the wonderful books, sadly long out of print, of Rachel Peden, an Indiana

farmwife. The same delight in rural virtues and spiritual connection to the land. The same care with the tiny details which brings the smells and noises and sights of the country into the consciousness of us city folk. The same loving descriptions of family and friends that make every character come alive.

There are certainly differences between Rachel Peden and Jimmy Fox. Most obvious: hers is a female perspective; his, a male perspective. And Jimmy's life was harder than Rachel's. Rachel and her husband Dick owned their farm and could buy what they fancied whether they needed it or not. Rachel wrote of the present, Jimmy of the past.

But the real difference lies with Rachel's experience and ease with writing. Rachel Peden graduated from Indiana University and for twenty-five years wrote a column for the Indianapolis Star and the Muncie Evening Press. Rachel not only had a college education, she was a professional journalist, a seasoned writer. She died of cancer in 1975.

Jimmy beat cancer. He never went to college, struggled in school, and suffers debilitating dyslexia which makes reading and writing difficult. He was delighted to find that I taught Brain Gym® because this program helps dyslexic children and adults read. Yet without the help of Brain Gym® or any other program, he persevered to write a delightful and engaging memoir with laugh-out-loud stories about eccentric people, stubborn animals full of personality, and his own mishaps.

Along with the details of straw tick mattresses, hog butchering, and baking pies, we sympathize when his father shuts down Jimmy-the-entrepreneur's popsicle business, agonize with him at his first (and last) prom, and grieve when his dear friend Watty is killed in the Korean War. We laugh as he and his friends skip school to ride about in an old Buick, making themselves sick smoking their first cigarettes. Didn't help that they neglected to roll down the windows in the Buick.

How lucky Jimmy's grandchildren are that they have The Legacy of a Country Boy through which to know their Grandfather. And how lucky we are that he has shared his life with all of us. Experiencing Jimmy Fox's life on the farm in Maryland is a special treat.

MaryJo Wagner, Ph. D.
Marble, Colorado

Prologue

I have been in a lot of cities over the country and never saw one yet I would like to live in. I am proud of my country heritage. I'm one of those plain ol' country boys who still loves farm life with a big horse!

These memoirs and notes all began when my youngest son, David, needed help in preparing a social studies assignment. I researched the book, <u>Christian Overholtzer & His Father Jacob</u>, by Grace Overholtzer Milligan. From Grace's book, I could pull information that related directly to my family, and thus to David. After beginning this research, I learned I had contracted lymphoma cancer, so while undergoing chemotherapy treatments and re-analyzing my life, I thought it would be meaningful to my descendants to hear some of my favorite memories, allowing them to feel and get a flavor of their heritage. Knowing full well the angel of death can ride a fast horse, this book is dedicated to all those who come after me and care to know how family life was before them.

David Martin Fox - born November 7, 1977 (youngest of three sons)

Father: Francis James Fox - born October 9, 1937
Mother: Mary Martin Fox - born October 2, 1950

Half Brothers: Charles James Fox - born June 4, 1962
               Mark Wesley Fox - born March 12, 1966

Family Tree

I have two sons from a prior marriage
Charles James Fox and Mark Wesley Fox
Mary & I had one son: David Martin Fox

Francis James Fox
Mary Diane Martin

Mom had a twin sister, born three minutes apart,
Laura Belle & she married Robert Kemp.
Mom had two younger brothers:
first Bill, whose proper name was Charles Earl Cartzendafner,
married to Lettie Pauline Martin. The youngest brother was
Bud, whose proper name was William Donald Cartzendafner,
married Jeanette Olide Eyler. Neither had any children.

Mom had five siblings her older sister Carrie Grendaline
married Russell Lindsey.

Next older sister Edna Mae (Boots)
married Raymond Cain &
after his death she married his brother Virgil.

Father Russell Seiss Fox – Known to his grandchildren as Pop Pop
February 12, 1910 - December 7, 1993
Dad had one older brother George who was married to Grace Coe
Mother Mary Elizabeth Fox – Known to her grandchildren as Mom Mom
November 5, 1914 - February 5, 2001

Grandfather Norman Bruce Fox – Known to me as Grandpap
January 5, 1886 - September 7, 1940
Grandmother Elizabeth Susanna Overholtzer – Known to me as Grandma
September 28, 1868 - January 29, 1912

Grandfather George Christian Overholtzer
March October 10, 1856 - August, 1942
Grandmother Mary Virginia Overholtzer
January 4, 1860 - October 26, 1920
(Second Wife: Martha Anders Overholtzer)
December 7, 1877 - January 1, 1953

Great Grandfather George W. Fox
January 6, 1862 - April 9, 1948
Great Grandmother Sarah Ellen Fox
September 28, 1868 - January 29, 1912

Grandfather Christian M. Overholtzer
March 7, 1797 - October 24, 1865
Grandmother Elizabeth Shindledecker Overholtzer
August 6, 1798 - August 25, 1873

Grandfather Emanuel S. Overholtzer
March 18, 1827 - June 17, 1910
Grandmother Sara Sunsanna Overholtzer
1837- April 1918

Grandfather Christian A. Overholtzer
August 10, 1740 - February 15, 1819
Grandmother Christina Musselman Overholtzer

Grandfather Jacob Overholtzer
Grandmother Unknown

Acknowledgements

To my best friend and lovely wife, Mary: A special thanks for all her aid in accurate suggestions and blunt criticisms. Sometimes my grammar would cause her to have a raised eyebrow. Without her, there would not be a book.

For my dear friend, Pastor Helen Thrash Arminger, whose talents and suggestions have not been forgotten. She assisted me during preliminary stages of the book and gave it form, which it might not otherwise have taken.

Thanks to my mother and father for sharing their accounts of a lifelong story and for all the wonderful memories. My mother's detailed story of her life, with that lovely country charm of hers, was captured on tape in her very own voice. The stories told are straight from the horse's mouth!

And to my three sons, David, Mark, and Chuck, for their reassurance, support and encouragement, I am very thankful. Much appreciation and gratitude is given to Mark for his proofreading and comments. What a special blessing it was for me to have Dave use his graphic design passions and creativity in formatting this document. His patience in dealing with my constantly-changing mind seemed endless. I am so very appreciative of all my sons' faith that this book would come to fruition.

One awesome reward I received in writing this book was the generous kindness of people. The friendliness and wisdom of their hearts rest behind the lines. I'm grateful for the encouragement and inspiration given to me by so many to move forward with what appeared to be a seemingly impossible task. I also owe a great debt to all the characters that are no longer with us that played a vital role in my early years, and who will remain in my heart forever.

Dr. Helen Rose Dawson of Baltimore, Maryland, past vice president and dean of Villa Julie College, was instrumental with her encouragement. Dr. Dawson's insight rekindled my desire to publish The Legacy of a Country Boy.

Dr. MaryJo Wagner of Marble, Colorado, a Ph.D. in American History, Licensed Brain Gym Instructor, and true historian complimented me by serving as my finishing editor for this manuscript.

Christy Cliff of Colorado Springs, Colorado, performed skillfully as my final proofreader. Her clever means of personal observation and opinion, as well as suggestions for sidelights and artwork to clarify details, provided a deeper dimension to my memoirs. A special thanks is also offered to Craig Cliff, who brought the book formatting along in its process.

Dave Price of Valentine, Nebraska, a cowboy, artist and ex-rodeo rider, designed pen and ink drawings for various chapters. There is an old saying about cowboys like Dave, "What they dreamed we live; what they lived, we dream." Bruce Couture of Black Forest, Colorado, a rustic log cabin builder, created pencil sketches of old tools.

The most difficult chore in writing this document was filtering out the glow of the unfit on those delightful old Roger Howard stories. It would be totally impossible to use Roger's everyday words in re-telling his stories fitting enough for young readers. I do confess it seems to run better when it's all lit up. Nonetheless, I wish to give thanks to Roger for just being ordinary. His yesterday's rubbish is my today's treasured memory.

My thanks are offered to all, and to list them seems like a lame return for their talent and compassion, which they expressed for The Legacy of a Country Boy.

 *The Begats*

G reat-great-great-great-great-great-grandfather: Jacob Overholtzer
Great-great-great-great-great-great-grandmother: Unknown

No exact dates of birth or death are known for Jacob. He
came from Oberholz, Switzerland, which is thought to be the
home of the first Oberholz families. It is unknown whether
the village name or the family name came first. This
Mennonite family moved to Germany to escape religious per-
secution. William Penn had promised religious freedom in
Pennsylvania, which is why the family later moved to the
United States.

Great-great-great-great-great-grandfather: Christian A. Overholtzer
August 10, 1740 - February 15, 1819
Great-great-great-great-great-grandmother: Christina
Musselman Overholtzer
(Earl Township, Lancaster County, Pennsylvania) May
30, 1759 -? It is unknown when she died, but it is thought by
some that she was buried somewhere on their farm.

The birthplace of Christian A. Overholtzer is not certain:
some say he was born in Germany and some say he was not
born until his family reached Pennsylvania. Mennonites were
not drafted, but had to pay an extra tax for not serving in the
armed forces. Because Christian was a successful miller and
paid his taxes, his family, years later, were able to obtain much

1

information on him and his heirs. He and his wife, Christina, settled in Adams County and later moved to Hamiltonbann Township, York County. When the township was divided, they were considered to be living in Liberty Township.

Great-great-great-great-grandfather: Christian M. Overholtzer
March 7, 1797 (in York County, Pennsylvania) - October 24, 1865

Great-great-great-great-grandmother: Elizabeth Shindledecker Overholtzer
August 6, 1798 - August 25, 1873

Christian M. Overholtzer was born in Hamilton in York County, Pennsylvania. He married Elizabeth Shindledecker on October 25, 1818. She was from Frederick City, Maryland, where she belonged to the German Reformed Church. In 1819 Christian inherited half of his father's estate (several thousand acres). There he built a small log cabin, which was later made larger into a nice-sized two-story house and covered with wood siding. A large farm bell hung over the log portion of the original cabin. It was used not only for calls at mealtime, but also for a warning and as a signal for help during Indian attacks. Christian and Elizabeth lived in the house their entire lives. Both are buried in Carrollsburg Cemetery.

Great-great-great-grandfather: Emanuel S. Overholtzer
March 18, 1827 - June 17, 1910

Great–great-great-grandmother: Sara Susanna Overholtzer
1837 - April 1918

Emanuel S. Overholtzer married Sara Susanna Jacobs. They were farmers and members of the Lutheran Church in Taneytown, Maryland. Upon his death in June 1910, at the ripe ol' age of 83, he was the oldest living citizen in the community.

He had been paralyzed for three months before he died. Sara died at her daughter's house in New Midway, Maryland.

Great-great-grandfather: George Christian Overholtzer
October 10, 1856-August, 1942
Great-great-grandmother: Mary Virginia Overholtzer
Jan. 4, 1860-October 28, 1920
Second wife: Martha Anders Overholtzer
December 7, 1877-January 1, 1953

My Great–great-grandfather George Christian Overholtzer was born October 10, 1856, the son of Emanuel S. and Sara Jacobs Overholtzer. George married Mary Virginia Heck, who was born January 4, 1860. He was a farmer and at retirement moved to Taneytown. Mary died October 28, 1920. George then married Martha Anders, who was born December 7, 1877 and died January 1, 1953.

I remember my father telling me that his grandfather (George Christian Overholtzer) made a waterpump from a hollow log. He also made a watering trough that was cut from a gum tree and hewed out by hand. This took all winter to accomplish. Until the sale of the property in 1967, this water pump and watering trough were used at my great-grandparents' home outside Taneytown. Before George Overholtzer, died he had given this farm to his oldest son, Maurice Motter Overholtzer. He gave his oldest child and only daughter, Elizabeth Susanna Overholtzer (my grandmother), a smaller farm plus equipment for a wedding present. He also gave his youngest child, Emanuel Nathan Overholtzer, a farm, which was approximately the same size as Maurice's, 156-3/4 acres.

Emanuel was a farmer in the Taneytown area. When there was a fire in the large barn, some cattle were killed. Although some horses were rescued, they were so severely burned that they died later.

3

Maurice married Beulah Bankard. Beulah was born on May 15, 1890, and died January 12, 1953. Maurice was born on September 4, 1884 and died March 8, 1967. He was a farmer on the same farm where he was born. Upon his death, a public sale of the farm, equipment and household was held. His two children, Robert Maurice (born 1913) and Helen Beulah (born 1918), received all the proceeds from the 1967 sale.

At the sale, I purchased an aqua-colored mustache cup for $25 and a fancy mauve and white teacup trimmed in gold for $37.50. My grandmother told me these cups were from her grandfather, Samuel S. Overholtzer.

Grandma and Grandpap Fox

Also at Uncle Maurice's sale, I purchased a four-legged stool, which my father told me his grandfather always used when sitting at the table for meals. He didn't recall if he used the stool because of back problems or maybe leg problems, but he did remember that he sat on this stool. Next to his place at the table, a smaller plate with a raw onion and a paring knife was placed alongside his dinner plate. He would slice the raw onion and put slices on everything, mixing them with anything on his plate. My father said, "He HAD to smell like a Billy goat!"

Great-grandfather: Norman Bruce Fox
January 5, 1886-September 7, 1940

Great-grandmother: Elizabeth Susanna Overholtzer
August 1, 1880-August 24, 1972

 # Life with Grandpap and Grandma

Grandpap Fox

Grandpap Fox was a farmer and part-time carpenter. At one time, he worked at a cement factory. I was not quite three years old when Grandpap died of pneumonia. I recall three special memories of my grandfather. On one occasion, my grandfather was plowing and I was riding his black plow horse named Jerry. I must have enjoyed riding and that is why I remembered this so well. Grandpap was plowing the front field by the driveway along Feeser Road.

I remember that Grandpap had a rocking chair, which used to sit close to the wood burning cookstove in front of the window. I used to rock by standing in the front of the rocking chair with one foot on each rocker and both hands on the armrests while Grandpap sat in the rocker with his hands around my waist. My grandfather would make up songs about Jerry and sing to me.

Another precious memory is when Grandpap and his neighbors were making hay using a white horse named Doll. I would ride Doll forward to lift the hay up from the wagon and then she would back up to release the hayfork back to the wagon again.

Grandma Fox

My grandmother was a short, stout woman who enjoyed laughing. It seemed she always found something funny. She was the boss, not because she was the oldest person around or the one with gray hair and many years of wisdom, but because of her personality and leadership. I wasn't very old when I learned that I couldn't push her around. If I went too far, the only thing she had to do was stomp her right foot down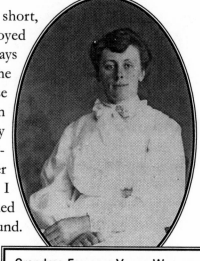

Grandma Fox as a Young Woman

firmly on the floor. I knew it was time to get myself in order. My grandmother always wore her hair in a bun and covered it with a bonnet. She had a variety of bonnets from which to choose. Some were saved for Sunday; sometimes her aprons would match. She often worked in the fields. When she did, she would take a pair of ladies' silk stockings, cut off the feet and then pull them up over her arms and use safety pins to attach them to the sleeves of her dress. I asked her why she did this, and she explained that a sweater would be too hot and she had to keep the sun off her arms, "Because a lady never gets suntanned. It's not decent."

My grandmother used to say to my mother, "My God, Mary, doesn't Jimmy look poor." I was very thin. My mother would say, "Oh, I think he'll fill out." I did. Back then kids grew up fast. I remember that, when I was nine or ten years old,

Grandmother would give me coffee. She always pronounced coffee, "caffee." She figured once you were old enough for coffee, you could call her "Lizzy." Everybody did. This would put you on a person-to-person basis rather than grandson-to-grandmother basis; friend to friend. It was great and made me feel grown up.

I stayed with my grandmother often and for long periods of time, because my mother was very ill and had many operations. I was very little and don't remember that much. Once, my mother and father came to pick me up to take me home, and I didn't know my mother. She cried because I didn't know her, and I cried because I didn't want to go home with her for a visit.

Just about everything we ate on the farm, we grew or raised ourselves. We bought very little at the market, and both my mother and grandmother spent a great deal of time in the kitchen preparing the meals. The food we ate was hearty and filling—necessary nourishment for working in the open air from sunup to sundown. Every day, three times a day, Grandma ate fried potatoes. First thing in the morning she would fire up the cookstove and peel and slice potatoes to put on the back of the stove in a large cast-iron frying pan half full of lard. She would then go to the barn to do the milking. When milking was finished, she would come back to the kitchen and finish preparing a breakfast of fried potatoes, home-cured ham, eggs, fresh butter, bread, plenty of jelly and King Syrup. Grandma would buy King Syrup molasses in one-gallon tin buckets.

I was particularly fond of a treat my grandmother would make in the wintertime. She would take time out of her busy day and make something special for us—"snowcream"—which became a winter tradition. We didn't have things like Little

Debbie's oatmeal pies or Twinkies or Oreo cookies—they were much too expensive—and nearly everything we ate was from the land, literally. Grandma would mix a little vanilla, some sugar, and a lot of fresh fallen snow and then bury it in the King Syrup can in the snow so it would harden. It was delicious!

Out on the Town with Grandma

I also remember Grandma hooking up a horse named Sam to her buggy to go to Taneytown. We would first stop and visit my Great Aunt Marthie (nee Anders), who was my grandmother's step-mother. (She was the second wife to my Great-grandfather, G e o r g e Overholtzer.) Aunt Marthie had a big red velvet settee. I loved to sit in  the middle of the sofa with my arms out to each side and rub my hands over the soft material, while Grandma Fox and Aunt Marthie would talk. I was also intrigued with the trundle bed in Aunt Marthie's bedroom, which she used for overnight guests.

After Aunt Marthie's, we would stop at the feedmill by the railroad tracks. We would pull up there by the side door and the miller would come out and say, "Hey, Lizzie, how's it going?" After the miller heaved a couple bags of chicken feed into the back of our buggy, we went up the street to the general store where I waited outside on a bench while Grandma did her shopping. Ole Sam would just stand there untied for the whole hour. When Grandma finished she called me in to get my favorite candy, chocolate with vanilla cream, and we would each get a pint of ice cream and hop back in the buggy, heading home, eating our ice cream as we rode. I never could eat all of mine, but Grandma would finish up what I couldn't.

One time we walked to a neighbor's farm, where we got a big red boar hog. All the neighbors used this boar hog for breeding. Grandma drove him home with a stick. When we got tired, she just tapped his nose with the stick and he'd stop. We sat down under a tree and she pulled something out of her apron pocket to eat. I can't remember for sure what we ate, but they were probably peppermint lozenge candies. Anyway, Grandma always had treats in her apron pocket.

Mail

My grandmother would try to meet the mailman every day at 11:00 a.m. She liked to hear the news from around the country and what was happening with the neighbors. The mailman was never in a hurry. They would carry on conversations like, "Lizzie, did you hear that Atwood Fizer's mule killed that calf that was born the other week?" She would reply, "Ha! I never did like that old mule—wouldn't have him on the place! I told him so, too!" Then he'd say, "Well, I guess I'd better be gettin' on now. She'd say something like, "Well, tell Ally Shank I'll be coming over in the next few days." This mailman carried the news and not all of it was in his hand.

Sleeping with Grandma
A Roll in the Hay

My grandma had been widowed for many years, and my mother was very sick for a long period of time, so I lived with Grandma. I always slept with Grandma on a cozy comfortable straw tick. The covering of the tick had black and white stripes and was made of a sturdy, canvas-like material, designed as a large bag stuffed with straw. It was a homey mattress, a style that was popular at the time.

In the fall, after the wheat had been harvested, it was time to change the ticking. The tick would be taken off the bed, carried to the hen house, unstitched on the bottom end, and emptied onto the floor for new litter. With good homemade lye

soap, the tick was washed and hung out to dry. By late afternoon it was hauled to the straw stack to be tightly refilled. With a "sail-needle" that curved almost in a complete circle, the bottom end was carefully hemmed shut. By the last twinkle of light the new ticking was set in place and ready for bedtime.

Shortly before it became full dark, Grandma lit the kerosene lamps on the kitchen table and read the Bible as I lay on the bench behind the table. Following the clock striking nine,

Grandma began banking the fire in the cookstove and closed the damper down for the night. She gently picked up the lamp and held it high. I followed in the soft shadow of the light up the narrow winding staircase to her bedroom. As I changed into my night garb, Grandma pulled the covers back and with her hands she rubbed the sheets to soothe the coldness. When she was ready she said, "Come on, jump in here."

After I curled up in bed, Grandma would take her hair bun down and brush it out straight. She blew the lamp out, took off her glasses, and put her teeth in a glass of water. With the moonlight reflecting off the mirror to brighten up our room, she looked pretty scary to a little boy.

Her sweet voice was a comfort, as she put her arm around me and told me how much she liked having me there to help her on the farm. She told me what a big help I was to her by feeding the horses, milking the cows and tending to the chickens. We lay there and talked about what we had to do the next day. She always ended our conversation by saying that my mother was going to be just fine, and that she didn't know what she would ever do without me. Grandma made me feel really important, wanted and needed.

The straw in our mattress was intensely "squeaky." The tick was puffed up high in the center. With every roll I quickly slid to the outside of the bed. I would grab onto Grandma's nightgown and pull myself back up. Once in a while a single piece of straw would stick up and poke at me. With that, I'd sit up in bed and take a good smack at it until it moved. Straw ticks can be a little prickly and itchy for the first few weeks, but the smell is great!

As the year wore on, the straw crumbled and sank down, making us both roll to the center of the bed. Then I would sleep very close to my grandmother. I could almost taste the freshness from the smell of the wheat; the aroma filled the whole upstairs. On cold winter nights, Grandma heated up flatirons, wrapped them in a cloth and put them under the covers at the foot of the bed to keep us warm. The weight of the heavy irons sank down in the tick, causing warm air pockets to come up to our feet.

Our house didn't have any form of insulation. The wind blew in from around the window across our bed. A large brown and white "cowhide" (actually a guernsey steer-hide, from a steer that previously had been butchered for beef) lay across the top of all the covers and quilts on the bed. Sometimes snow would drift in the window onto the cowhide. The chamber pot was kept on my side of the bed for convenience in the middle of the night.

I have plenty of fond memories of my grandmother from the 1940's, and although many times the bedroom was cold, sleeping with Grandma was warm and wonderful, a treasure that I am not likely to forget.

Grandma's Hen House

It seemed to me that Grandma had a very large hen house. In the wintertime, she set corn fodder around the chicken house to help insulate it. She had a brooder house with a coal stove in it and when she got peeps, she used the stove to keep them warm. I would go in there on a very cold day where it was nice and toasty warm.

Grandma Fox purchased what was called the "straight run of baby chicks." That means when she received her litter (a large group) of peeps, there were 50% cockerels and 50% pullets. A cockerel is a male chicken; a pullet is female. It cost more for sexed pullets. Grandma always bought leghorns, which are a rather small chicken but known as the queen of the layers. Most of Grandma's chickens were used for laying eggs.

Grandma tried to keep the brooder house 95-100° and two inches from the floor the first week, then reduce it 5° a week until the chickens were about half grown. If they get chilled, they pile up on top of each other in one big bunch and the ones on the bottom could smother to death. So if they started to huddle around the stove, she knew it was time to spruce up the fire. I could tell if they were happy because I saw them

spread out and lying around in a deep sleep one minute, and the next minute they'd be up running and mingling around with the others.

Sometimes little chicks had a hard time learning to feed themselves. So if there was something shiny mixed in with the feeder, like marbles, they pecked at it and learned to eat. After they were old enough, the young pullets were put in the hen house with the older hens. The first few nights, after it got dark, Grandma took a flashlight so she could see just enough to catch the young pullets. While placing the pullets on the roost, we used a flashlight to keep it dark in the hen house so the old chickens would stay on their roost. Grandma picked them up one at a time and set them in their place. I was the flashlight holder, flashing it on and off. My simple commands were "on" and "off." On the "off" position Grandma reached down and grabbed the chicken while it was good and dark. The "on" position was to find an empty spot on the roost to place the pullet without taking too long. Some learned after the first night to get on the roost by themselves, but for others, it took two or three nights to learn.

It is a natural instinct for a chicken to want to sleep on a roost. The roost is a form of protection for the chickens; it gets them off the ground and out of predators' reach. Sleeping on a roost is as normal to the chicken as it is for them to peck their way out of the shell to be born. However, chickens from a brooder house loose some of their natural instincts since they don't have a mother communicating with them. Since the young chickens do not have their mother to teach them to roost, we teach them.

A roost is an area in the chicken house or coop made of a round stick like a beanpole. A chicken has three toes plus a spur with long curved nails for gripping, which hold them steady on their roost while sleeping. Generally a roost is situated on the inside of the back wall facing a row of windows. That way they can see out the windows and feel safe and secure. At our house we had eight rows on a diagonal about twenty feet long and two and one-half feet up off the floor. The diagonal allowed each chicken to see over the ones on the front row.

In the wintertime they sit closer together for warmth. During hot summer nights they space themselves for more ventilation. They like to sit in the same spot each night by their best friends. Chickens are called to roost at the last twinkle of daylight and off the roost at the first drop of light.

Young pullets are about twenty-six weeks old before they start to lay. Then they will lay for about three years. We had some that laid for four years. This is the time to cull out the older hens. The best way to tell if a hen is laying is by the keel bone.

16

The keel bone is the two bones that you can feel in the back of her legs. If you can place three fingers between these two bones she is a good layer. If not, the bones have gotten hard and will no longer spread; she has finished laying for life and is ready for the pot.

Sometimes you can spot an old or unhealthy chicken just by looking at it. If the cone and wattles are yellow or whitish, it isn't healthy. If her feathers are ruffled and misplaced, and she has her head down and her eyes aren't clear, she is an unhappy chick. It's important to remove her from the flock. If her cone and wattles are a nice red color and she is walking around cackling, that's a sign of a healthy chick.

It is necessary to keep plenty of feed and fresh water in the hen house at all times. Chickens require grit for their craw. Grit is little tiny stones that have been ground up. Chickens don't have a stomach, so when they eat their food, it goes into the craw and the grit grinds up their food, which then lodges in the gizzard and is digested from there. Laying hens must have a lot of calcium. They get that from eating ground-up oyster shell. The oyster shell is needed to make the eggshell hard. If she lacks calcium in her diet, the eggs will be soft with a skin of a shell that is not saleable.

The chicken is also given scratch either on the ground or on the floor of the hen house. This helps their leg muscles, their craw and their feathers. Scratch is a mixture of whole grains like wheat, corn, and barley.

It is natural for the older hens to want to set in the spring of the year, that is, to lay their eggs in a place where they will not be disturbed in hopes of hatching out their young. It takes 21 days to hatch a brood. A hen that is going to set is called a "clook" or "broody" or "setting hen." We called them a "clook." When she has all her eggs and incubation is under way, that is called a "clutch." You can check to see if there are any unfertile eggs in the nest by candling them. To candle, hold an egg in front of a candle, flashlight or any bright light. The little red lines you see are the blood veins starting to form in the embryo.

When you break an egg into the frying pan, you see the yellow yoke standing up in the center of a mass of clear liquid. That clear stuff circling around the yoke is called albumen. It provides nutrition for the embryo. The two little white strings flowing on the top are chalaza (ke la' za), which are spiral chords of albumen. When the shell is broken, the chalaza (which are attached to the inside of the egg shell to the yoke) pulls away from the egg shell and comes to the surface of the yoke. This is much like a large ship tied up in a harbor. The job of the chalaza is to hold the embryo in the center of the shell during incubation. A setting hen has a slightly curved beak and is able to turn her eggs several times a day throughout the incubation period, which prevents the embryo from sticking to the side of the shell, causing a deformed chick.

In the days before band-aids, the membrane, that rubbery substance inside of an eggshell, was pulled out of the shell, placed over your cut and tied with a clean cloth. It was sterile and as the membrane dried, it pulled your cut together. The yoke was stored in a cup with a saucer on top for a lid and set in a cool section of the icebox or springhouse for later use. Whole eggs mixed with turpentine were used for rusty cuts from barbwire, nails and so on. Many old-timers during my era carried a wealth of information in their head about such remedies that almost no one needs to know today. However, there is a certain

18

amount of grace that comes with the old-time home-style doctorin' that some of our youngsters missed out on.

Once all the eggs are hatched out, that is called a "brood." After the hen takes her brood to the hen house with the rest of the chickens, they'll be called a "flock." Chickens occasionally build their nests in a hayloft or under a manger in the stable. Sometimes aggressive hens will steal a nest. They'll wait and watch for the setting hen to leave her nest. Then she'll find her chance and take over her nest. When the first hen returns and finds a stealer setting on her nest, she'll try to drive her off. Sometimes she'll leave and sometimes she won't. If a hen is off her nest and another hen tries to steal her nest, it will sometimes cause her to stop setting.

Grandma sold her eggs to a huckster named Shriner. Sometimes she traded her eggs for bread. To tell if the eggs are good to eat, put them in a bucket of water. If an egg floats, that means the egg is old and has a lot of air in it. A fresh egg will dive right to the bottom. Grandmother kept her eggs in the cellar where it was cool. They stayed fresher longer there. Grandmother pickled eggs and stored them in a stone crock as a way of preserving them. Pickled eggs will keep for about a year.

Hens will molt in the summertime. But not all breeds of chicks will molt at the exact same time. To molt is to lose their old feathers and grow new ones. While waiting for the new feathers to come in, these girls are not the prettiest things you have ever seen.

To pick chickens, my grandmother put a bucket of water on the stove and took it off right before it started to boil. While she was waiting for the water, she killed some of her half-grown cockerels. The cockerels were always used for meat. She dipped them in the hot water one at a time. The skin was very tender. If the water wasn't just right, the skin would tear. The older culled chickens weren't much of a problem. They were a tougher bird and used in pot-pies or chicken and dumplings.

Grandmother Cartzendafner also kept geese in the henhouse during the night. They were allowed to roam free during the day. She raised Toulouse geese, which are some of the largest gray geese there are. She actually had one for dinner every now and then, but the main reason was to raise them for the down. The male goose is called a "gander" and when provoked he hisses at you. The female is called a "hen" and she honks. The babies are called "goslings." A group of geese is called a "gaggle."

The outside feathers of a duck or goose are long and flat. They are large and wide, waterproof and tough, with a hollow shaft. On top of the tail there is an oil factory that distributes oil to the outside feathers as needed. This little factory is known as the oil sack and it must be removed before cooking.

The underneath smaller feathers are called down. Down feathers are short, fine, soft and silky, hairy locks clustered on the same little shaft that looks much like a dandelion in full bloom. That is why the old timers called goose down, "goose hair." All of these tiny little shafts of hair under-lap and overlap each other locking in the warm air in the winter and locking out the hot air in the summer, which explains why wild ducks and geese can swim in icy water without getting cold. During these times when waterfowl come together for warmth, that is called a raft. While actually touching one another and treading in a circle, they churn the water all night to keep it from freezing; the movement also keeps their blood flowing faster.

Down feathers are not only well-suited to keep geese and ducks at a comfortable temperature, they are used in ticks and pillows. Of course, before including the down in people bedding, it is important to clean it. This is done by placing the down in a pot of hot soapy water and washing it gently. After rinsing thoroughly, it's placed in cheesecloth or an old sugar or salt muslin bag and hung out in the shade or in the corner of the kitchen. It must dry very slowly and needs to be fluffed up as it dries to keep it from sticking together. Now it's ready to be stuffed into a pillow or tick.

My mother said that in the spring of the year, when it started to get hot, she helped catch the geese to pluck them of their down. Mom said that the older geese like to have this done. With the goose's head stuck under her arm, Mom started at its neck using her thumb and four fingers to push the down towards its feet. There was a washtub between her feet, and the down feathers fell in the tub. Then she did along one wing and that goose turned itself so she could get the other side with ease, followed by the back of the goose. After that, the goose raised up so she could get to its belly. Mom said, "I guess it made the goose feel cool or maybe it itched and that is why they liked it so."

Often a young goose didn't know what was going on and tried to get away. But after its head got under Mom's arm, it calmed down. Grandmother washed the down and saved it to make pillows and tick mattresses.

Grandmother's guineas were fed along with the chickens in the henhouse. Guineas, from the pheasant family, come in many different colors, but the pearl was the most popular. The little ones are called "keets." The males are cocks and the females are hens. They stand up on their toes and stretch their heads in the air to make their cry. The cock has a one-syllable holler, "Kee Kee Kee" and the hen has a two-syllable holler, "Buckwheat Buckwheat." Guineas are excellent watchdogs. When they holler, it is so squeaky, it sounds like they need

WD-40 oil. They see and hear everything that is around, are very active, and like to be busy all the time. They're free rangers and like to pick at grass and catch bugs, so they're easy keepers. The all-dark meat of the guineas is quite delicious. Their eggs are very good but smaller than a chicken egg. The cock and hen look almost the same, with the male having a little larger wattles under his chin.

Guineas are excellent flyers and like to roost in high spots or trees. A guinea will always come to roost in the same spot at the same time every night. It takes them about five minutes to settle down. For five minutes they are screaming at each other and moving from one limb to another. Then, as if someone had just blown a whistle, they stop. But if something comes around, they soon start squawkin' again.

Grandma's Chores and Fun

The Otterdale Mill was located on Big Pipe Creek not far away from her farm. Grandma took her wheat to Otterdale Mill to be ground into flour. It was really something to see that huge waterwheel and those gears and belts in motion. A few days later, we'd go back to pick up the flour. She'd haul it in a 100-pound sack and store it in the flour barrel in the summerhouse.

During this era many family farms had a summerhouse situated very close to the main house, and which is a small one-room building with lots of windows for light and ventilation. It usually had a large fireplace or a cast iron wood or coal burning cookstove. Summerhouses had a variety of names depending on its principle use, such as a washhouse, summer kitchen or butcher house. A washhouse is used for doing the family's laundry; a summer kitchen is used during the hot summer months so as to keep the main house cooler for dining and sleeping; and a butcher house was used for butchering chickens, steers or pigs or for canning fruits and vegetables.

One Sunday afternoon around 1945, we kids went to the barn, got out Grandma's old workhorse, Sam, and walked him up to the step of the corncrib where my brothers and sister and I hopped aboard. The four of us rode Sam toward the woodlot. It all started out okay, but before long Sam had another idea: he made one nice big buck and we were all off! Although Shirley landed on the side of a stone pile and hit her head, she was fine. We all survived Sam's change of heart!

Gus Shank was a good neighbor. He came over and split firewood for my grandmother. I'd sit on a stump and talk to him while he worked. I asked him if he liked to split wood, and he said he'd rather be eating my grandmother's mincemeat pies!

One thing I remember that was so different from what we do today is that Grandma would always have her kitchen table set ready for the next meal. When the dishes were washed and dried, everything was placed back on the table and a dust cover was placed on top of all the dishes on the table. I presume the reason for this was that there were so few kitchen cabinets that this would act as a space and time saver. She'd pull the dust cover off the table and she was ready for her meal. You could drop in at any time, and she'd be ready to feed you.

Many times I have heard my grandmother say, "You have to own two farms before you can put two spreads on a slice of bread." I asked her, "What if a fellow owned four farms? Can he use butter and two kinds of jelly and all the molasses he likes on top?" She laughed and answered, "Oh my land, child, I can't even imagine that anybody would even want to."

Grandma had five meals a day: early morning breakfast; at 10:00 a.m., a light lunch including pie, coffee and snacks; dinner between 12:00 and 1:00 p.m.; supper around 6:00 p.m.; and a light snack before bedtime (around 8:00 p.m.). For a time when I was around two years old, our family lived with Grandma. I remember my brother Richard and sister Shirley attending the one-room Otterdale Schoolhouse. They'd ride old Kit, our mule, to school in the morning.

When they got off the mule, the mule would go home and my father would work the mule during the day and then when the school bell rang, my father would go to pick them up in a buggy drawn by the mule. (That mule really wanted to work, to go home after taking the kids to school!) Then, when report cards came and it was a short day (and visitors could attend), I got to ride the mule to school with Richard and Shirley. In preparation for me to attend first grade the following year, I was allowed to ride on the mule to school all by myself on visitor's day.

After a time, Grandma sold the farm for $3,000 and moved to be a housekeeper for a nice man named John Starr. My youngest brother, Marvin, went for two days each year to help her make mincemeat pies. She made her own mincemeat out of chopped lean neck meat from the beef and raisins. I don't remember how many pies she made, but it was somewhere between 50 and 100 pies. He brought pies home by the cardboard box full and stored them in our attic steps where it was cool. (And we ate them all year long.) Good pies? Yes! (If, of course, you like mincemeat!)

Later when Grandma was no longer able to work, she spent six months with my parents and six months with Uncle George and Aunt Grace. My sister Shirley would come over and sit with her in her room and read the Bible to her. All the days of her life from cradle to coffin were spent on a farm. Potatoes fried in lard kept Grandma alive for 92 years! I remember asking Grandma if she was afraid to die. Her reply was, "Heavens, no, but I don't like the job of doing it."

 *My Parents*

Father: Russell Seiss Fox
February 12, 1910 - December 7, 1993
Mother: Mary Elizabeth Cartzendafner Fox
November 5, 1914 - February 5, 2001

M y father, Russell Seiss Fox, was born in a house on a farm along Otterdale Road just before Feeser Road, north of Otterdale Schoolhouse in the Taneytown, Maryland area. My mother, Mary Cartzendafner Fox, was born in a house on a farm in Union Bridge, Maryland. In 1917 my mother's family moved to a 136-acre farm, which her father purchased for $9,000 in New Windsor, Maryland. They drove 6-8 head of horses and 20 head of cattle from Union Bridge to New Windsor when they moved to their new farm. My grandfather, Charles Henry Cartzendafner, was known as "Pap" to his children. He was a Percheron horse farmer, breeder and trainer and was known for breaking and training Percherons. He had grays and blacks and my grandmother told me that all of his horses were curried every day.

As the end of my grandmother's life was approaching, she told me the story of Grandpap's purchase of a Percheron stud horse for $1,000. (That was a lot back then!!) The horse bred one mare and then one night during a "lightning storm" he reared up in the stable, hit his head and killed himself. They had one bred mare to show for the $1,000. He said to her, "Well Byrd, that's the way it goes." Grandpap called Grandma, "Byrd," so my first Percheron mare was named "Byrd."

My grandmother said Grandpap was a gentle man. She said that's why he was so good at breaking horses. He liked to harness a young filly or colt and let it stand in the stable for a few days so they got used to the harness; then he tied them to the off side of his team and let the youngster walk along without pulling. For about a week he continued this training so the young horse would get used to the team as he worked them. Then Grandpap put his young colt in the team and started working him; the horse didn't even know that it had been "broke." Grandma said when no one else could break a horse, they would bring the horse to Grandpap and he could do it. I feel very close to Grandpap Cartzendafner; I can identify with him, and I hope in some small way I am carrying on his tradition with Percherons and other horses.

My grandmother, on the other hand, was rather stern and not a particularly warm person, but while she was on her deathbed she shared stories with me and that made me feel much closer to her. When Grandpap died in 1929 from a ruptured appendix, she was left with six children and a farm to operate to make a living. Times were hard on her, especially since this was during the Depression, but my grandmother was a strong woman. When the authorities from Westminster approached her with the possibility of putting her five children (who at that time were under age) in foster homes, she didn't cry. She just stood wringing her hands over and over again as if her hands bore the burden of her fear and sorrow. She responded to their suggestions of removing her children to different families by saying, "No, I've got to try." With the help and support of neighbors, her oldest daughter Grendaline, Grendaline's husband Russell Lindsay, and their family, my grandmother

28

remained at her home, and raised all her children, until she died, with dignity, on February 23, 1959.

Grandpap Cartzendafner's Farm, New Windsor, Maryland

My Cartzendafner grandparents lived in a two-story, old-time house with two-foot thick walls made of native fieldstone covered by a tin roof. As my mother would say on those 'beezely' (as my mother called it) hot days, "Close the shutters and it will be pleasantly cool." Their house had a finished attic with plastered walls and a full cellar. From the cellar within a few steps there was another building that was built to be a washhouse. The washhouse had a huge fireplace that was large enough to hold a sixty-gallon cast iron kettle to boil water for laundry. There was also an upstairs. Behind the washhouse was the smokehouse, made partly with fieldstone and finished with square logs for smoking meat. A white picket fence bordered the house and the nearby buildings. The yard was frequently mowed by the half-dozen sheep, which were kept for wool.

My mom would help with the laundry by building a fire and then filling the kettle with water. There was a crane that the kettle hung on after it was filled. She could easily push it over the fire until it started to boil. After it was boiling good, she pulled it out, placed the clothes in and pushed it back. She had a long flat board with holes in it that was called a whaling stick that she used to stir the clothes around as they boiled. If there were some extra dirty ones, they were pulled out and placed on a wide laundry trestle and whaled (pounded) with the whaling stick. Mom said, "I guess that's how it got its name." After boiling the clothes for a while, she pulled them out with the stick, picked them up and put them in a tub of cold water for rinsing, and then carried them to the clothesline for drying.

Mom told me that Grandpap would clean all his horse harness the same way about twice a year, spring and fall. Then it was

hung out to dry. After it was well dried, Pap would get out a can of Blue Ribbon neatsfoot oil compound and rub it all over the harness. This would soften, water-proof and preserve the leather. After the harness was thoroughly dry, it was taken back to the harness shed and hung on hooks. They also did their butchering in the washhouse. The wash-house had many uses.

My Grandmother Cartzendafner did not have a summerhouse, but used their large screened-in back porch to eat on during the summer months. I recall staying at my grandmother's in the summertime and eating breakfast on this big long porch. When local cantaloupe was in, she would serve it for an after-breakfast treat. You'd see the bowl of peeled cantaloupe in the

30

center of the table, ready to be eaten. But first, we had to eat all our breakfast of puddin' and hominy, sausage and eggs or whatever hearty breakfast she had prepared for us that morning, before we were allowed to pass the peeled cantaloupe treat around the table.

One hot, sizzling summer morning we were eating breakfast on the porch. The large bowl of peeled cantaloupe had been passed to my Uncle Bill, when it slipped out of his hand. Sticky cantaloupe juice went all over the red-checkered oil tablecloth. He jumped up, slid his plate to one side, grabbed the corner of the tablecloth and pulled it up into a little pocket so he could suck up all the juice before it hit the floor. My grandmother went for a tea towel, but Bill had the juice up before she had a chance to take care of the mess. Grandmother was really aggravated at Bill for his impudent ways at the table and kept repeating his name in a manner that only Grandmother could (Bill being pronounced, Beel). Grandmother said it three or four times, but Uncle 'Beel' did not care. He just said, "Byrd, sit down and stop worrying about it. Now you don't have to wash the floor."

My grandmother was a slender lady, who had a cute twitch with her nose and wore tight-fitting golden wire-rimmed glasses. It was my understanding that her twitch came from St. Vitus's dance, which she'd had as a child. She was a respected widow, very much admired in the community for her role in raising six kids on her own.

Hearsay had it that one of the prominent farmers, Mr. Jessie Trite, lived the uttermost way from the Cartzendafner farm, but joined land in the next valley. He had become properly widowed and had admiration for the Cartzendafners.

Mr. Trite was always a good neighbor and would come calling

on Grandmother just to see how she was getting on. While he was married, his visits were never questioned, but after he became a widower, my Uncle Bill would tease Grandmother shamefully.

Bill would see Mr. Trite coming down the lane and he would call for Grandmother to get ready because, "Here comes Jess. He's comin' to see you." Grandmother liked Mr. Trite as a neighbor, but could not take Bill's badgering and unmerciful teasing. She would say, "He's doing nothing of the sort." Then she would hide in her bedroom with the door closed until he left. I couldn't say for sure, but it seemed to me Grandmother was not of the quarrelsome kind, so I reckon she found it better not to argue and just stay away.

Grandpap's Way with Horses

Grandpap died when my Uncle Bill was only nine years old, in 1929. He claimed he didn't remember a whole lot about Grandpap, but when I went to visit my Uncle Bill (Charles Earl Cartzendafner) just before he died, he told me some great stories about my grandfather that I hadn't known. He remembered one story about horses that he thought I might find interesting. Sometimes Grandpap would hook up six or eight horses to a wagon, and on these big heavy loads, he would ask Bill to go with him, as he needed someone to attend the brakes in the back of the wagon. Their long dirt driveway was exceedingly steep and had become rutted with wagon tracks from the weighted loads and much hard use; it took a lot of "umph" to get to the top.

In the heat of summer when the horses started the long climb up the narrow road, Grandpap always liked to give the horses a break halfway up the hill. The second portion of the hill reared up better than the first part before they got to the top. Uncle Bill rode on the brake-board in the back of the wagon and jumped down and drew the brakes as soon as it stopped. Grandpap had a specific place in the middle of the hill where he liked to stop the wagon and let the horses take a blow. He got off the wagon and knelt down and picked up a handful of gravel and began shaking it around so as to sift the sand out through his fingers. With a light handful of gravel he hurtled himself back up into the wagon, telling Bill when to release the brake. As the brake was being released, Grandpap threw the gravel up high and far so it could gently fall down over all the horses at the same time while he simultaneously yelled, "Come up." This simple and effective gesture insured that every horse in the team was doing its fair share of pulling at the same time as the brake was being released. Uncle Bill said that my grandfather had a way with horses, and knowing how much Grandpap loved them and how deftly he handled them, his team always worked hard for him.

In the early 1950's I had been working at St. Thomas Church. During a lunch break with other contractors, an elderly gentleman came by, sat alongside me and began telling me horse stories from his childhood. His name was John Coe. John was then in his sixties and I was seventeen. John told me in a spirited voice that when he was just a pup at the age of fourteen, he worked for Charlie, an old man on a farm near New Windsor. Early one morning in the late part of winter it was cold and dark, and low clouds massed the sky. They hooked the horses to the corn wagon and began filling it up with corn to haul into town. They had to shovel the corn out of the corncrib hard and fast to beat an upcoming ice storm.

The farm sat deep in the bottom of the valley. Their sheer driveway was sunken well below grade level between two abrupt walled banks equally high on both sides. The natural grade rolled smooth as the driveway stabilized into open fields on top of the hill. The fencerows were barricaded with dry honeysuckle that appeared to sparkle as if each strand were set in tightly bound glass from the freezing rain. The old man was in front driving a flashy hitch of beautiful Percherons. At the same time, John Coe was riding in the rear of the wagon, sliding around on top of rolling ears of corn.

The old man had a great big, long black snake whip. He knew that when the horses approached the struggling part of the hill, they couldn't stop where they usually did. He stood up in the wagon and cracked the whip above the heads of the six-horse hitch; all six of those horses dropped to their bellies to draw that wagon up the harsh grade to the state road.

That day the state road carried little traffic for such a good road. Along the grove, tree limbs hung heavy with the burden of ice. Old Charlie was a bit of a show-off driving his team through town when all the other teams were at a standstill. You couldn't help but hear the chains jingling and the clamor of his high-stepping team and watch their snowshoes pound the road and spark the cement at a lively gait. The sweaty team was happy to be on the easy side of gravity. As they passed John Strine's general store, people walked to the edge of the porch to get a better look. As stable as a "drag-sled," old Charlie stood up and took a little bow as he wheeled his horses into the narrow alley to the back end of the feed mill. On the sharp turn the wagon screeched and rumbled from under the heavy load.

34

A small crowd gathered in back of the mill that day to watch Charlie back his team up to the door. It was a tight and slippery spot for six big horses to move about. Old Charlie never did use any forwarding tongues, just a fifth chain hooked to the wagon tongue. He figured his horses would have more maneuverability with a chain rather than with wooden tongues hanging in between them. He also kept the single trees tied up high on his horses, halfway between the back knee and the beefy part of the butt. That assured avoidance of any possible tangles or messes that could occur. I was told this was known as the "Conestoga Hitch."

After he was comfortably backed up to the mill door on the first try, he commanded the off-side horse to step over the fifth chain, then the lead horse came around to him. All the while he remained seated on the wagon. Then he reached into his overcoat pocket and pulled out a lump of sugar and gave it to the lead. That action was a crowd pleaser. Then habitually ole Charlie spit some of his "Picnic Twist" chewing tobacco juice over the wagon wheel and said "Well boy, let's go to work!" They climbed down the freezing wagon wheel to go to work unloading their corn, but not until he had given the other horses their fair share of sugar.

John Coe said, "You've never seen anything like it before, boy." So I asked John who this old man was. He said, "Awl, you wouldn't know who he was. He was old Charlie Cartzendafner of New Windsor." I said, "Well, that old man was my grandfather."

My Way with Horses

Whether to use a tractor, horses or mules for power is a decision that most people don't have to make. My feeling is, if there were more tractors left sitting in the barn and more horses working in the fields, there would be less stress.

Is horse or mule power more cost efficient than a tractor? It all depends on what level of capability you are looking for.

Jimmy and His Percheron Mares

For me, disking with a team of my horses beats the heck out of using a tractor in my garden. In my mind and heart, a tractor isn't comparable to a team and its cost. After all, a tractor decreases in value whether it is being used or sitting idle. If you were working mares and they were foaling every year, they would be increasing in value. You can double your work force in about three years.

There is no doubt that a tractor is faster and easier, but if we follow through with this logic it would be easier just to go to work in town. Then I wouldn't have to split wood or fix fences, repair barns or have animals to feed and take care of every day of the year. I would be free of all labors required of me. But I enjoy taking time to do things in a simple way. The faster pace is not for me. Whether riding the disk or the mower in the hayfield behind a pair of horses, that's what it's all about for me. When it comes time to rest my team at the end of the field, I can sit there and see all of God's creations.

The Fandangle Machine

One evening at suppertime, Pap was telling the family that he had purchased a new machine (a car). Mom couldn't recall the year, but said it was a Velie. She said that when Pap got their first car, he didn't need a driver's license, but did need instructions on how to drive it. She wasn't sure if he needed instructions because of his age, or just because a car was something completely different from what he was accustomed to.

Mom said that he had trouble driving the car because of the timing with the clutch and the gas pedals. When Pap let the clutch out, the car bucked off. When he changed gears, the engine would stall and then he would call it a "fandangle machine." Mom said that when she thinks back on it, it must have been awkward for Pap, an excellent teamster, to experience such a big change from driving horses to driving a car, so he didn't use the car very much.

One summer evening, Pap drove the car to Barn's Store in New Windsor. Barn's Store was a general store that carried groceries and dry goods. She remembered seeing a sign that read, "Ready-to-Wear Women's Clothing." You'd be lucky if there was anything in your size, but what a luxury it was to be able to purchase something already made. Mom's mother made all the bloomers for each of the girls in the family, as well as their petticoats.

Anyway, as Pap was returning home, Mom's older sister, Boots, yelled out, "Here comes Pap back from town!" Mom went to look up the steep fieldstone lane and Pap was coming down lickety-split, bouncing from one side to the other. She said that she'd never seen Pap drive so fast and that there must be something wrong. Pap didn't stop at the house. He just kept on going right down past the house into the wagon shed and out the other side. Pap was unhurt and the unstoppable machine was plenty tough, so it was okay too.

Pap came shuffling across the porch looking all flustered. He was carrying an apple box full of groceries. He had some of his Picnic Twist Chewing Tobacco seeping out of the corner of his mouth onto his mustache, and he was looking a mite ruffled. Mom and Boots ran to the porch to meet him.

As he walked into the house, he explained how this fandangle machine had run away with him. He said, "It got to goin' too fast comin' down the hill and wouldn't whoa." Pap didn't remember which pedal to push in to get it stopped, so he pushed the first one and that was the clutch, which made the car go faster. He didn't know if he should let it back out or what. He just sat there and held on. Mom said that Pap didn't drive it at all after that. She said, "I guess he figured that he couldn't manipulate it after all." He went back to driving his horse Lady.

Uncle Bill told me that after Grandpap died, that old car always seemed to be in the road. He said that Grandmother told him to hook the horses to that old fandangle machine and put it in the ditch out there in the pasture field out of the way. I guess it's still buried out there today.

Uncle Bill and the Straw Hat

Uncle Bill told me another story about one time when they rented some property on the other side of State Road, across from where the farm was located. His mother told him, "Bill, I want you to take that young pair of mares over and bring that wagon back that we left over there." At the time he was just a young fellow, around 10 years old, but since his father had died he considered himself the man of the house. Uncle Bill thought he knew everything there was to know about horses, so he went over to the property on the other side of the State Road and hooked the young pair of horses up to the wagon.

What he didn't realize, however-
er, was that he'd made the
chains too long on
the   wagon

tongue
for the yoke. He
started out and every-
thing was fine, but coming
down the driveway, the wagon ran up
behind the horses. The horses, being young and inexperi-
enced, didn't realize what was happening, so they got scared
and took off running. They came down that driveway, "hell-a-
belt-in!"

Back in those days when they made wagon beds, they used 12" wide boards for the bed or floorboards and they weren't nailed down. While coming down the stony driveway, the boards started flopping up and down and jumping all around, and unbeknownst to Uncle Bill, his straw hat flew off his head and went in between the boards and down through the bottom of the wagon, landing in the road.

My Uncle Russell was working behind the barn. When he heard all the commotion coming down the driveway, he ran out to see what was happening. He saw a pair of horses running with Bill pulling back on the lines as hard as he could. Bill thought he could stop them, but there was no way he could stop a pair of horses, especially when they were running away.

As they neared the barn, the horses started to slow down and Russell ran out and grabbed them. Bill said the only thing that he could do at that point was bawl. He just sat there and cried. Uncle Russell said to him, "Well, if you're just going to sit there and bawl, you might as well just go to the house." When he went in to tell his mother, she, as is typical of many mothers, wanted to know where his straw hat was and, of course, he had no idea. Poor Uncle Bill. This was not a good day for him. He looked everywhere for that straw hat, both inside and under the wagon.

After his family had done their milking and all the chores, Bill was still bawling—he hadn't found the straw hat. The end of the story was a happy one, however, because Bill's mother walked up the road the next morning to get the mail and spied the now infamous straw hat lying on the road where it had so carefully landed the day before. Bill got his hat back and a bit of his hurt pride, and I guess he finally stopped crying.

Wagons Rumbling and Chains Jingling

My mother said that in the wintertime, my grandfather had a woodlot located someplace that they called, "down in the barrens." Grandpap was in partnership with my Uncle Ham (Hamilton Fritz) and they'd go down there and work in the woodlot cutting wood. I guess it was probably hickory because they would haul it in to Meyers Meat Company and sell it to them. My mother said she'd wait on the porch in the wintertime when dusk arrived early and it was quiet and still. She'd run out on the porch and listen for my grandfather. My grandmother would have supper ready, and they were waiting for my grandfather to come home to begin eating the evening meal.

When he arrived, of course, he would have to put his horses away and feed them. She said she would never forget the sound of the horses coming up the State Road, the only paved road into Westminster. My grandfather always had shoes on his horses and you could hear the chains and the metal wheels of the wagon rumble, especially in the cold crisp air. My mother said she'll never forget the sound of the horses on the road, the wagon rumbling and the chains jingling on the horses, and to this day, it's a fond memory she has of her father.

My mother grew up on a farm near New Windsor in the days when people milked cows by hand. Each sibling was responsible for milking specific cows. In the spring the cows were turned out on stubble-ground. Stubble-ground is where the field of wheat, oats or barley had been harvested, and the cows ate everything else that was growing in between the rows. Somebody had to mind the cows so they wouldn't wander off to another field where they weren't wanted. This was a boring job that no one liked, but everyone had to take a turn.

41

Everyone on the farm helped out with the endless chores that helped keep the farm running and the animals healthy. As a young girl of 13 or 14, my mother helped with all kinds of jobs around the farm. In the summer, she'd ride the binder, help to get in hay, and stack wheat. Most of the wheat crop was planted to be able to pay for the following year's property taxes. Planting corn and cultivating were her favorite jobs, and in the fall of the year she would husk corn. The summer chores ran right into the fall and that's why she was unable to return to school in September. My mother started school each year in late October or early November, but only after all the crops were in and the winter snows had begun. Then my grandfather often took my mother and her sisters to school in a one-horse sleigh.

My Lady

Mom told me that Grandpap always had a hired man to help him on the farm. There were two she remembered: Gill Hill and Oss Hammond. Both were black men. At this time, Oss was slightly under middle aged and Mom thought she was around ten years old. The year was 1924.

Oss didn't have much in the way of family, so he lived with Grandpap's. In one corner of the kitchen, a table was provided for Oss's meals. Mom told me that the table was about three-feet wide and two-feet long. He had his own silverware and place setting. I asked why he had his own table, and Mom said that at that time it would not have been decent for a colored person to eat from the same table with the family that he was working for.

Mom said that she could remember Oss sitting at this little table at dinnertime (which was in the middle of the day). Oss would push his chair back and say to her mother, "Yes in deedy, Miss Byrdie, that was some kinda good eatin'. Yes in deedy, it was." Grandpap would tell Oss, "If a feller works, he has to eat." Oss would laugh and say, "I declare, yes sir, Mr. Charlie, he surely do, I declare, he surely do."

Oss slept in the finished-off attic. Grandpap would ask him if it was getting too hot to sleep up there, because if it was, he would find a place downstairs for him. Oss would say, "No sir, Mr. Charlie, you know me and my kind, it never gets too hot for me."

After dinner every day, Grandpap would take a little snooze during his dinner hour. Oss would lie out under the tree on the back lawn. One day my mother and her twin sister Belle, were outside talking to Oss. Oss was lying down lazily under the shade tree with his head propped up against the tree and his straw hat pulled down over his eyes. Mom said, "I'm not proud of this, but Oss was not paying any attention to us so I asked him if he was a nigger." Mom said that he jumped up and started to run after them, and they screamed and went to hide in the outhouse.

Their father came out and the naughty girls overheard Oss telling their Pap about the incident: "Mr. Charlie, those twin girls went and called me a nigger, now they got themselves penned in the toilet." Grandpap said, "They did?" "Yes sir, Mr. Charlie, They surely did! And they ought not do that." Grandpap said, "Well you are, aren't ya?" "Yes sir, Mr. Charlie, I is, but those girls don't got no business calling me a nigger." "Well, if that is the worst thing they ever do they will be just fine." Grandpap called the girls out of the outhouse and gave them a good enough scolding. Mom said they really felt bad about doing that because Oss was real nice.

It was getting cooler weather closer to winter, and after payday

Oss asked Grandpap if he could have off on Monday to go to his cousin's funeral, and that was okay. On Monday night well after dark, Oss returned home. Everybody in the house was sitting around in the kitchen when Oss walked in looking a little sheepish, and was acting funny like he was sick. Grandpap asked what he was doing out tramping around after dark. He muttered something that nobody could understand. The next day Frank Stitely stopped over and told Grandpap, "Old Oss was really drunk over the weekend, wasn't he?" That was the first time anybody in the family had ever seen a person drunk.

Mom told me that some of Oss' kind of people lived in New Windsor and were holding down some kind of trifling jobs, and Oss went to see them now and then. They would get together and go to this little dinky bar down by the railroad tracks and tap on the back door. The barkeeper would ask what they wanted, bought whiskey or local. They would say moonshine and the barkeeper would say he'd be back in a bit. They'd stand out behind the closed door while he went to fetch the moonshine. Directly he would return with a jug and they'd all go down in the grove and drink it. Back in the 20's, black people were not allowed to go inside the bar.

This all came to surface later and the truth came out that there was never a funeral. Grandpap enjoyed all the pleasantries of life and he couldn't help but needle Oss about the cousin's funeral. As soon as Oss would ask off for a day, Grandpap would question, "What cousin's funeral is it?" Oss didn't think this was too funny, but would get a grin on one side of his face. Grandpap was an early-to-bed and early-to-rise person. If he had company that stayed too late, he would tell them, 'Stay as long as you like, but I'm goin' to bed.' He liked to be in the barn by 4:00 a.m. That way he'd have his milking and other morning chores done and be ready to light out for the field by 8:00 a.m.

I asked Mom if she could give me a definite, detailed physical description of her father. She replied, "Oh yes! I have many rich memories of Pap." Her description of Pap was from her recollection at the time when she was about ten years old, around 1924:

Pap was wise and a charming well-bred man who was thin and stood six foot, three inches tall. He walked in a straight line, but on the outer edge of the heels of his boots. He had broad square shoulders and sparkling hazel eyes with a gleam, and a neatly trimmed, fashionable man-sized mustache that turned up on the ends. His thinning brown hair was becoming a grizzled-gray. His tough, leathery, dark skin and muscular hands showed many years of sun and weather exposure. I tell you, I thought of Father as a real eye-catcher! He was a soft-spoken man until provoked. He had his own thoughts regarding religion and politics. He was not timid or diplomatic about his point-of-view, and stood his ground. He liked to jive and tease you!

Mom said that Grandpap was a well-known haggler. One Sunday evening, a horse and mule dealer called Grandpap on the telephone and was putting on a right good spiel about a driving horse. Mom said she overheard Pap. He wasn't being any too neighborly, for it was the custom of good country people not to do business on Sunday. Pap told him in a strong, stern voice that he was not going to indulge himself in any kind of conversation like this on Sunday. If he would like to call back later in the week that would be okay, and if not, he could suit himself.

A few days later, Mr. Dealer called back. Pap was haggling over a driving horse named Lady. Mom asked him if they were going to get the horse and Pap said, "Only at my price." About an hour later, Mr. Dealer called again saying that he'd had an offer on Lady, did he want her or not? Pap got off the phone, was standing in the middle of the doorway to the kitchen, backed up to the door frame, scratching his own back and answered, "I told him if he's going to give you the best price, then sell her." Mom said they were all upset. Pap told her that he didn't believe that Mr. Dealer had a better price, but he got him thinking. Sure enough, the next day Mr. Dealer came driving down their lane in a roadcart with Lady trotting along behind.

Lady was a beautiful red sorrel driving horse with good breeding. She had a narrow white blaze from the top of her pole running down to the tip of her nose. The first thing they did was to put shoes on her. Mom said that she held the farrier's box for Pap, and Mom's twin sister, Belle, held Lady by a short lead rope while Pap nailed shoes on Lady.

I went to the sale of Grandpap's farm after Uncle Bill and Uncle Bud sold it, and there I met Randal Spoerlein who had lived in New Windsor all his life and at one time served as the Mayor. He told me that he knew Grandpap well. Mr. Spoerlein agreed with Mom that Lady was an outstanding road horse. He said that Charlie (Grandpap) referred to his horse as 'My Lady.' Charlie would dip Lady's harness of soft English tanned leather in the watering trough before harnessing her up, then wipe it off and shine the buckles up. He had Lady's head reined up high when hooked to his runabout cart.

Grandpap would make this kind of sucking noise from the backside of his mouth with his teeth tight against each other (like a cluck). At the same time, with his right foot, he stomped flatly on the floor of his runabout. With no words spoken,

Lady would take off like all get out, leaping forward to her fast road trot, lickety-split. Mr. Spoerlein said, "Charlie was one heck of a teamster with a great deal of pride. He'd be sitting up straight holding those lines, letting people see his splendid road horse at her best, coming through town not looking right or left until he stopped at the square. While waiting for his command, Lady began to prance, doing a high two-step with her front feet, making a show for the onlookers. With a cluck and a stomp, Lady would jump right back into her trot. It looked like her feet never hit the ground. Townspeople would walk to the edge of their porch just to get a glimpse of Charlie passing by."

Mr. Spoerlein invited me up for a visit, but unfortunately he died before I got up to see him. I'm sure that if I had met with him, there'd have been more stories about Grandpap that I could have shared. I hadn't gotten over the bashfulness that country boys are sometimes afflicted with. Rather, I would make excuses or appear too busy to go see Mr. Spoerlein. At the time I simply didn't realize my shyness.

Baloney Skins and No Gas

In his mid-teens, Dad and some of his cousins went on a picnic to Gettysburg, Pennsylvania. They had a wonderful time at an area known as Devils Den. And then long before it got dark, they thought it would be wise to head down the road.

Dad said that he had one of those gas gauges that didn't lie—he carried a rule to check the gas in the tank of his car. He said it seldom ever read much over an inch. This was on a Sunday, and in his day, service stations didn't open on Sundays. He said he must have misread the rule earlier, because he was almost out of gas.

Back then, most stations were only a gas pump in front of somebody's house. Folks thought that was okay because customers could knock on the door and ask for gas. Not thinking he would be turned away, Dad knocked on the door, and nobody answered. There were no lights on either. There were two pumps in front of the house. Dad had stopped in front of one of the pumps. In those days the gas pump had a long hose. The gas was cranked up into a glass bottle and gravity made the gas flow into your car. He checked the hose and it was full of gas so he drained that hose, then moved to the second pump and drained that hose. Figuring he got a good half-gallon out of each hose, they returned a few days later to pay for the gas.

After starting down the road, he had a flat tire. He and his cousins jacked up the car, pulled the flat tire off and put on the spare. After going about two miles over some rough roads, another flat appeared. Having a second spare, they put it on.

By now, they were almost out of gas again. He said when he got to the top of one hill, he would shut off the car and let it coast down the hill to save on gas. Because the car had no fuel pump and operated by gravity flow, they would have to back up the hill to be able to use the little bit of gas that was in the tank. Before too long there was another gas pump, but by now it was getting late, so rather than bother anybody, he just coasted the car up next to the pump, drained the hose, and pushed the car a little piece down the road.

It was pitch dark when the third tire blew out. He said all of his tires were bald and nothing but baloney skins. They pulled it off and, using a tire repair kit, which he had carried with him, they repaired the third tire. He said it was that way all the way down the road, first gas, then a tire, they must have had six or seven flats that night.

It was customary for country people to take care of the public roads that ran along in front of their property. In the winter, they would remove the snow; in the spring, they would fill in the mud holes with stones from the field and grade the roads. Throughout the summer, as often as needed, they would cut up fallen trees and take off tree limbs that would keep a teamster from hauling a load of hay to town, and soon the boundary lines mostly ran from the mailbox in both directions. This kept the mailman, grocery truck, bread trucks, and egg man from getting stuck.

That night was in the spring and the roads were full of mudholes. Dad hit one hole so hard that the battery fell out and he didn't know it until the next morning. He figured that it must have been that doozy of a hole close to the mill, but it was only a mile or so. So he walked down there and there was the battery lying in the middle of the road.

After getting the battery home, he put it in the car, but there wasn't enough gas to start the car. He said it was a short night. By the time he got everybody home and himself in bed, it was daylight and time to get up. I'll bet Dad was relieved when he finally got new tires and a full tank of gas.

The Courtship of My Father and Mother

When he was a young man, my dad started a trucking business with a one-horse spring wagon. He would go to different farms, pick up milk, and deliver it to the cooling station for the dairy farmers. Although my father liked his new business, it was very cold work in the wintertime. During his rounds he sat out on the spring wagon with no protection against the cold. There were times when he thought his fingers would freeze and drop off, so he stuck his hands between the horse's hind

49

legs. I asked him if he ever got kicked and his reply was, "Not yet." After a while he was able to save up enough money to buy a farm truck, which was not only faster, but warmer.

Sometimes when Dad would arrive at the cooling station in New Windsor, he would see a young woman named Mary Elizabeth Cartzendafner, who was later my mother, there. She'd be driving a beautiful sorrel horse named Lady, who was pulling a spring wagon with her five-gallon milk cans. Dad was happy to help Mother unload her milk cans. He'd place the heavy milk containers on the conveyor, which would transport the milk inside the cooling station where it remained until the train arrived to carry it to the Western Maryland Dairy in Baltimore where it was processed. Dad said he thought Mother was a pretty girl, and he didn't mind helping her. Mother thought he was very handsome with his dark hair, and that he was also strong and had very nice manners.

Mother's Sunday school class made plans to go on a field trip to the amusement park at Tolchester on the Eastern Shore. They hired Dad with his big farm truck for a hayride to Baltimore Harbor, where they would board the boat to Tolchester. After Dad delivered everyone to Baltimore Harbor, he joined the class on their field trip. They ate their picnic dinner at the Pavilion Building. This was followed by horseshoes, ball games, swimming and lots of fun events. Dad hung around with Mother all day. They had a wonderful time and after that day they began courting. It wasn't long after that my mom considered Russell Fox her beau.

Dad had already been friends with Russell Lindsay who was working on the Cartzendafner farm. On Sundays my father would come to help out on the farm. But sometimes they'd have fun too. They made homemade ice cream and he'd stay for dinner. After dinner Aunt Grendaline, Uncle Russell, and my mother and father would play games like Dominoes and Rook. On special occasions, my father would borrow his brother's new car and take my mother for a ride after dinner. In November 1931, Mother got scarlet fever and the house was quarantined. No one was allowed in or out of the house for three weeks. Uncle Russell and Aunt Grendaline chose to stay out of the house so that they could take care of the farm chores and the milking. Grandmother had a herd of dairy cows, and in order to continue shipping milk, someone who was not living in the house had to be responsible for the milking. During the quarantine period, Uncle Russell and Aunt Grendaline lived with his parents (Florence and David Lindsay) in New Windsor. Their pay was small, the times were hard, and the work was plenty. This was something few sons-in-law would do, but he must have felt that he was helping his wife's family through hard times. My mother had to remain in her bedroom upstairs, and my father would go to the backyard and talk to her through an open window.

Absence must truly make the heart grow fonder, because my parents were married on February 13, 1932. Although my mother was only 17 years old and had not completed high school, they made arrangements to elope. My father had just turned 21 the day before. They left for a date together, and my mother didn't return home that night. Reverend Sutcliff at an Episcopal Church in Taneytown married them. I believe they spent the first night of their honeymoon at Grandma Fox's and that my mother called home to let her mother know what they had done—gotten married, that is.

The Young Newlyweds

The first winter that my parents were married, my father got a job clearing hedgerows on a farm in Finksburg. Dad toted his tools—saw, axe, wedges, and grubbers—in a granary sack along with a sandwich, which my mother made for him. At lunch time he would crawl back in an area of the hedgerow which was thick with honeysuckle. The hedgerow would break the wind and the bright sunshine kept him warm while he ate lunch. Nevertheless, it was still very cold so he never took long for lunch. I guess it was kinda like sitting behind a barb-wire fence in a wind storm. His pay was almost nothing and if it hadn't been for my mother's good tomato gravy they probably would have starved. Dad was one of the rare few who were always ready to spring up to responsibility, even for an empty job. When my father told me about this, he said that he always thought of that first winter whenever Mom made tomato gravy.

Dad and Mom's 50th Anniversary

The following spring my parents moved to Stevensville in Eastern Shore. My father took a job working a farm for Dr. Legg. The farm was located on the hinterland of the Eastern Shore near Stevensville. The land was low, flat and fertile, where a farmer can raise everything but the price. The farm was largely surrounded by water. The tidal drip-edge flowed up close to the back yard.

Henry Singer had lived at the farm a month before Mom and Dad arrived there. He was a passing acquaintance of Mother's from her high school days. Henry was a wiry foot-loose individual that stalked the setting sun. He was of an average height

52

for his 22 years, well talented in art, farming, and in calligraphy, and a master at breeding and raising game birds and waterfowl. He was a senior when Mom was a sophomore. Dad had not met Henry, but they knew Henry would be living with them when they reached the farm.

Dad told me,

"Yep, Henry was there when we pulled up to the front porch. He came out hollering "Get out. Come on in. Glad to see you", and all of that kind of welcoming stuff. He really made us feel at home. We all become friends right off. In the early mornings we breathed the fragrant air of moist pine. The smell was something different than we were accustomed to; it burned off in the course of the day. With the oncoming sunset, the moisture returned again for the night."

A "milk-pitcher," as milk cows are commonly called, for milk, cream, butter and cheese or what-have-you, and a pair of 'rooters' pigs were all there as part of our salary. The usual tending stock were a few head of dry stock (cows not being milked), several teams of heavyset pulling horses, broilers for the table and laying hens (the girls) for eggs. Doc kept a "book count" of all the undercurrents to make sure it all divvied up at the year's end.

At seventeen, Mother was an attractive young woman who cast a pretty shadow. Doctor Legg had been a friend of Mom's family for many a year; he thought highly of Mom, much like a father looks after his daughter. Doc thought Mom, Dad, and Henry were a good team for his little "shirttail" farm. Dr. Legg came to visit the farm occasionally, and Mom provided dinner for him when he came. The main meal was served in the middle of the day, "high-noon" at 12:00 p.m. sharp. The good Doctor would always leave a quarter inconspicuously by his plate, to cover the cost of the meal.

Dr. Legg loved all the wild waterfowl that trolled the waterfront of his property. There had been some trouble with poachers shooting his White Chin geese (named so by the Indians for Canadian geese). Dr. Legg didn't like poachers and they returned the favor. Doc instructed Henry to get Dad to drive him to Stevensville to the courthouse to be sworn in as a game warden.

Mom, 1931

Henry came back with a nice shiny badge. A few days later Mom informed Henry that she'd heard some shooting down around the next cove. For sure it must be a "River Sniper" in Doc's ducks. Mom had made a sail for Henry's rowboat out of a bed sheet. He set sail for the cove, the wind blowing a steady gale, his homemade sail galloping along as smoothly as a Sunday horse through a meadow.

With a shy heart, Henry told me this story himself: "I rounded the corner, stood up in my boat, and yelled, 'Stop that shooting in the name of the law!'" Henry said that they shot one more time and blew a hole in his sail. He was hoping that that was their best shot. Unharmed, he jumped down off the seat he was standing on and pulled the sail down, making himself a smaller target, and started paddling back out of that cove as fast as he could. He never stopped until he got to the barn. He said, "Russell, take me to the court house." He hurried into the courthouse, breathless and a tad surly, and threw that game warden's badge on the desk.

The judge asked, "Why Henry, what on earth is the matter?" Henry said, "Those poachers shot at me, and here is your badge!" In his openhanded disposition, Henry said, "Any money I have coming, just keep it, I'm all through with this game warden business." The judge said, "Oh now Henry—" but Henry interrupted, "You can go have them shoot at you, that's fine with me, then you'll be the one sitting on blisters, not me."

Having thousands of ducks and geese around the farm, Henry asked Mom if he shot a duck, would she fix it. Timidly she replied okay, but said Doc wouldn't like that if he ever found out about it. Henry said boldly, "Don't you worry yourself about Doc. What he don't know won't hurt him." There was no disrespect intended. Doctor Legg was a mighty nice man and well thought of. Dad teased Henry, saying he was going to call the game warden.

Henry got his duck, and Dad helped pick it. They thought it might be a good idea to burn the feathers. That evening they ate like pigs, gulping the duck down. As soon as supper was over, Mom said that Henry and Dad jumped up from the table and gathered up all the evidence and buried every last bone, not knowing when Doc might drop in unexpectedly. Mom laughingly told me, "Those boys weren't scared of Dr. Legg, no they sure weren't. Doc never showed up and their secret was buried."

I have an enormous amount of respect for the hard-working people that know how to fend for themselves. My father was a tenant farmer without any other source of income. Tenant farming deprived him of personal liberties and put him under a financial strain. My mother never got used to the many luxuries in life that most people considered necessities. But working together, they made do. It seems to me that some of the downtrodden folks always had at least one foot slipping in the mud trying to get ahead.

There's a trick that I heard about that I think is absolutely amazing. That's the jelly jar. It was common practice to collect old beer or pop bottles along the river for the purpose of making jelly jars. Dip a string in kerosene. Take the bottle of your choice, tie the string at the desired height for the jelly jar, then cut off the long ends and light it off. Let it burn out, pour cold water on it and it will break where you tied the string. Throw the neck part away; now you have your jelly jar. Sterilize, fill up and pour melted paraffin wax on for a lid. Then you have your jelly, ready for winter. It's meaningless for me to say that these were the days before bottle cutters.

While my parents lived on the farm, a black family lived nearby: Bertha, a simple lady, and Jake, a plain man with a pleasing disposition. They were much older, getting well along in years and had lived in the area all their lives. Mom said "nicer people you will never meet, but as poor as Job's turkey." Their house was an old shack with the front porch almost to the ground. Jake had a pig running around in the yard and a house full of chickens. Mom could see they were down on their luck—it beat all she'd ever seen. One Saturday evening Bertha invited them over for a dose of Eastern Shore hospitality; after supper they went down to the water, knocked around, playing ducks and drakes, the name we used for the game of skipping stones on the water. That was the beginning of a pleasant friendship. They all had many enjoyable visits.

Jake was attuned to the ways of the water, and he invited Dad and Henry down to the river and showed them how to catch crabs. With their bib overall pant legs rolled up to their knees, they waded into the water, pulling a small wooden washtub. They had a light three-foot rope attached to the handle of the tub. Then the other end was tied around their waist. This would give both hands free for holding the net and yet hold the tub from floating away. The Maryland Blue Crab has excellent eyesight and can swim as well as any fish. The crabbers would glide along slowly, quietly, then stand still and watch the crabs swim to them. With a swift dip and one smooth sweep, they grabbed the crab in the net, and turned and dumped their catch in the basket. In less than no time there was enough for their meal. This must have been a beautiful sight, these guys in their bib overalls.

Jake said that he only caught jimmies; he always left the sooks for breeders. The best time for softies is low tide. Walking along in the water slowly, looking at the bottom, you can see a little hump. The soft crab hides on the bottom of the low tidal waters, camouflaged with a dusting of river settlement. The little bump that you see on the bottom of a smooth riverbed is probably a softie; just reach down and pick it up. A jimmy has a long narrow inverted flipper on his belly; the bellies of a crab are known as aprons. The female, sometimes called a sook or a snook, has a u-shaped inverted flipper. A juvenile female is called an Sally or she-crab; it has a v-shaped inversion. Both of the female's grasping pincher claws are red on the tips, while the jimmies are blue. A sook carries her eggs under her apron, and from a distance, it looks like a sponge. She is called a sponge crab. Crabs are ugly buggy-looking creatures, but the little devils are romantic lovers. The jimmy gently cradles his sook beneath him holding her delicately with his pincher claws as they drift around on their honeymoon. Soft shell crabs are known as softies. Several times during a season, they actually outgrow their shell molding and during this process, they are called peelers.

Bertha showed Mom how to clean and fry the crabs. There was a recipe that had come from Bertha's family and had been passed through the many generations. Being from the country on the Western Shore, none of the three thought much about eating anything like a crab. Jake said, "The way Bertha fixes these softies up, they are some kinda good, it's nuf'n like'um." I was told there were lots of times when they didn't know where their next meal was coming from, whereas softies and "sea-plums" (oysters) were always there. Pennies were few and far between, but the couples made do. It's been my observation that this marriage was not put together for its monetary bounty.

Bertha and Jake introduced Mom and Dad to the most patronized store in Stevensville. It was originally a big manor house that had been transposed into a mercantile. The great room in the front held groceries, with 55-gallon wooden barrels of sugar and flour sitting on the floor. On the counter was a 5-gallon white porcelain bucket trimmed in red with ice water. A dipper hung on the handle. It was kept there during the hot weather for all customers to share the same dipper. The scullery was fixed up to store cow feed. Steel traps for catching muskrats hung on the walls—a real delicacy on the shore. Fishing gear and so forth were all placed about in corners.

Mom said, "This is where your father and I saw our first hot dogs. Together we came up with the 15 cents and could hardly wait to get home to eat. We ate the whole pound of all beef dogs," Mom said. "I guess that was being a little gluttonous. What in the world would they think of next?"

My mother grew up working with horses and was considered a good enough teamster. Mom offered to cultivate the cornfield while Dad and Henry took care of other farm chore needs. She made several rounds and was coming back to the end near the barn. The team didn't want to turn away from the barn; instead, they wanted to go to the stable. She could tell these horses meant business about heading for the barn. Their heads went up, necks arched, and with tails slattin' they took off in a run. Mom, knowing what to do, pulled them into a circle. Then they started raring and bucking, first one, then the other, kicking up the dust. Mom suspected she was going to be thrown for a flip. She began hollering, "Russell, Russell." Dad heard the clamor of all the commotion coming from the field. He knew right off Mom had surprisingly gotten herself into a tizzy.

Dad was one of those ol' country boys who knew his horses. He ran to the field without attempting to do any hazing and jumped on back of the cultivator, grabbed the lines, gave the horses a good snatch, and gradually pulled them into a tighter circle to where they couldn't run. That took awhile: this team could turn on a dime and give you nine-cents change. The last few bucks were high and hard. Then they came to a stop and stood steady with some fiddle-footin' for a few minutes; it was cowboy country. By now Henry had seen the smoke signal and was giving Dad some hurrahs for the grunt of his courage. In the old days there weren't too many first-rate teamsters, and without prejudice, Dad was exceptional.

Dad held the horses while Mom got off with trembling hands and wobbly knees. She said, "I was scared half to death." Then he took the horses to the other end of the field, socked the cultivator in the ground good. That took some of the fire out of them. He came back, handed the lines to Henry and told him, "They are as touchy as teased snakes." Mom was still bewildered and bushed as she asked, "Which way's the house?" Very "knightly" for his gallantry, Dad put his arm around her for comfort. Instinctively he knew her spirit was seeking his shelter. Mom was a pure extract of her mother, and reading her thoughts, he walked her to the house and fixed her a hot cup of tea. Mom's thought was "I could have gotten hurt." The "All American Country Boy" is often imitated but seldom equaled.

Dad, with his expert opinion on horses, asked Doc what he had paid for those hard heads. Dad said that they weren't worth the money. Dr. Legg asked what they were worth. Dad did some fast country boy arithmetic in his head and replied, "You paid 50 dollars apiece too much." Doc, a little astonished at what he said, replied, "Do you think you can teach them to do what they need to know?" Dad replied, "Only if I can get seed to grow on a rock, I can."

Doc, an up-coming physician, came to Mom spreadin' the news about the way Dad spoke to him. I asked her what happened then? The whole kit and caboodle was that it didn't amount to doodle squat. Her only reply was, "When Russell is running full tide, he does have a little bit of a temper." There were no intentional plans of being belligerent; it happened more by accident than design. I'm sure Doc couldn't draw much comfort from such a reply.

Dad's only thought on the matter was Doc's knowledge on horses was hopeless. He might as well try to teach a sittin' hen how to cluck. Dr. Legg's beliefs on farming were petrified and would not or could not change. Neither was willing to change, but both sides were willing to set aside ill feelings and continue their arrangement.

Mom pulled her fair share of freight around the place. She planted flowers along one side of the house and mowed the yard. Dad said she was always keeping "the place prettied up." Mom took care of the chickens, gathered the eggs, or 'hen-fruit,' which Dad jokingly called 'cackle-berries,' her responsibility. Orange crates and bushel baskets were used for the laying hens to nest in.

One afternoon Mom went to gather up the eggs. She checked next to the last nest, and a huge black snake rose up with its head in the striking position. Mom jumped back and started screaming. As she told me the story, she said, "Jimmy, I was half-scared to death. He was a fierce-looking thing with his tongue sticking out at me."

We all know a black snake will not eat you. In my country boy buffoonery I said, "I'm not exactly certain just how many times a feller can be half-scared to death and still be alive." My grammar is sometimes at the mercy of the old country. I can't tell you the what for's or the why, but teasing Mom was something I always enjoyed. I got a little "cackle" out of her, but she sharply and abruptly said, "Your father came on the run; he saw my dilemma, went back to the house, got the gun and shot the snake. That's all!"

Dad asked, "Are you going to tell Jimmy about the "brooder-house rat?" She said, "No, I'm not telling him anything else. He acts too simple." Dad seized the moment and continued, "One afternoon your mother walked into the brooder house to feed the peeps. As she opened the door, over on the next wall there was a rat moving very slowly towards one of the baby chicks." He said, "Guess what? It scared her half to death. Yup! I got the gun, I got the rat, I blew a hole right out through the back wall, rat and all." Did you ever wonder what would happen if you were to get half scared to death twice? Mom herself, in her usual confident and firm voice, replied, "That's not exactly how it happened." Dad, grinning, said, "Okay you're right, I'm wrong, any mistake is yours." One of his favorite sayings: "Okay, you tell me what I did." Mom changed the subject and told this story:

Like any other 22-year-old boy, your father and Henry always took time out of the workday for a little play. They both were told that they were expected to be in the barn by the time the top peak edge of the sun was coming up; for most farmers that would be called first light. So one day before lunch after a long morning in cahoots, Henry and Dad each got a fresh horse out of the barn and thought it might be time to check the mail. At 11 o'clock, it was thought to be time for the mail to arrive, although nothing you could depend on. But it was worth the try. The lane was so long that it was necessary to ride a horse and save on gas.

They reached the mailbox and the mail had not come. These boys sat on their horses waiting for the mail to arrive. The horses were getting antsy and were pawing, wanting to move on. Around the turn came Dr. Legg; he pulled up, stopped, got out of his 1930 Roadster and walked up and asked, "What are you boys doing?"

Dad explained that they had come for the mail but it hadn't yet arrived. Doc said, "It doesn't take both of you to get the mail," and he gave them a bringing-up lecture that only fathers usually do. Dad told him right fast that they would be back at the farm on the double.

Mom continued, "We were all embarrassed. Can you imagine Doctor Legg didn't know that the usual amount of mail for us was less than one letter a week?"

One day Doc sent another pair of young horses from his office location in Union Bridge for my father's use on the farm. These horses were, as my father described to me, "crazy and half-broke." Later Dr. Legg stopped by to see how the plowing was going and was very disappointed to see how little had gotten done. He boasted to my father that he could drive from Union Bridge to Stevensville and back to Union Bridge and still do a day's work.

In Dad's early years he could pitch wits with the best of them. Dad explained to Doc in a quick response that he had already promised better pasture with greener grass to his horses if they would work. Without stopping for a pause he continued, if these "crazy half-broke horses could plow 40 miles an hour, it wouldn't take so darn long to get the plowing done." Dad was not always politically correct. He spoke his mind and didn't care if you liked it or not. It was simply the truth the way he saw it.

Dad told me Doc was a good physician and a mighty nice man but he was a 'milk-skin' farmer, an employer who didn't pay his laborers very much. Well my parents didn't stay long after that. In the kindest manner and as discreetly as possible, they thought it was more mending to tell Doc that Mom was homesick, and she wanted to move back over to Baltimore. That shouldn't ache him too much. Together they broadcast various goodbyes among friends and neighbors and headed back to the Western Shore. They both agreed that the times that they spent working and living on the shore were happy ones, much like a long honeymoon. Their light of memories shone clear while the pain of sorrowful ones vanished with the past.

For Henry, his loss was a sorrowful one. Riding a hot, wet plow horse bareback down a dusty lane to get the mail alone wasn't nearly as much fun. Henry thought Dr. Legg was a fine person but had some peculiar ideas about farming. Doc sat just a little too heavily on Henry's shoulders, and with the loss of his two friends the days became long and trying. Henry couldn't work long enough or hard enough for Doc. He figured if that was the case, then he couldn't do anything long enough or bad enough to get fired, and decided he'd have to quit. Unselfishly, Henry decided to give Doc the "full-choke" privilege of farming for himself.

Henry decided to move out of the flat country and back to the hills of Uniontown, Maryland, about 250 miles away. His only possession was a golden pheasant. He had saved up enough money for the ferry ride back across the bay so at first light, he stuck his pheasant under his arm and started walking up the road to meet the ferry. He got on the ferry and took a seat on the floor of the deck and in an hour he'd reached the Western Shore. He got off, looking around to see of any possible free rides; holding onto his pheasant, he continued walking. It was very near night when he saw a truck approaching; he gave a friendly wave. Being out in the middle of nowhere, the driver stopped.

The driver asked, "Where are you bound, boy?" Henry told him he was going to Uniontown. The drivers asked, "Where?" He replied again, "Uniontown!" "Where in the heck is Uniontown?" He told him that it's outside Westminster. The driver said that he was going to Westminster. They arrived well past midnight. Henry climbed out of the truck and thanked Mr. Truckdriver, set his pace for Uniontown hanging onto his pheasant. He was heading to his mother and father's farm in Uniontown. It was dark as Henry rounded a turn in the road and headlights came up from behind him. The car stopped and the driver asked Henry if he would like a ride. He replied, "Sure would." It was first light when Henry dropped off his pheasant in the chicken coop on his way to the house. According to Dr. Legg's standards, it was time for Henry to start to work. In the summer months it would now be 4:30 a.m.

Shy about his skill, Henry has probably forgotten more about birds than most people ever knew. Henry turned out to be a world-renowned breeder of waterfowl and other game birds.

Life at
Twiford Farm

My Birth and the
Move Back to Twiford

Mom and Dad moved from the Eastern Shore to Twiford Farm in Stevenson, Maryland. At that time, however, the farm was called Glen Cairn and was owned by William Horatio Whitridge. This is where my oldest brother, Charles Richard, was born on December 24, 1932. His name, Charles, came from my grandfather, Charles Henry Cartzendafner. My sister, Shirley Belle, was born there on July 25, 1934. Her middle name came from my mother's twin sister, Aunt Belle Kemp.

For some reason, perhaps Mr. Whitridge died, my parents moved to Glen Arm, where my father worked for Dr. Eleden. My father got a job as a herdsman on a dairy farm. This is where I was born on October 9, 1937. I wasn't named after anybody; they just called me, "Jimmy." I never knew my name was Francis until I started to school. The teacher called me Francis and I didn't know she was talking to me. In the fourth grade my teacher called me Jimmie, but told me I was spelling my name wrong because it should be Jimmy with a *y* for a boy and *ie* for a girl. I told Mom and she said it didn't matter to her how I spelled it; it can be spelled either way. My sister mostly called me Jimmy James and still does.

Then when Grandpap Fox died in 1940, we moved in with Grandma Fox because she needed help on the farm. My younger brother, Marvin Bruce, was born there on December 24, 1940. He was named after my grandfather, Norman Bruce Fox.

In July 1942, my father returned to Twiford Farm as a gardener, and our family moved back to Stevenson. He worked for Martha and Clarence Wheelwright. We moved into a house in the back of the farm. There was no electricity, no running water, and we had an outhouse out back. As well as receiving a house for us to live in, he was paid $45 a month; six ton of coal a year; kerosene for lights; one dozen eggs, two chickens, and a pound of butter each week; one-half gallon of milk each day; vegetables and fruit which were raised on the farm, and two hogs a year. This was a fair salary for its time.

My father used to milk cows by hand. After moving to Twiford Farm, he had already built up a lot of forearm muscle from milking cows. On a rainy day in the shop, the other farmers were working on machinery and clowning around. They were testing each other's strength by picking up an anvil when they started teasing my father that he was too skinny to compete. He showed them when he picked it up with one hand and then asked why they needed two hands and suspected they couldn't do it because they had "too much belly." Then they all laughed.

The Manor House

The Wheelwrights had previously owned a farm in Howard
County that was called Twyford. After moving to the farm in
Green Spring Valley, Mr. Wheelwright kept the Twyford Farm
name but changed the y to i. Twiford was a 220-acre gentleman's farm with five tenant houses. When we lived there, the
other tenants were the Stairs, Schaeffers, Joneses and Scarbers.
Bernard P. Hoge, of 705 Title Building, Baltimore, Maryland,
was the owner's agent in charge of selling Twiford Farm to St.
Timothy's School in 1949. The listing included two barns, a
chicken house, a brooder house, a vegetable cellar, a corncrib,
a granary, a milkhouse, a smokehouse and a workshop.

I always found it amusing that Mrs. Wheelwright referred to
the workshop as the "smitty" because a lot of blacksmith
work was done there. There was a quarter-acre concrete goldfish pond, which was drained and scrubbed thoroughly every
spring, and a several-acre garden with an overhead sprinkler

system. In front of the garden were a dozen ten feet
by three feet hotbeds,
which were used for starting plants. There were
hotbed blankets made especially for these hotbeds to
cover them up during the
wintertime to keep the
seeds from freezing. This garden was so big that it had its own
house, called the seedhouse, where the seeds were kept.

The old manor house had been destroyed by fire, so Mr.
Wheelwright had a new house built before they moved in. It

took three years to build his new house and it was completed in 1938. The new house had 30 rooms, eleven bathrooms, four oil-burning furnaces, an electric elevator, which ran from the basement to the third floor, and a ballroom 35x45 feet with huge fireplaces at each end. Above the fireplaces, Mr. Wheelwright had a marlin at one and a sailfish at the other, which he had personally caught. On either side of the fireplaces he had trashcans made from the feet of an elephant, which he had shot. At one fireplace he had the front feet and at the other fireplace he had the hind feet.

There was a flower room for arranging fresh-cut flowers daily and a bar finished in knotty pine. A fireplace was in the large dining room as well as in the breakfast room. The house also had a living room and a library. Beyond the foyer was a lavatory and a powder room on either side of the hall. Mr. and Mrs. Wheelwright each had a personal office on the second floor, but the farm office where Mrs. Gough, the secretary, worked was on the first floor. Mrs. Wheelwright called her office her "writing room." Toward the back of the house were five rooms called the servants' rooms. The house also had a huge kitchen with a working pantry.

New Twiford

From the front door, there was a wrought-iron spiral staircase that led up to Mr. and Mrs. Wheelwright's room, which was referred to as the master wing. It was like a private apartment with bedrooms, fireplaces, fitting room, bathrooms and study. Mr. Wheelwright's room had a large bed with a big canopy. The bed was so high that he needed a stepping stool to get into bed. The first step on the stool was designed to enclose

70

his night garments. Off the bedrooms was a sun-porch that overlooked the formal gardens. Past the lawn area was a peach and apple orchard; beyond that were the woods, bordered by dogwood trees. Between the orchard and the dogwood trees were the domestic honeybees. They were fed molasses bread (King Syrup on a slice of bread) and sugar water. This was a good place to stay away from!

Also on the second floor was a game room, which was 35 feet wide and 45 feet long. There were seven bedroom suites plus four additional master guest bedrooms, each with private baths and sleeping porches. In addition there was a nursery suite with two bedrooms and two bathrooms on the second floor. There were linen and cedar closets throughout the entire house.

The basement housed a wine cellar with an automatic thermostatic control to maintain the correct temperature for the wine. Just inside the door was a little desk where the wine and spirit log was kept. The log showed the aisle, row, and bin number for each type of wine, as well as providing an inventory so Mrs. Wheelwright would know when to have wine reordered. There was also a bowling alley in the basement. From the wine cellar was a five-car garage off to the left. Above that was a five-room apartment where the chauffeur and his wife lived.

Upstairs—Downstairs

I remember some of the help who took care of the house: My friend Harrison was the cook; Mrs. Hennessy was Henry's governess; Mrs. Gough was the secretary; the well-liked Mary Balou was the head housekeeper; there was a downstairs maid and an upstairs maid, whose names I can't remember; Mr. Wheelwright had a valet; Mrs. Wheelwright had a personal maid, Irene; a laundress; pantry-help; and the chauffeur,

Lester. Additional people would come in for fall and spring housecleaning times and for canning season.

Sometimes Henry would ask my mother if he could stay for dinner at our house. She would always say, "Yes, but ask your mother if it is okay." Then Mrs. Wheelwright would call my mother and ask if Henry was invited for dinner. And of course he was and we would have a good time with Henry at our house. When Henry was going to be eating alone at his house, he would invite Marvin and me to have dinner with him. It was a very special treat to have the butler serve me. The butler would carry each bowl around the table so we could help ourselves to the quantity we wanted. Once everyone was served, the food was taken back to the kitchen. If you wanted a second helping, you would push the buzzer on the floor to call the butler back. Sometimes I requested a second helping just so I could push the buzzer. I would always thank the butler very much for bringing the food and serving me.

Once Mrs. Wheelwright decided she would have a party. When she told my father, he said, "That's okay, but right now we have all this hay down and we need to get it in before it rains." She said, "We can always buy hay. I want to have a party now." All the men came from the farm and started hanging Japanese lanterns around the house and down around the pool. She had Rosa Ponselle come and sing at her party. This lady could really sing. She lived across the valley from us and when she had a party at her own house, we could hear her powerful voice when we were home. After I started into the landscaping business, she called me up and asked me to come to work for her.

Daggum Bee Tree

My father and Cooper Dorsey worked together on the farm. Cooper was lots of fun to be around. He was always into something. Cooper made a lot of different kinds of wines. He had barrels ranging from five gallons to 55 gallons in his cellar, all filled with wine.

This was some time in the late 'thirties, and it was hard to get sugar. Cooper had a large family and did everything he could to provide for them. Dad said, "Yes, poor Cooper did everything." He even did the laundry most of the time. His wife was kind of a sorrowful soul, either sick or pregnant.

One day they were getting in hay in the backfield and walked over to the edge of the woods to sit in the shade until the next wagon came out to the field to get loaded. Cooper said, "We have plenty of time before the next wagon comes. I know of a little drippy spring down over the hill where we can get a cool drink."

There was a little stream that fed out from the spring about ten feet away from the spring-head. They took their hands and pulled enough sand out of the bottom to catch a little pool of water. They let it run to where it was clear, then got on their hands and knees and sucked themselves up a refreshing drink. After they had their fill, Cooper said, "Let's wait here. It's a nice breeze coming through here." They leaned back against a nearby tree, took off their hats and really got into resting for a spell.

Dad said, "Look over there, Cooper. See all those honey bees going back and forth, to and from the hayfield? They're gathering pollen from the clover." Cooper said, "I bet that will make darn good honey." Dad replied, "I'm not crazy about all these deerflies around here anyway. They liked to eat you up. Let's see if we can find that bee tree." They grabbed their hats and eased over to investigate the bees' flyway. The way the sun was shining through the trees at that time of day helped them follow the bees through the woods.

It wasn't long before the tree was spotted. Cooper said, "There's that daggum bee tree." The curly-que grain in a gum tree is slightly wavy and intertwines together, which makes it hard to split. The grain is so hard to split that it was used to make hubs for wagon wheels, watering troughs and other things that would have to hold together without splitting easily.

Dad and Cooper decided to wait until cold weather before taking the honey. The bees would be a little drowsy and not so much a threat, so in the cool weather the men would have an easier time. It must have been late fall or early winter when the two of them went back since all the trees were bare and the leaves were pretty flat on the ground. It was real cool and moon-bright. This bee tree was dead and had been struck by lightning. The bark had a scab running from the top straight to where the lightning had blown a fair-size hole in the ground.

It was Saturday night and Dad had been to town early that morning and purchased a new three-and-a-half-pound pole axe. He had saved awhile for this axe and was well pleased with it. He said that he had only made two or three licks into the tree when a piece of metal about the size of a quarter broke out of the razor-sharp edge on his axe. It came flying toward him. He said, "It made me flinch a bit but I felt like bawlin' like a baby."

This old dead bee tree was leaning pretty good, so it was no trouble to decide where to throw it. They chopped and chopped. Dad had a determined personality and kept telling Cooper that, "She is weakening. Yeah, she's weakening." Finally, it went over.

Cooper scrounged around and found or made a smoker out of a funnel. Dad wasn't sure whose it was. They put a box of blue-tip stick kitchen matches in it, mixed with some dampened straw chaff, and lit it off. Striking the matches put enough sulfur in with the smoke to completely stun the bees until the tree was on the ground. They split the tree with a lot of hard work. Bees were crawling all around on the ground and trying to climb up their pant legs. My father told Cooper, "Beware there are bees everywhere." The befuddled bees had been knocked silly and no one got stung. With wedges, they got this old gum tree pulled apart and walked out of the woods well past midnight with a washtub full of fresh, sweet clover honey.

After they got back to Cooper's house, they took a boning knife and cut the honeycomb into pieces, and hung the pieces of comb from a string attached to the kitchen ceiling with the honey dripping in wash pans. They didn't have a honey extractor that anybody knew of. This seemed to work just as well, but took longer and nobody was in a hurry anyway. Dad said, "Whoever eats the most honey gets the most wax." We had plenty of honey for the table and Cooper had a batch for his wine.

Beeswax is nontoxic. Use it to preserve homemade jelly by pouring melted beeswax on top to seal it like a lid. Beeswax candles have a wonderful aroma. Properly made beeswax candles burn a bright smokeless flame that doesn't sputter. A cake of beeswax is handy for a carpenter; it can be used to coat those hard-to-drive nails. For ease in threading needles, ladies pull the thread through a cake of beeswax to stiffen the thread. Beeswax is also good for waterproofing. For a sure start, just rub blue tip kitchen matches in a cake of beeswax. Beeswax also makes delicious chewing gum.

Did you know that holes in a honeycomb are six-sided? The octagon shape is stronger than a round or square hole. It is amazing what we can learn by observing nature. For me, nature is the sweet nectar of life.

One Good Mule

My father told me that he would rather care for one good mule than two horses. If a mule should get out and find his way to the corncrib, he'll only eat until he is full. But if a horse gets out and finds a bag of feed, he won't stop until it is gone. This can cause a horse to founder, which is a chronic condition of lameness in the front feet or all four. The same is true if a horse gets overheated from work and is given too much water at one time. A mule will drink a little, then stop and go back later for more. If a horse is worked hard and gets overheated, it must be cooled down or it will founder. On the other hand, it isn't necessary to cool down a mule. The heaves is also caused by overheating, but it affects the lungs, making it difficult for the horse to breathe. Horses with the heaves are called wind suckers.

Mules' smaller feet require very little attention. Horses' feet require much more; the frog must be kept clean and trimmed. If not, there is a chance of thrush. Horses can stifle, which means the stifle joint is displaced. Displacement of a stifle joint cannot usually be treated, but if the horse happens to get spooked and jumps a certain way sideways, most of the time it is corrected. Stringhalt (some call it "stringhaltered") is when the leg is jerked upward at each step. It appears as though a spring is on the foot and as the foot comes up, the horse's head jerks up. Dad told me a lot of neat stories about his mules. He even owned some horses in his time, but he still liked mules best.

It wasn't long before Dad thought that he needed another pair of mules. He bought a matched pair of gray mules named Kit and Kate. Dad preferred gray mules over any others. (The Amish like only black horses or mules because when they curry a white or gray horse, their black clothes would be hard to keep clean.) This pair of mules liked to work together. They would rear up on their hind feet and put all their weight into their collars to get a big heavy load rolling.

Kit had a bad habit. When you would walk in the tie stall to put the harness on, he'd squeeze you up against the side of the stall. Dad said that he thought he'd had enough of that, so he got a stick that was as long as he was wide. He sharpened one end down to a point, then as he stepped into the stall and old Kit would lean up against him for his morning squeeze, Dad placed the flat end of the stick up against the boards and the pointy end up against Kit. Well after a few times of that, old Kit soon learned to move over and give plenty of room. After that he turned into one good mule.

You could get two sticks, one in each hand, go down in the pasture, find Kit, climb on him and drive him by tapping him on the neck to go right or left or on the rump to go straight. If he didn't get tapped, he wouldn't do anything, just stand there.

One evening Richard was leading a mule in after a day's work. Right inside the door in the first tie stall was a horse named Doll, eating. As Richard entered, Doll kicked him with both feet and sent him flying up against the side of the barn. It was hard enough that he knocked the boards loose on the barn. To me it's amazing that you can get kicked by a 1,600 pound horse with both feet and not get hurt. This is Richard's side of the story. Perhaps it's just a misunderstood myth that comes from a frightening experience. However I do know horses or mules do not like any other horse or mule near them while they're eating, and they mean it.

Dad was not happy with this type of stable manners. He got a locust fence post and hung it about a foot off the floor with two chains from the ceiling. So when Dad was leading Doll in and out of her stall, she'd step over it. It did not take long before she made another kick. This time she hurt herself. Doll was not able to work the following week, but she never tried to kick again.

Some of the local farmers would put out a couple acres in peas for a cash crop. They all helped each other to haul the peas to the vinery. The farmer that they were helping would cut the peas with a horse-drawn sickle bar mower like you'd cut hay. The peas were still on the vines. Some people put them in small piles, gathered them up to be put on the wagon and hauled to the vinery. There the peapods were stripped from the vines and hauled to the cannery. My father hooked the hay-loader to the back of the wagon. The loader straddled the row and pulled the peas up onto the back of the wagon. This was the easy part. After the peas were on the wagon, you had to fork them around to get an even load. Pea vines that have grown together to about two feet high and tangled together are hard to pull apart.

My dad took two wagons and two teams of mules to help out. Sometimes the pea vinery would be two or three miles away. He drove one team of mules and the other team of Kit and Kate followed along behind until they got to where they were going to work. They filled up Kit and Kate's wagon and Dad drove them to the vinery for their first time. After that, they knew the road and drove themselves. The workmen at the vinery would see Kit and Kate coming and unload the wagon when it got in front of the vinery.

There were many wagons coming and going at the same time. When Kit and Kate arrived at the vinery, they got in line with the rest of the teamsters. As the wagons were being emptied they pulled up a little closer to stay in line with the rest of the wagons. They knew just what to do. After getting the wagon unloaded, one of the workmen sent them back to get another load.

The neatest thing was that, as these mules were traveling back and forth, they had to pass oncoming wagons. They'd find a place along the road to pull over. Then, they'd pull in and stop until the oncoming wagon had passed. Kit and Kate pulled back out and continued on down the road.

Dad said the amusing thing was when Kit would spot an oncoming team, he'd choose his place to pull over and let them pass. He'd stand there until they passed, but that could take maybe 15 minutes. As soon as he saw another team, no matter how far away it was, he was ready to stop and wait for it to pass. If the field that Kit and Kate had left was finished by the time they got back, they'd stay there and wait until someone came to get them.

There was another mule that we all heard a lot about; that was Hambone. Hambone was an unusually good Army mule and movie star. He was a gray mule that liked to jump. An Army Sergeant bought him in St. Joseph, Missouri for $210 in 1940. He was foaled in May 1932. He had a respectable (mare) mother but his father was a jackass. Some muleskinner said, "It took a couple pounds of spit and sweat and a ton of

cussin' to turn him into a first-rate Army mule." Hambone
went overseas during the war. Mules were the best way of getting through the mud, jungles and mountain trails because of
their surefootedness. Mules were reliable and rugged.

Hambone returned to the States and after several years he
found himself at Fort Carson, Colorado. He was always
known for his jumping. On his day off he'd be entered in
jumping contests. He out-jumped in the mule contests and
out-jumped in the finest thoroughbred horse contests. This
made a lot of the top horse breeders unhappy, so it was said

 that Hambone could no
longer jump with the hors-
es, mainly due to a name
like Hambone, because
that was degrading to the
horse jumping class. It did-
n't take the Army long to
give him the proper name
"Mr. Hamilton T. Bone."
After a little protesting and
a lot of laughs, it was decided to let him jump with the best of
them. He was entered in the national jumping contest at
Madison Square Gardens in New York and took the Grand
Championship, with a frown from the competitors.

One time Hambone carried 300 pounds of weapon parts for
a howitzer to the top of Pikes Peak for the Fourth Artillery
Battalion. Hambone was well known, and there was even a
demand for him in Hollywood for the next three years to make
movies. He also won at the International Stock Show in
Chicago and the Pikes Peak Rodeo in 1954. The Army called
him the "jumping fool" and had official marching songs that
they sang about him.

On December 15, 1956, Mr. Hamilton T. Bone and Trotter, a beautiful slick black mule with a roan nose who was known for his fast gait, along with three-hundred other fine mules, were given a special ceremony for their retirement. The pack mule era had come to an end. Trotter went to West Point Military Academy to be their mascot. He died in December 1981 at the age of fifty-one.

Hambone went on to be a Colorado celebrity in the Pikes Peak Rodeo for the next 14 years. He was never out-jumped. Finally he was turned out to pasture. He died on March 29, 1971 at the age of 30. He took with him a long line of unbroken championships.

Daily Routine at Twiford

In the house at Twiford Farm, Mom and Dad did their own wallpapering. Mom pasted the paper on the kitchen table, which was covered by an oilcloth. Dad would then take it and stick one end up to the ceiling and use a floor broom to sweep across the paper to make it stick. If the paper didn't come close to the ceiling that was okay because a border would be placed at the ceiling to cover the mislaid paper. You could always tell the skill of the paperhanger by the size of the border around the top. Every room in the house was papered, with the exception of the kitchen, which was painted. All rooms had linoleum on the floor.

We had a very old four-door car and a long bumpy driveway. One day my father took Marvin and me to Biddison's General Store in Stevenson. (There's a flower shop there now.) We were returning home, driving back on the bumpy driveway, and Marvin was in the back seat by himself. Without Dad and me knowing it, when we hit a bump, the door flew open, and

Marvin rolled out. (You see, the car made so much noise, doors could open and shut and you wouldn't even know any-thing had happened.) When we got home, Dad looked around and, seeing that four-year old Marvin was missing, said, "Oh my word, what happened to the kid!" We drove back the bumpy drive-way and there was Marvin, unhurt but crying for all he was worth as he was heading toward home.

Mom had a gasoline engine washing machine, which was kept on the front porch. I called it the front porch because that's where you drove up to when you came from the barn. However, if you wanted to go to the front door you would have to go around to the back of the house. Everybody told me that the back was the front, but I didn't agree with that. Anyway the front porch, as I call it, is where Mom did the laundry.

The engine for the washing machine was at the bottom, and in order to start the machine there was a pedal like that used on a motorcycle, which would need to be pumped. A long lever like the old gearshift levers in cars needed to be thrown into gear to get the agitator of the washing machine started. If the clothes were particularly dirty Mom would use a washboard on collars, knees of pants and so forth. She was the proud owner of two washboards: one made of tin and the other one of glass. She'd stop the agitator and slide the chosen washboard into the tub and after the scrubbing was finished, she'd remove the washboard and throw the agitator back into gear. It would jump and dance all around with water splashing out all over.

A long bench held two round washtubs, which were used to complete the task. One tub was used for the clear rinse and the other was used for the blue rinse. Bluing was a liquid that came in a bottle and was used as a brightener. A basket caught the clothes after they came out of the wringer.

Washing clothes was not as simple as today. As a matter of fact, it could be a little dangerous. One time Richard was helping Mom, and as he was putting the clothes through the wringer, it caught his hand, and before he knew it his whole arm was stuck in the wringer up to his shoulder. He started hollering and bawling so Mom ran out and threw the wringer in reverse to run his arm back out again.

In the wintertime, washing clothes was a long, rough, cold job to be done on the front porch. After the clothes were washed, they were hung on the line with clothespins and it was not uncommon for the long johns to become stiff as a board.

I can see Mom now with her flowered, feedbag apron, Dad's dark gray woolen button-down sweater with the sleeves pushed up, and a red bandana tied around her head, hanging up clothes and singing one of her favorite hymns, "Amazing Grace." Mom really was basically a very happy person. She was always singing or humming. Dad would say she's as happy as if she had good sense. Mom was a happy person by nature, but let me tell you, don't ever say anything bad about her kids or she'll get madder than a wet hen.

For light, we used kerosene lamps. We could adjust the brightness by turning the wicks up or down, but if we turned the wick up too much, it would smoke. My grandmother said a good rule of thumb was to turn the wick up enough to push the shadow back into the corner. These lamps usually would hold enough kerosene to last for about a week.

Times were hard and we were very careful not to waste anything. When we finished the cereal, my mother would take the wax paper liner out of the box and use it to wrap our sandwiches for our school lunches. We would use and re-use the wax paper for a week until it just couldn't be used anymore. I believe we recycled long before it became fashionable. I remember helping Dad fix Mom's pots and pans with Men-z-it. Men-z-it was a little kit about the size of a matchbox. In this kit were two little wrenches and different sizes of bolts with metal washers, which Dad would insert into the holes in the pots and pans to mend them. You see, we never threw anything away! Men-z-it could be purchased at hardware and drugstores. It seemed that everybody had it.

Dad had a shoe lathe that stood about two feet high. He had four or five different-sized shoe-irons. We would slip our shoes overtop those irons so he could repair the heels or soles of our shoes. At that time we could buy heels and half-soles for our shoes. It wasn't the disposable society that we live in today.

We listened to a lot of radio, operated from Dad's car battery. If we wanted to hear our favorite show we would have to wait until Dad got home with the car. When Dad arrived home, we'd run out to the car to unhook the battery, bring it into the house, and hook it up to our big tabletop, stationary radio. When we finished listening to our program, we'd have to immediately take the battery back out and hook it up to the car. Some of my favorite shows were Sgt. Preston (and his dog, Yukon King), the Fatman (which was a detective show), Henry Aldridge (about a young boy growing up), the Lone Ranger, and the Grand Ole Opry (on Saturday night). We could hear the Grand Ole Opry only if the weather was good and clear because the reception would fade when there was weather interference.

There was a running spring fairly close to the house where we kept milk and butter when we couldn't afford ice for the icebox, which was most of the time. We made a trip to the spring twice for each meal, which meant six times a day—at least. So we had a path between the house and the spring. In addition we had a water pump outside the kitchen door, but when the pump wasn't working, we had to carry water from the spring for drinking, bathing, laundry and dishes, as well as for giving water to the chickens and pigs. I had a little wagon I used for hauling the water, but by the time I got close to the house, the full buckets of water would be nearly empty due to the splashing and spilling as the wagon went across the bumpy path.

"Movin' On Up"

The day came when my father was asked to be the Farm Manager, and we moved from that house to the main part of the farm into the Farm Manager's house, which was the best house on the farm. (We felt like we were living uptown!) We still had a wood-burning cookstove, a coal stove in the living room for heat, but no heat upstairs. The heat upstairs was provided through a register from the coal stove in the living room. We would get up in the morning, grab our clothes, run downstairs to the kitchen, stick our feet in the oven door and get dressed in front of its warmth. We had a 15-watt electric bulb in each room, running water in the kitchen and a bathroom in the house! This was really living. No more going back to that spring!

Later, my dad bought a hot water heater. He hooked it up in the basement and ran hot water to the kitchen sink and to the bathroom. No one could really believe it would work, but it did! We had no idea how that hot water got up from the basement to the kitchen and the bathroom without anyone carrying it, but we sure were glad it made it!

After Dad began the position as Farm Manager, the first thing he did was talk to Mrs. Wheelwright about his idea of raising pigs. Pigs and hogs are known as swine; the males are boars, females are sows. A young weaned pig is a shoat. An immature sow or young female pig is a gilt, and a pig which has been castrated before maturing is a barrow. A group of baby pigs are called a litter or a brood. A group of hogs is called a herd.

There was an area in the back of the farm known as hog hollow, and that area was fenced off for pigs only. These pigs were very mean and would even charge you. I was told never to go inside the area unless with an older person. About three or four of the tenant houses were falling down. Sows went inside the basements, under the porches and even inside the houses to have their young. They ran wild and lived off of acorns and berries, along with brewer's grain. There was a distillery in Gwynnbrook. George Stairs, who was the youngest farmer at Twiford, ran the slop truck most of the time. The truck had a large tank on the back and it was used to haul the brewer's grain from the distillery to the hogs. Sometimes if I was behaving and George was in a good mood, he took me along.

Dad told Mrs. Wheelwright that if he had 20 sows and a boar instead of 100 brood sows, it would be cheaper and more profitable to raise pigs over at the barn and he could do it in a more orderly fashion. She agreed to give it a try. He made plans to build the hog house below the tractor shed with sycamore floorboards, three-inches thick and twelve-inches wide. These boards were so hard we needed to use a drill to get a nail started through them. Dad said that the sycamore never rotted.

We rounded up the old skinny-looking razorback-type pigs, sold them, and then purchased a better grade of hogs—Yorkshire sows, and a Hereford boar hog named Ed.

You could drive Ed around by pulling on his tail either right or left. "Driving Ed" was a lot of fun until one day poor old Ed died from a heart attack while out in the pasture field.

My father always referred to Mrs. Wheelwright as "The Madam." He had an enormous amount of respect for her. She also had respect for him and his honesty and integrity. One day when we were still at Twiford Farm, Mrs. Wheelwright stopped by to see how the butchering was going. Perhaps I was there at the time, but I didn't hear this story until the 1950's after we had moved on to Beaver Brook Farm. She walked around looking at the newly sliced pork chops on the table and bent over to inspect the fresh sausage in the large kettle. Without her knowing, someone hooked a pigtail to the back of her coat. This was followed by a lot of snickering as she continued to examine their work.

When Mrs. Wheelwright was satisfied with the butchering, she left the shop. The chuckling continued until they saw her get back out of her car, pull her coat around and unhook the pigtail. With a stern look on her face, she very slowly walked back into the shop and placed the pigtail on the big table. With that she turned on her heel and said, "I hope this never happens again." She walked directly back to her chauffeured car and left. After she was gone, there was a big sigh of relief and everyone was quiet the remainder of the day. All the workers were wondering who had put the pigtail on her coat; and it wasn't until later years that the truth came to light. After three decades of silence, Ida Mae Stairs, the youngest of all the tenant farmers' wives, then only in her early twenties, confessed to Mom that she was the pigtail-pinning villain.

Life at Twiford Farm Seen Through the Eyes of a Young Boy

The house at Twiford Farm had a wraparound porch, which covered two sides of the house and included a railing and banister. On the south side of the house there was a good-sized wisteria vine that ran up to the roof along the rain gutter. Next to the middle post there was a perfect spot for a bird nest. One day I noticed that "Mr. and Mrs. Robin" were building a nest in that ideal location. In an attempt to help them build their home, I gathered up materials I thought they could use. I think my carefully chosen pieces just weren't good enough for what they wanted, though. They might have used something, but I'm not sure. They did, however, build a fine nest, and there Mrs. Robin laid three eggs for incubation. I watched every day and the robins became very friendly.

Robins' Nest

Finally, the robin pair hatched out three of the ugliest little birds I had seen in my entire life. They were so ugly I was sure the mother and father would not come back, so I started digging up worms and feeding them. My father noticed what I was doing and told me that the babies had good parents and he didn't think I should be doing that. But since that was not a "No, don't do it!" I continued feeding the babies. It wasn't long before they started jumping out of the nest. I would catch them and return them to their home again and again. Most of the time when they jumped down, they would stay in the yard anyway. After a while, they stayed out of the nest altogether and they would remain in the yard. I could still feed them. I'd put little pieces of worms in my hand and they'd pick it off. Late that fall, they left and I was sorry to see my friends go. When they returned the next spring, they no longer knew me. (I guess that's where the term, 'bird brain,' came from!)

At that time, the manor house on Twiford Farm was the largest single family home in the state of Maryland, with twelve-foot high ceilings and very long hallways. One day a bat got into the first floor hallway. We were all called to the house to capture this bat. It flew up and down the hall with everybody smacking at it with tennis rackets, brooms, sticks and so on. Then the bat finally flew very slowly behind one of the large chandeliers, which hung from the inside wall. Richard, with his big barn broom, knew that he just couldn't miss this perfect shot at the bat. Well, he got the bat and 90 percent of the chandelier with it. Mrs. Wheelwright said, "I'm not worried about the chandelier as long as you got the bat."

There's another story about three little baby skunks that Watty Wheelwright (Mrs. Wheelwright's oldest son, who was a few years older than Richard) caught. He loved these little skunks and took them with him wherever he went. He took them to bed with him and he let them run up and down the halls of the manor house. The maids were all scared to death of these little skunks. When he was served breakfast at the very large table in the breakfast room, the skunks ran on the table and he would feed them off his plate. He'd divide his scrambled eggs up in little pieces and feed the skunks with his fork while he ate. One of the maids, Mary Belou, couldn't take this any longer. She offered Richard 25 cents each to kill the skunks. Being an old trapper, he didn't hesitate to take her up on the offer. At that time he made only ten cents an hour, so that was a good deal! One of the skunks had died earlier, so Richard's gain was 50 cents.

Lester, the chauffeur, thought this was the funniest thing he had ever heard of until Watty found out what had happened. Then Watty came looking for Richard. He found Richard down at the barn filling silo, walked up to him and told him he was going to have to kill him. Mother heard Richard and Watty hollering and screaming, so she went out to see what was the matter. Watty, very much like a gentleman, told Mother that he was sorry, but he was going to have to kill Richard for killing his skunks. Mother said, "Before you kill him, let me call your mother." He said that would be fine, call her, but he was going to have to do it anyway. Mrs. Thompson arrived and since Richard is still celebrating birthdays, I guess everything turned out okay.

I started working at the farm when I was nine years old and thought I was a top hand until I got my first paycheck. I said, "Dad, I thought I was a top hand. Don't top hands make more than a half a dollar a day?" He said, "Yes, they do." I said, "Oh," realizing I was not a top hand although I worked a ten-hour day from 7 a.m. until 6 p.m. with an hour off for lunch. Half a dollar a day did not seem like it was very much for all that work, but I guess $3.00 a week was not bad for a nine-year-old boy in June of 1946. (That still doesn't sound like much, but I didn't have other jobs from which to choose.)

In the spring, I would help with the whitewashing in the dairy barn. This was done for sanitation reasons. The white wash was lime, which would help prevent diseases and brighten up the barn. Whitewash was made by mixing lime, salt and water together; then you would apply it much like you would paint. We also whitewashed the glass on the hotbeds that helped to keep the direct sunlight off the new plants.

In the fall, we would take down the stovepipes, pull the three-foot sections apart that slipped inside of one another, and use

90

a long-handled brush to clean out the soot. There were elbows for going around turns. Behind the stove you usually started with an elbow, then a straight section and then another elbow into the chimney. If for any reason a section would be too long, you could cut it by using a pair of tin-snips. Then everything was put back in its place for the next year.

Milkin' Time

In the summertime, I didn't always wear shoes, so by the end of the summer my feet would be pretty tough and calloused. When fall first came, I continued to go barefoot, although it was getting colder. In the morning I would go down into the pasture field to bring the seven-grade (common, not registered or purebred) Guernsey cows up to the barn for milking. Without my shoes, I realized just how cold it was running through the frosty grass to bring the cows up, so it was wonderful to be able to jump on the spot where the cow had been lying and warm my cold feet!

If I was lucky enough to get a cow to stand still, I hopped on and got a ride back to the barn. It helped with the cold feet but believe me, its not all that much fun. They have a long sharp backbone and if you ride a cow very far, before long, it hurts so bad you can hardly catch your breath. If she tries to run to catch up with the rest of the herd, you're better off to fall on a rock—that won't hurt as much. You have to decide where you'd like your bruises.

I was not very old when I started milking cows. At milking time I would go to the dairy and get a milk bucket. The bucket was a special one. The top was made much like the bottom with the exception that there was a half round hole cut out of the top, about a quarter of the size of the whole top. This way

91

the milk could go in the bucket, keeping the dirt out at the same time. Well, at least I had a better chance of something not falling into my milk. But then there was the problem of hitting that hole . . . .

I'd carry the bucket to the barn and let the cows into the stable. Each one knew her stall. They would stick their heads though the stanchions and start eating. I'd close each stanchion to catch the cow's head so she couldn't back out while I was milking.

Then I'd take a rag with a solution of warm water and dairy disinfectant and wash their udders. This was important for health reasons. Our cows were checked over daily, and once a year the veterinarian would come to give shots and inoculations.

I'd sit on a three-legged stool to milk the cows. A three-legged stool would more readily sit in a good position under the cow, because you could get it level in the stall on the straw easier than you could with a four-legged stool. A four-legged stool was more apt to upset.

During fly season, I'd spray the cows. We had a hand pump sprayer that worked just fine. I'd sit on the milk stool, grab the end of the cow's tail and open up my left leg, put her tail behind my knee, and close it again. It didn't take me long to learn this trick, for when the flies started bothering her, she was ready to start swatting. That would mean that her tail would come around in my face. Boy that was nasty stuff! Those cows had a fly swatter that really worked.

Sometimes a cow might be a kicker. If one of those big horseflies started buzzing around and biting her on the belly and she couldn't get her tail loose, she would knock the bucket over or put her foot in it, trying to get at that fly. Sometimes I could pull it right out, and then another time, I might have to ask Dad for help. If she got her foot in the bucket, then I had to waste that milk, re-wash the bucket and start all over.

In the spring, if the cows were turned out on pasture, we had to be careful. The spring grasses often contain garlic, and a cow eating it will flavor the milk with garlic. Milk or butter that tastes like garlic is most undesirable. We'd hold them up in the barnyard until it was safe to turn them out. They were not happy campers about this. But what was worse? Their eating the garlic in the meadow could give them the scours. And then, when that tail got full of manure, look out! If you're sitting on that milking stool and the tail hits you in the face, it not only hurts, it tastes bad.

My brother Richard worked on the farm with the rest of the men. He was well-respected there for one thing: being the best butter maker. He just seemed to have a knack for it. Sometimes Richard would make me help just so he would have somebody to boss around in the dairy for a while. Making 30 to 50 pounds of butter a week, we'd form butterballs for the manor house by using two paddles to shape them and then dropping the butterballs in ice water. Using two wooden butter mold prints: one for a half-pound and the other for a pound, we'd squeeze the butter through the molds onto waxy butter paper. The designs on the prints were flowers. Everybody always told him how good his butter was. Maybe we should have called him "Butterball."

Mostly I worked on the lawn at the manor house. It was not

only the largest private home in Maryland, but it seemed to have the largest lawn in the world, complete with sticks, leaves, limbs and all other debris for me to pick up. It felt like I never got done—and I didn't!

Then there were some days that I didn't work too hard. At that time I had an Irish Setter named Reds. She was a family dog, everybody's friend. I would take her up to the lawn and sometimes we would play when I got tired of picking up sticks. After school started, she spent her day in the field with the farmhands, but they always knew when it was 4:00 p.m. because she would leave the field to meet us at the bus stop. The farmhands would say, "There she goes. It must be close to 4:00." She was their clock. She never missed a day.

Ol' Reds was well aged when he got paralyzed. My father saw that she was pulling herself with her front legs and dragging her back legs to get to the bus stop to meet us. My father tied her and that evening he called the veterinarian across the street, Dr. Stewart, to come take a look at her. He said she was paralyzed, that there was no help for her, and the most humane thing to do was to put her to sleep.

Beefin' It Up!

In the spring, my grandmother would purchase a young bull, generally around two-years old, which is just old enough for service. After the bull had sired all my grandmother's cows, she had him castrated. Now as a steer, he grazed with the cows in the pasture until late fall. Grandmother penned him up in a box stall in the barn and grained him good until sometime during the full part of winter. He'd get a thick layer of fat from that grain and be ready for slaughter. This was a common practice among country people. It was considered "a penny saved is a penny earned."

94

One time Dad butchered a steer for Grandma and found his lost gold pocket watch among other strange remnants of wire, nails and so on. A bovine has four stomachs and one of them is for collecting foreign objects that are accidentally swallowed. The stored items will remain in the cow for life. How did it get there? Maybe he dropped it while making hay, possibly it got picked up and hauled to the barn and fed along with the hay without anybody seeing it.

The steer was butchered and hung in the wagon shed to cool out. The wagon shed had a roof and was closed in on three sides. The corncrib was on the far side and the barn on the near side. With rope and pulleys put together (called block and fall), the butchers hooked a horse to the pulling end of the rope and hoisted the two halves of beef up close to the rafters. Each side was hoisted one at a time and left there for about a week to cool. You had to make sure that this wasn't near the same place that the pigeons were going to roost. The steer weighed anywhere from 1400 to 1800 pounds live weight and was close to three years old or so. The ideal weight was 1600 pounds. Anything less was not good finished aged beef.

Some people did not have room under cover to put their beef. They hung the beef on a tree limb high enough to be out of reach of the dogs and wild animals. I've seen beef hanging from a tree limb in the front yard next to the entrance of the house, simply because that was the only tree around with a limb large enough to withstand all that weight.

One time we had a dwarf steer on the farm that just would not grow. Dad asked Mrs. Wheelwright what to do with it, since it wouldn't bring a good market price. In response to Mrs. Wheelwright's query whether this dwarf steer would be edible, Dad stated that it would make good beef. Mrs. Wheelwright wasn't finicky about what happened to the steer. She thought that it might be fitting to divide it among the families living on the farm.

It was late fall when we butchered this three-year-old steer weighing only several hundred pounds. The seed house that stood just behind the gardener's house was empty that time of the year. This was in the days before the luxury of refrigeration. The steer was quartered and put in the seed house to cool out. Cool out it did—the temperature dipped down to freezing and stayed there.

The families on the farm were ready for some fresh beef and didn't want to wait any longer. Dad decided that he would leave his meat cleaver in the seed house and whoever wanted a piece of meat could cut off a hunk. Mom would give me a pan and send me to the seed house to chop off a chunk of beef in whatever portion she wanted for supper. That turned out to be some kind of superb beef. I think it must have been my meat whacking ability that made it so good. Dad would say, "I have never seen meat cut like this before."

By the end of the 1940's the term "aged beef" had made an unnoticeable change in meaning from a mature animal to the length of time refrigerated. The beef no longer had to be full grown and weighed in at only 1,000 pounds. This was done by force-feeding in dry lots (a fenced area with no grass). The beef was then slaughtered at half the age. The term "baby beef" (meaning small in size) was inherited. Big steers were on the way out. Others apparently realized what good beef a small steer would make.

Education 1942

My family and I were living in the house at the back of Twiford Farm when I started to school. In September 1942, my mother enrolled me in Pikesville Elementary School. It was a small school with less than 150 students in first through seventh grades. Mom had gotten me some new school clothes and I forgot to put on my undershirt and socks. Mom checked me over pretty well that first day and then said, "I declare Jimmy, get back upstairs and put on your undershirt and socks. Don't be wearing shoes without socks when you are going to school. You can't be going to school looking like a rag-picker." I went to our bedroom and did what I was told, came back down, grabbed my lunch and ran to catch up with my brother and sister.

I walked about a mile or so to meet the school bus with my older brother and sister. On very cold or hard rainy days, Dad would drive us to the bus stop. This area of Greenspring Avenue and Hillside Road was known as Rogers Station. Back in the thirties, Dad would put butter, milk, eggs, and the like on the train at this same station and send it to Mr. Whitridge's winter home in Baltimore.

There was a wood stove in the station and when the train came through, the conductor would get off and put more wood in the stove to keep the fire going. It was important to keep the fire going just in case some passengers or cargo would have to wait for the next train. Sometimes while waiting, passengers or locals would help keep the fire going. The station had burned down by the time I was old enough to start school. It was suspected that a passenger, while waiting for the train, filled the stove with wood and opened the damper. Then when the train arrived, the passenger boarded the train, forgetting about the fire. It grew out of control and the station burned down.

The train was still running when I was young. One day my friend Walter Dorsey placed a penny on the track and we waited for the train. After the train had passed, he picked it up. It was so flat that you could not read or see any inscriptions on it. Walter told me that this would be a lucky penny. (It wasn't lucky for the penny!)

This was during the Second World War, and the battles were in full swing. Gasoline was in short supply and most people needed gas stamps to buy gas for their cars. Farmers were the exception, in that they were allowed to have all the gas they needed for running their tractors. A ration officer would come around and count the number of tractors on the farm and compare that against the number of stamps being used. This government ration officer was often referred to by some of the local people in his district as the dumbest donkey of the neighborhood. There were always problems with the number of stamps and how much gasoline we and all our neighbors were allowed to get.

Frequently my father walked the half-mile each way to the barns from where we lived behind the farm headquarters to get to work. He let the car sit in order to save gas so it was a real treat when we got a ride to the bus stop. It had to be a heavy, steady rain before we got a ride.

The only bus for the whole school was kept in the white clapboard shed next to the schoolhouse. This shed was made just large enough for the bus and was never locked. Mr. Crouch was the only driver, and he was always right on time. The bus ran only one route, though several years later there were two routes, known as the early bus and the late. We rode the early bus.

In the winter it was better than dark as we left the house. We walked along the edge of the woods, and I could hear the

98

rustling of the crows and the dropping of dead branches as they moved about on their roost. Then we crossed over the road and into an open field past Mr. Wheelwright's exclusive shooting trap, which was made of red clay bricks and was a more prominent construction than most modern-day commercial shooting traps.

As we continued, we passed by the Manor House, walked between the farm buildings, on to a back road that led down over a hill to where there were beautiful rounded cut rocks laid in two elegant entrance pillars that stood there very stately on either side of the road. A big heavy chain was anchored into each pillar. I jumped the chain onto Greenspring Avenue and took a short jog on a hard-surfaced road to Hillside Road. After a full day at school, it would be "purty" dark by the time we got home. Later our route was cut in half after we moved into the farm manager's house by the barns.

Richard and I were fur trappers. We'd lay a trap line in the evening. The next morning we would get up early and check the trap line before going to school. This was popular among most country boys in order to get a little extra money. One morning, along with some foxes and a 'possum, we caught a polecat (also known as a skunk). My older brother didn't take the necessary precautions when dealing with the polecat, leaving himself wide open to get a good spray from his bomb. His vanity instantly changed. The stench was awful!

When we got home, Mother was most unhappy about our successful trapping. Richard was told to get out of those clothes. He didn't have to go to school that day but stayed home and took baths. The next day Mom covered him with Sloan's Liniment and sent him back to school. The teacher said that she didn't know if the liniment was a better smell than the skunk or not.

We skinned our hides out and put them on homemade stretchers (a wide board with a v-cut at the top). We'd pull the hide over the stretcher with the hair inward and salt them down. I suppose there will be readers who think this was barbaric but it was fitting for the times. About twice a year, Dad would take our hides to Merle Devilbliss, a dealer in Taneytown. However, if we could get a better price for our hides in Hanover, we'd go there instead.

Trapping wasn't the only way for a kid to make a little extra money. A school friend of mine was proud to tell me that his momma told him he was the "Number One Bootblack" in Pikesville. The only means of getting his lunch money for the week was by working after school and on Saturdays shining shoes. I preferred trapping although it was a little harder work and I had to wait for Dad to find time to take our hides to market before getting paid, but if the price was up, it was well worth the wait.

I remember seeing my good friend and neighbor, Sonny Biddison, in the first year at school. His father was a storekeeper in the neighborhood. At lunchtime we'd swap lunches. He always carried tuna fish or baloney and mayonnaise sandwiches and a Kooster pie. I brought country ham, home-cured bacon or scrapple sandwiches with some butter that was made there on the farm. Some days I carried a cold fried egg sandwich. You had to be really careful when you bit into the yolk so you didn't make a mess on your pants. I don't ever remember having peanut butter and jelly sandwiches like a lot of kids have today. Whatever was plentiful on the farm was what we carried in our lunches. I thought Sonny's lunch was the best and he thought mine was; we had great times.

Our dentist worked out of his home across the street from my school and down four blocks past the Pikesville Fire

Department. One afternoon after school was out, I was supposed to go to the dentist for a checkup. As I was walking past the firehouse, I slowed down and looked in the open door. While looking at the trucks, I spotted a dog, named Sparky, lying on a mat in front of the coat rack. I asked if Sparky rode the fire truck. The fireman replied, "Oh yes, he rides between the driver and the bell clapper."

Then one of the firemen asked me if I'd like to come in. I just shrugged my shoulders and said, "I don't know." He knew I really wanted to come in to see the trucks. I was a do-gooder and too shy to say yes. He said, waving his hand "Come on in." I did, and he showed me all around. Then he asked if I would like to see upstairs where the firemen on duty sleep at night. So we went upstairs and looked around. He told me about fires and how the men jump out of bed into their boots, pull up their fire pants, flip their suspenders over each shoulder and jump on the brass pole to slide down to the fire truck. I thought that was neat.

They asked me if I would like to slide down the pole. Sure I would. The fireman upstairs yelled to the fireman downstairs, "Man on the pole." I felt like a big guy. He helped me to reach the pole by holding me around the waist. Then the fireman downstairs caught me as I reached the bottom. What a nice treat! I was having so much fun that I completely forgot about the dentist.

I got to the dentist and who was there before me, but my mother. I must have fooled around for over an hour. She was not happy about my visit at the firehouse. Mom said that she was worried about me, and if I didn't start listening better I would surely put her into an early grave. I didn't want to be responsible for anything like that. (Mom lived to be 86 years old, so I guess I must have really straightened up.) Dr. Piven, a young man who understood small boys, laughed about it. He was just starting up his practice and didn't have very many patients yet. He took me right away. After I was finished, he gave me a pack of Dentyne gum, which I was happy to share with Mom.

I was in the second grade when Franklin Roosevelt died on April 12, 1945, before he finished his fourth term as President of the United States. He was well liked by many people. President Roosevelt used to say, "I want to see a chicken in every pot!" I figured it was going to take him a while to check out all those pots, and now it was a shame that he'd died before he finished.

I had to repeat the second grade because I couldn't master the alphabet. Many times Mom was at school talking to the teacher about me and my trouble with schoolwork. My parents began to get more and more concerned, thinking that there was a deeper problem. My teacher kept saying that it's okay because lots of boys have trouble with so many new things coming to them at one time. She told my folks not to worry, that I would be all right.

In the third grade I was not doing any better, so by mid-year my mother knew I was going to have to repeat that grade too. She talked to the Baltimore County Supervisor, Mrs. Eckhardt, about my being in the third grade and still being unable to learn the alphabet, as well as having difficulty with syntax. After a lot of talking and meetings and testing me, nothing was happening. By the time Mom got all these things taken care of, she was on a first-name basis with Mrs. Eckhardt and all the educational specialists in Baltimore County.

To excuse themselves in the situation, the teachers who met with us were trying to convince Mom that I was not ready to start to school (when I was already in the third grade) and that I was too immature. They went on to say that I was lazy and

that I would not try; that I was trying to be a funny man by repeating things backwards just to get a laugh. Mrs. Draper continued by telling everyone, "Yesterday, I asked Jimmy to come to the blackboard and print the lower case letter h. He was thinking about what to do." I said, "Jimmy, remember how to make a lower case l and an n; then just put them together."

Jimmy and Marvin

Naturally…to me, I put the n, then the l in my attempt to print the h, but it came out nl—which was backwards. As I stepped back to show the teacher, I heard the whole class giggling and snickering, which didn't add any to my ego. I was so embarrassed that I laughed too.

Thinking that I was purposefully being funny, the teacher angrily sent me to my seat, where I laid my hands out on top of my desk and patiently waited for my good morning smack with the yardstick on the knuckles. By the way, yardsticks back in the 40's were made out of oak and a lot harder and a lot heavier than today's light balsam wood. On hearing this story, Mom asked, "Jimmy, did you do that?" I said, "Yes Mother, I did, but I didn't mean to, it just happened."

There were whispers cropping up around the table, and I was getting a little fidgety. Finally Mrs. Eckhardt suggested that perhaps a private tutor would help, though they were not any too plentiful in those times. Mom made a few phones calls and spoke to Mrs. Offutt. She was one of the headmistresses and English teachers for The Garrison Forest School, a well-known private girls school in Green Spring Valley. Mom thought she had a better chance of finding a tutor there, and sure enough, Mrs. Offutt knew of a part-time teacher who had helped a pupil with a reading problem. Mrs. Eckhardt called and checked out her credentials and skills and they met with her approval.

I was introduced to Mrs. Annin, a qualified tutor for readers. We were a perfect match for each other; she was from way South with a slight drawl and in no particular hurry, and I was the little country boy from way out in the country who wanted to learn how to read and couldn't. She knew at a glance that I was a country boy. I never had much desire to be something different. I don't know if she ever noticed it or not, but I was proud of it. The way I figure it, God dropped me in these boots and this is who I am.

After going to public school in the morning, I walked over a mile to Mrs. Annin's house. I worked there and then hurried back to school to catch the bus. I really got my exercise in for the day. That year I passed to the fourth grade with good marks . . . for me. It took a lot of extra effort.

Back then teachers didn't know specifically how to help their students with dyslexic problems. Nobody'd ever heard of dyslexia. After several weeks working with Mrs. Annin, things hadn't improved for me. However, Mrs. Annin started to get a good feel about the problem She told me, "Jimmy, I believe you're reading from right to left and that's why your sentences are reversed. You really aren't trying to be a funny man— you're reading the sentence backwards word for word and in some instances letter for letter." One afternoon she said, "Jimmy, let's try something." We took a blank piece of paper and I held it under each line, then I used my finger on top of the paper to point out each word and studied it in depth. She said, "We're in no hurry. If we read one line today successfully, then tomorrow we will read the next. We needn't hurry." She had the patience of Job.

"Now Jimmy," she said, "take your time, read each word carefully, be sure to stop and listen to hear it clearly, then read the next word until we finish this line." Reading the word clearly made a difference. Sometimes, because I was reversing my letters, I tried to make the sound out of a word that was not a word at all. "Now move the blank paper down one line and read that." Sure enough my eyes didn't move back to the beginning of the line. They automatically wanted to start on the right side instead of going to the left of the page. Many years later a doctor told me that your eyes are the windows to your brain. There are mirrors in the brain and one of those mirrors is not reflecting back; that's why it is getting reversed. This was his explanation in layman's terms.

Not knowing anything about dyslexia, Mrs. Annin had the instinct to know that I had a very short attention span and after a few lines we took a break, worked on arithmetic for ten to fifteen minutes and then back to reading another few lines; took another break, did some spelling, then back to reading and so on, until I was able to do a whole paragraph, then a page, and so on.

This training exercise continued with the paper for many months. After that I used my pointer finger to keep on track without the blank paper. Mrs. Annin bought me a little book on Indians. After I read it aloud to her, she gave me the book to keep, which I read over and over. What a great reward to have that wonderful feeling of finishing my first book. I was so proud. Mrs. Annin said, "Let's only read fun stuff!" Her secret was to keep me reading as much as possible to train my eyes and brain to read left to right. Without a doubt, she must have been at the top of her child psychology class.

Three days a week for two hours a day, twelve months a year for three years, I labored to learn how to read and write. All the while my friends took off for summer vacations, spring breaks and Christmas holidays, but I continued to study. Do I have any regrets? HEAVENS NO! I don't read aloud very well, and I read very slowly, but with concentration, I can read. Today, only when I'm tired and trying to finish a chapter in an enjoyable book will my eyes land on the right side of the page. When writing, I still have to go back and untangle the words in a sentence that have become reversed, or the thoughts in a paragraph that have jumped ahead of themselves.

In the summertime I continued with my tutor two hours a day, five days a week, just to keep up with the other kids. Things were beginning to look up with all the help from my tutor and the extra study time; I was just making it, but did pass to the fifth grade without sore knuckles.

These tutoring sessions started to lay a little foundation as I continued to buck along over a number of rough roads. Mrs. Eckhardt was at school to see me and talk to my teacher at least once a week.

I remember one day during the middle of harvest season, my father was supposed to pick me up after my session with Mrs. Annin. He was at least two hours late and lunchtime had been long gone. Mrs. Annin said, "Your father hasn't arrived. Can you eat a piece of my homemade apple pie?" as she handed it to me. This was back in the day before they ever realized that you can get more than four slices out of a pie. I told her, "There ain't nothin' I can't eat!" She seriously said, "Jimmy, there isn't anything I can not eat!" I said, "Yes ma'am, me either." She gave a nice sociable laugh and said, "I was hoping you might enjoy it." Mrs. Annin had misconstrued the aim of my remark; in a country-like manner, and of course right off, I didn't hesitate to thank her and tell her how good it was. I didn't see any use in embarrassing her or myself by making a point out of the fact that I was as hungry as a bear. Then she announced, "Oh, here is your father now." She laughed about the pie some more and waved good-bye, saying that she would see me on Wednesday.

I was learning a great deal in the public school through eyes and ears, but because of the difficulty in my reading and writing they had no way of testing me to see what I had learned. Today, lucky students no longer have to go through that treacherous finger-smacking ordeal. Now kids are given the option of oral testing that wasn't available to me.

It wasn't until our youngest son started to school (I was then 46) that I learned about the word dyslexic. It was David's misfortune to have inherited that from me. Dave was tested and today they have ample help for dyslexic kids in the public schools. He even graduated from Westwood College in Colorado with a degree in Graphic Design.

No provisions were made to help children who had any learning difficulties during my schooling. I knew some kids that just dropped out. Today there's an abundance of books written on every level that any kid can learn to read and enjoy. I have found that teachers today are well-informed about dyslexia and reversal reading. As elementary as it might seem, using the alphabet is still my most troublesome task.

I guess my parents must have felt that I was feeling a little futile in school, so they wanted me to join the Cub Scouts. Watty Wheelwright was teasing me about being a big Cub Scout and asked me what we did. I told him that this week I was supposed to bring something in for show and tell. He said, "Jim-Bo, I have an idea." He went home and came back with some nice 10" x 12" photos of fighter planes. He said that I could have them and explained to me what they were. It was the perfect show and tell at the perfect time, when everybody seemed to be talking about World War II, and the kids were interested in all the modern things like ships, planes and canons.

This was my second Cub Scout meeting. My show and tell went very well. All the kids liked my photos. After the meeting, we had refreshments. When I laid my photos down so I could have some cookies and juice, someone picked up my pictures and kept them. I told the Scoutmaster what had happened and that I wanted them back. They were never returned to me, and I never returned to Cub Scouts.

Watty's favorite trick at that time was to walk up behind you, and then with his right hand, pat you once on the back; then using his left hand, pat you once on the chest; followed by quickly tapping you on the top of the head with his right hand; and as he did this, he would be saying, "Glad to see you're back from the front, old top!" Then he would laugh.

During the war, patriotism was high. There were posters everywhere of Uncle Sam in his high hat dressed in red, white and blue with stars and stripes, pointing his finger and saying, "I need you!" One sunny Saturday morning, Mom was going in the station wagon to Pikesville to pick up some things. She asked Watty, Billy Whittridge, me and my siblings if we wanted to go. We all piled in and arrived in Pikesville safe enough. Since I was the youngest and the one who always helped Mom carry things, she told me I had to go with her and the rest would meet back at the car in an hour.

This pack of kids let Pikesville know that they had arrived in town. They were first in one store, then another. Watty, Billy and Richard wound up in the Five & Dime Store. Watty saw a set of American Flags for his bike with a little bracket and a thumbscrew to hold it on the handlebars. There was a large flag in the middle and two smaller ones on each side, with two smaller ones yet on either side of them. Watty didn't have any money, which was nothing new for us kids, so he picked it up and stuck it inside his shirt. We got home and Richard told Mom that Watty snitched the flag for his bike.

Watty was riding around on his bike making a breeze so the flags would wave. Mom called him in on the porch so she could speak to him alone. I ran around the house creeping up close to the porch to find out what the big secret was all about. Mom said, "Watty, the lady who works in the Pikesville Five & Dime Store just called me and said that you took those flags without paying for them. Don't you ever pull a trick like that again or I'm going to tell your mother." "Oh, Mrs. Fox, don't tell Martha," Watty pleaded, referring to his mother as Martha. He said, "You can pull my hair, kick me, but don't tell Martha!" Mom said, "Watty, you should be ashamed of yourself! The idea of you doing something like that!" "Oh I am, Mrs. Fox, I am! I am ashamed!" Watty exclaimed. He was a character, but all heart.

Hunting and Other Country Sports

Hunting was a favorite sport of many country boys both old and young. Coon hunting was my first experience with hunting. I wasn't yet 10 years old in 1945 when I was invited to go on my first hunt.

Mr. Harry Keller asked me if I would like to go with him. I was allowed to invite all the friends I wanted. He said, "The more the merrier. Tell them to dress warm with hats, gloves and galoshes." I was pleased and excited to be asked to go on a coon hunt. We all met at my house after dark.

Before I continue on this first coon hunt story of mine, here's some history and background on coon hunting.

Mr. Keller used four dogs. One was a cold tracer. He was used for scouting around to see where the coon had been early on in the evening. Then after he made a strike (that means to pick up the scent where the coon had been), he signaled by giving an occasional choppy short bark. The remainder of the dogs followed.

The barks are different when dogs are cold tracking. They give single, delayed howls and keep on tracking. If they lose the trail, they stop barking altogether until the scent gets hotter (closer to the coon). If the dog goes the wrong way, that's known as backtracking. It usually doesn't take a good dog long before he realizes it.

Then there was the hot tracker. This dog had a faster, more rapid bark, showing a lot of enthusiasm. The howls were closer together until you could hear one howl after another, coming louder and faster the hotter the scent. Then all the rest of the dogs followed the hot tracker and the race was on, with each dog wanting to be the first to get to the coon. Each dog tried to outrun the other, barking louder than the rest of the pack.

A tree dog was needed next. That is a dog that is trained to stay by the tree no matter what and keep barking. He stood by the tree with his front feet up on the tree and did not stop barking until the coon was on the ground or the handler pulled him away.

Sometimes it could take hours before the handler got there: crawling through the underbrush, going around marshland, looking for a low part of the stream to cross during the middle of the night, following the sound of the barking dog. If that dog stopped barking, you might never find the tree with the coon in it. I have seen dogs stand there for hours barking with saliva drooling down to the ground, waiting for someone to come get the coon.

Sometimes a dog is so eager to get to the coon that he will try to climb the tree. I've been told that a good tree dog would stay there all night. That doesn't mean that the only thing a coon will climb is a tree. One time we ran a coon into a nearby resident's garage. This was a good neighbor that everybody called Uncle Louie. It was late at night, and with four or five dogs barking not more than 50 feet from his bedroom window, he didn't know what to think. But when he appeared on his front porch with his 12-gauge double-barrel shotgun ready to fire, we couldn't explain what we were doing fast enough. Well, with all that excitement and the hollering over the dogs barking, the coon slipped away through a hole in the back of the garage.

There is also the kill dog that is usually the biggest and the strongest. It's important that all the dogs work together. You can tell by the bark what dog it is and what it's doing: whether he's a cold-track dog, with barks short and delayed; a hot-track dog, where the yodel picks up the tempo; a tree dog, where the monotone bark is persistent; or a kill dog, with its aggressive sounds. If you are within hearing distance, you know what your dog is doing and where the coon is.

There are many different breeds of hounds. In my area of the country, the Walker Dog, Blue Tick, Red Bone, and my favorite, the ole black and tan Coonhound, were the most popular. Names for these hard working dogs are not always endearing. If the dog is a Blue Tick, then there is a good chance that he or she will be named Ole Blue. A Red Bone will

111

be named Ole Red, unless he is missing a tail or part of an ear or leg, then he would be called Stubby, Shorty or Hoppy. If he barked a lot, he may be called Rattler. These dogs didn't have romantic names to them at all. They were named for their purpose. Big prices are paid for these dogs. If the dog has won the title of "Night Champ" (achieved at a coonhound competition), its value could easily be several thousand dollars.

Sometimes more than one hunter would get together and use eight to ten dogs in the same pack. They needed to watch that the dogs didn't get jealous and fight with each other. Then on the other hand, I've heard of people taking only one dog out. I don't know how many coons they caught, but I guess they felt that their dog could do it all, and I do believe that there are some dogs that can.

Coons are rather intelligent, and they like to play annoying pranks on the pack. They'll cross over streams to get dogs off their trail. If that doesn't do it, the coon will go back to the stream and swim down a ways further and then get back out. While on a hunt on Eastern Shore, one of Mr. Keller's dogs chased an older more experienced coon into a river. The dog jumped in and swam out to get the coon, but the coon circled around behind the dog and before the dog realized how close the coon was, the coon had climbed up on the dog's back and sat on his head. Mr. Keller said, "That darn coon is trying to drown my dog!" The dog was working furiously to stay up. The water was ice cold, but Mr. Keller didn't care. He ran right out into the water and waded in up to his chest to get that coon off his dog. The dog was a little shook up to say the least (and so was Mr. Keller), but it didn't break his spirit: he was still ready to go.

Using another popular trick, the coon will climb several feet up the tree trunk and then jump far out on the ground and take off running again. When in a pine grove he will climb up one tree, find a good limb and crawl to the next tree. Then he'll go back down to the ground without even stopping. This can fool the smartest dog. I guess this is where the old saying came from, "You are barking up the wrong tree." A lot of tree dens are located along streams. Sometimes the hole to a good den will be at the trunk, with part of it hanging out over the water. That makes it easy for "Mr. Coon" to swim in the stream and then escape right into his house without the dogs sensing where the coon went.

I'm not sure why, but coons don't come out to feed during a full moon. Rather, they will simply lie in their den with their head hanging out the hole looking at the moon. The hunting season starts in the fall, around September. Although at that time their young are about half grown and able to care for themselves, they stay with their mother until breeding season. When a pack of dogs strikes a she coon with four or five little ones, it would be obvious that they would give the dogs a fit with many tracks running in all directions.

It is difficult to hunt coons with leaves still on a tree, because a coon is hard to find in the top of a tree that is full of leaves. Coons will lie in the crotch of the tree, and among the leaves and shadows, they're very hard to pick out. I had a five-cell flashlight that gave off a strong beam and it was still hard to find the coon. Sometimes you could only see two shining eyes staring at you. Animals in the dark will mostly look toward a light. If there's snow on the ground, dogs are unable to follow the scent, so all conditions have to be just right for a successful hunt.

On my first coon hunt, we left my house at dark, around 6:00 or 6:30 p.m. and headed for the woods. It wasn't very long before the dogs caught the scent of a coon. Mr. Keller said, "That's Ole Blue tonguing now." Then the rest of the dogs started to follow and he said, "They're off!" We had about a four- or five-mile chase. It was pitch dark. We all had flashlights except Mr. Keller, who carried a lantern which gave off more light than a flashlight.

It was a clear, cold, crisp evening. As we crossed over our neighbor's meadow, I could hear the frosty grass crunching beneath my feet. I could feel the stillness of the night as we reached the woods. After a hearty chase, the coons arrived at what turned out to be a den tree. If a coon reaches his den in time, then he is usually safe. So we had to leave them there. Oh well, sometimes that happens.

Well, it was around 9:00 p.m. by now. The five-mile chase took close to three hours. We all had worked up an appetite, and much to our surprise, Mr. Keller pulled a thermos, hot dogs and rolls out of that big hunting coat. We all gathered sticks and cleared off a spot in the middle of the trail, sat around the fire, and roasted hot dogs. What a wonderful treat for my first hunt! We didn't catch any coons, but I caught a pleasant memory.

Mr. Keller was an elderly man. I continued hunting with him for over a decade whenever he felt up to it. He had a son, Louie, who was 15 years older than me. I also went hunting with Louie numerous times until the fall of 1995. Louie is a delightful person who had a fondness for the woods. During hunting season, he went out hunting every night with or without any company from the human race. He continuously and consistently had good dogs, and in his more recent years was the noble owner of a reliable mule. Mules are noted for their sure-footedness. Their eyes are set out further on the sides of their heads than a horse, which enables them to see their hind feet. They know where their feet are at all times. They can see quite well at night. In the dark woods this is very important.

114

Louie rides the mule through the woods during the hunts. He carries his dogs in a dog box on his pickup truck. Before he leaves home, he saddles his mule and leads him to the truck. Then he tells the mule, "Up, up." And the mule jumps up into the bed of the truck and rides to the hunting grounds. Then Louie tells the mule, "Come on, get out, we're here." The mule jumps off the truck and is ready to go on the hunt. Louie says he has walked so much during his lifetime that he has had two hip replacements, so now he needs the mule to continue his coon hunting.

I don't remember how my family ever came by a baby coon, but I do remember bottle-feeding him with one of my sister's play baby bottles. Perhaps Dad took a den tree down by mistake. We raised the baby in the house against my mother's better judgment. He was so cute and cuddly. He didn't have a mother, so he was allowed to stay with us. He ran all around the house, hid in the darnedest places and climbed on top of the couch. He followed me to the barn and climbed on the rafters in the hay mound. If he was left outside, he clawed at the screen door to let us know he wanted to come in. (Mother really thought that was cute!) Someone would open the door (but not Mother!), and he came in and made himself at home. He was used to jumping up on my lap and being fed. It was funny when he got hungry: he'd come running as hard as he could and jump up on my lap to get fed.

Early one morning, we were having breakfast. Mom was sitting at the table in her faded cotton gown, when this little guy got hungry. He came running into the kitchen and took a nosedive for Mom's lap. She didn't hear him coming, but suddenly felt that little ball of fur on her bare legs. With an ear-splitting war hoop, she jumped up from the table: sausage, pancakes, coffee and juice flew all over the place! I want to tell you partner, we all thought she'd really lost it and we were in BIG trouble. She was standing there shaking, asking, "What

115

was that?" When we saw how frightened the little coon was, we all knew what had happened.

I think Mom did hold a grudge, for we had to build a pen to keep the baby coon in outside, and after that, he was never allowed inside again. He was bigger by then, so that was okay. He liked living around people and got along with the dogs. We would leave his door open all day and shut it at night. By the time he was full-grown, we left it open all the time. Late that fall he started not coming home at night. After some time he stayed away for a week or so, until finally he didn't return at all. I really enjoyed him while it lasted, but he was born wild and I wished him the best.

One time we raised an opossum in a cage in the brooder house. He was a nice pet and didn't bite or claw you, but he didn't have any personality at all. The only thing he liked to do was curl his tail around your finger and hang upside-down. I could walk around with an opossum hanging upside down on my finger. That's not a bunch of fun. Besides it's a little hard on the finger. The older he got, the stronger the odor he had. By the time he was full grown, Dad said he must go. I wasn't too disappointed. We took him to the woods and released him.

The old saying of playing opossum (meaning playing dead) is a myth. I've got to tell you that that's not the way it is: he ain't playin'. As soon as an opossum senses danger, he gets so scared that he actually faints completely. He passes out from pure fright and remains unconscious for some time. If his predator is still around when he comes to, he actually collapses again.

My friend Louie was a contented owner of a greyhound dog. Some of Louie's pals had suggested that he enter his dog in the Valley Inn Races and knowing that his dog was exceptionally fast, he entered him. This dog could outrun any rabbit in Baltimore County.

Louie had a plan. He told his dog to sit, and after backing away several hundred feet with a hot dog in his hand, he called the dog. That greyhound wanted that hot dog bad, so this was the training exercise plan for the race. Race day came and Louie was ready. He backed the dog into the cage on the starting line —and gave him the first half of the hot dog! Then, Louie walked down to the finish line with the other half of the hot dog in his pocket. The shot was fired in the air. All the dogs took off except Louie's. His dog just sat there in the cage at the starting line. (I guess he was content with the first half of the hot dog!) The dogs were supposed to make one complete circle and then go to the finish line. After all the other dogs completed the circle, Louie's dog saw the rabbit and came out of the cage. He ran past all the other dogs, grabbed the rabbit and started chewing the wooden ears off. Mr. Hatfield, owner of the Valley Inn and coordinator of the race, got rather upset (to say the least!) and told Louie he had to pay for a new rabbit and never to bring that dog back there again.

Christmas 1946

I didn't know my Grandfather (Charles Henry), but one of his sayings was, "Being poor is nothing to be ashamed of but mighty unhandy." I grew up realizing that, but it didn't make much difference. I was used to wearing hand-me-down clothes. It didn't matter much if they fit because I didn't have a choice. I guess sometimes the way I was dressed, I looked like a little slave of want.

My older brother had a second-hand bike that he had outgrown. Dad was good at fixing things up so, without me knowing about it, he took it in the shop and made repairs on

117

all those past wrecks. Then he finished it off by painting it with Farmall red tractor paint. This was my big and special Christmas present that year.

At first I didn't realize that it was Richard's old bike. The nice paint job was so good, I thought it was new. But after a better examination, I determined that it sure did match those old Farmall tractors. Then I asked Richard where his old bike was. He said, "Well, you have it!" I said, "Oh, good!" I didn't believe he wanted me to have it. I think Dad was unhappy about Richard being so blunt concerning the truth and so unwilling to share.

It was a warm Christmas that year, making it an easier one to remember with the unusual summer-like weather. I felt the weather was a present from God. It was a wonderful bike and I enjoyed many happy hours on it. I can remember riding my bike in short sleeves I was so proud to have my own bike. I parked it next to the front step of the house so I could keep an eye on it at all times, just to make sure that my older brother didn't try to sneak a ride without my permission. So along with my Red Ryder BB gun, which I had tied onto the side of my Farmall bike, it was a swell Christmas.

For me, I think getting ready for Christmas was half the fun. I enjoyed going to Pikesville with my father. There were two fruit stands, one at each end of town. At the first stop he bought oranges, tangerines and grapefruits. Dad thought this stand was the best for the type of fruit he was looking for. I asked if I could help to pick out the fruit. What fun I had! Dad stood around talking to the owner about the happenings in town and a lot of other unnecessary conversation.

Everywhere I looked there were wooden orange crates full of fruit. The owner gave me a pasteboard box and I chose the ones I wanted. Each one looked better than the other one. This was a special treat—the only time we had oranges. Most of the time the only fruit we got was grown on the farm.

The next stop was for nuts. This fruit stand was inside a temporary tent. Dad liked all kinds of nuts. I thought it was neat walking around in this big tent. He got pounds of English walnuts, pecans, almonds, hazel, butternuts and Brazil nuts. When we left there, Dad was carrying a big bag. We got home and Mom asked, "What are you going to do with all those nuts?" Dad replied, "Eat-em."

I liked Christmas shopping with my family. We went down to 33rd Street in Hampden. The first thing we did was go to the movies. There were two theaters: one always played westerns and the other played love stories. Mom and my sister Shirley would enjoy the love story. Naturally the guys would go see the western. The show always began with a newsreel on the screen. Usually the newsreel included President Truman talking about how everybody was helping out after the war in Europe and about the Iron Curtain, which made me wonder how they ever put a curtain all the way across Europe. It sure must have been hard to hang.

After the movies, we would meet at the Five and Dime Store up the street. It was a neat store with two floors. Downstairs was kitchen stuff and all the womanly things, like housewares, for Mom. Upstairs along the back wall, they had garden items, pitch forks, shovels, handtools and brooms. They had bobby pins and thimbles to men's overalls—anything you would want. If they didn't have it, it must have been considered a luxury because they sure had all the essentials!

Just before Christmas we took a trip to the Montgomery Wards store on Monroe Street in Baltimore. Mom placed her order through the catalogue that they sent us every year. Then all we had to do was ride to the store to pick up our order. This saved some time in her shopping. I think shopping in the catalogue was as much fun as going to the store. I could sit there going through that catalogue for hours just wishing for first one thing and then another. That's why it was called the wishbook.

When we first arrived at the store, we picked up our catalogue order and tried our clothes on. If everything fit, then we took off through the store for more shopping and wishing. Montgomery Wards on Monroe Street had many floors. This was the first place I ever saw an escalator. Boy, that was a lot of fun. We'd go up and down until Dad said, "How about waiting in the car?"

Right under the first-floor escalator was a candy stand. Dad let me and my brothers and sister each pick out one kind. It was loose candy in a large jar and the sales lady had a little scoop, which she used to get it out.

At Christmas Mom did most of the decorating in the house. She sent me to the woods to get crows' foot, pine branches with cones still attached, holly and greens. She placed it around the doorframes, fireplace mantle and everywhere. Dad cut our Christmas tree down from back in the woods. We all were excited and happy to help decorate the tree.

On Christmas morning, it was a long-standing tradition in my family to have oyster stew. We were allowed to open presents first, but then everybody had to eat oyster stew no matter if you liked it or not. When asked why, I was told that it was a family tradition and I would learn to like it. I asked who started it and nobody knew. Being Christmas and all, I thought everybody was in a good mood and I could push it a little, so I said,

120

"Then, I don't think you'd mind if I didn't have some."
"Wrong!" now heard from the head of the table. "Eat your stew and dry up!" That was Dad's way of saying stop talking. I didn't look up but ate every last bit. I've learned to enjoy oyster stew and continue the tradition.

After breakfast we all played with and looked at each other's presents until mid-morning. Then the phone would ring. Mrs. Wheelwright was inviting us all to come there so she could give us presents. Dad would tell the other tenant farmers that Mrs. Wheelwright had called, and it was time to go to the manor house for Christmas.

Mrs. Wheelwright always gave nice presents so everybody was delighted to go. I remember her giving me a Navy pea jacket along with a sweater to match. It was wonderful. She gave all the kids all kinds of candy. The one that I liked best was the money candy. Each child had a little bag full to take home. I thought it was so real looking. I played with it for days before I ate it..

The Christmas tree at the manor house was marvelous. It must have been 12 feet tall! Mrs. Wheelwright's tree decorations were spectacular. I was told that some of the balls were even hand painted. All the farmers had a hand in putting up the tree and decorating it for the season. A garden was under the tree with trains running in all directions at the same time. The largest set was a great big yellow American Flyer train and then there was a Lionel train set and other train sets. It was really neat and something I had never seen before.

That year Watty got an electric toy canon that shot ping pong balls. When we arrived, he was in full swing. He was pretending that the tree was the enemy and Watty was shooting those beautiful balls right off the tree! He asked me if I'd like to try.

I was very shy and didn't know if I should or not. After looking around and catching my father's eye, I knew that he thought I shouldn't do it. Not Watty though; he wasn't shy. He saw Dad look at me with that expression and he laughed and said, "It's okay, it's Christmas." By that time Mrs. Wheelwright had noticed what was going on and said, "Oh heavens, Fox, I think Watty has already ruined your tree." I made a few shots but found it really hard to shoot those beautiful balls, especially with my father watching.

We always had lots of people for dinner on Christmas Day. There was Mr. and Mrs. Rever, their two sons George and Billy, aunts, uncles, cousins—just a house full of relatives. Mr. Rever was a salesman for Stebbins Anderson's hardware store. He did a lot of business with Dad. He brought all kinds of stuff to make eggnog. Dad supplied the eggs and cream.

They used a large bowl and started with one dozen eggs, whipped them up until they were all foamy. Mr. Rever said, "Pour in a little cream, not too much, Russell." Then it was Mr. Rever's turn. "Well let's see here . . . a little rum maybe . . . just a little more . . . okay, a little rye whiskey . . . Well, Russell, what do you think?" All the time he just kept on pouring! "Now a little brandy . . . not too much and a little bourbon . . . " And then he said, "We might as well fill it to the top." Mom and Mrs. Rever would be saying, "You don't need all that."

There were so many people there that we had to eat in two or three shifts at the table. The kids always ate last, first because we liked playing more than eating; and second because after we were finished at the table, no one wanted to think about eating at the same place. Holidays were lots of fun.

We always had a turkey that we killed from the farm. Mother prepared oyster dressing, candied sweet potatoes, hot slaw and lots of other goodies. And of course there was homemade butter and homemade pies. Being a little less fortunate made our family a lot closer. We were all dependent on each other during the hard times.

No Bull

I joined the Baltimore County Boys' 4-H Club in 1946. My first project was to build a waterwheel to show how water could be turned into electricity. If it were not for my father, I think I'd still be working on it. After that, my projects were raising Aberdeen Angus steers.

We didn't have money to buy any livestock, so Mrs. Wheelwright let me pick out any steer that I wanted from her herd to raise for a 4-H project. In early spring I selected one. I weighed all the feed and kept a record book from the time I started until the time my steer was sold. We were able to borrow the farm truck to haul steers to the different shows and fairs throughout the county. Then we showed at the Maryland State Fair in September.

The last show was the Eastern National Livestock Show and Sale, at that time held annually in November. The largest meat packing companies from the Eastern region would be there to support the 4-H and FFA kids. Every year that I was in 4-H, Esskay Meat Packing Plant held a banquet free of charge in downtown Baltimore at their processing plant for all the members.

123

They sent school buses to pick us up. They gave us a tour of the plant, served us a wonderful dinner and had lots of speakers telling us what a great job we'd done with our projects. We supplied the top packers with the best beef that money could buy. They knew it and praised us for it. Some of the other packing plants represented were Corkhill, Heintz, Swift, and Armour.

After the sale we went over our record books and added up the profit. Mrs. Wheelwright told us that she felt that we had worked hard and that 100% of the profit was ours. The Wheelwrights kept a good bloodline of cattle to start with, which gave us good show steers to work with. We earned prize money as we were traveling from show to show, and offered to give that to Mrs. Wheelwright. Her reply was, "Heavens no!" So we got all the profit plus the show money. Without the generosity of Mrs. Wheelwright, we'd never have received so many pleasures of good country living.

Cider in a Corn Shock

Before hybrid corn was developed, most farmers checkered their corn. Checkering is a method of planting in a crisscross pattern, making it easier to cultivate. The first thing you need is a slow pair of gaited horses. The horses should have an even gait of about three miles an hour. Anything faster could drag over the hill of corn that was just planted. Then you'd find a continuous row of corn, not hills, just so far apart.

I never did checker corn, but I did use a John Deere No. 999L corn planter. The one I used had a head to hold the checker-

124

ing wire on a reel under the seat. The checkering wire was necessary to create straight rows of corn and to trip the planter to drop the corn. To lay out the wire, you staked one end down and put the rest of the reel on the head under the planter seat. There were many different types of planters, and they all worked differently.

This reel of wire had little loops every 18 inches called buttons. Every time the button passed through a guide under the planter, it hit a place called a striker. This tripped off a chain of reactions of sprockets and shafts going to where the plates were in the bottom of the corn hoppers. The plates we used dropped two kernels of corn to the hill. Some plates dropped up to six kernels.

Checkering corn was a skill not every one could master. It took a lot of hard work and planning how you were going to plant your field. Our rows were 30 inches apart and the hills 18 inches from one to the other, planted one to two inches deep. At each end of the field, we stopped to stake down the wire. Then after three or four rows you had to rewind the wire to start over.

Dad didn't like to plant field corn until after the 5th of May. If it was still a little cold, he might go ahead and plant, but he planted it two inches deep. That way it took longer to come up. If planted close to the top of the ground, it would come through faster, and then if it turned cold, it could get frostbite. The thing that most farmers worried about as soon as the corn came up was the crows. Crows will start along the edge of a field near the woods and hop along straight down the row, pulling each hill of corn up and eating the small kernel on the bottom. This was known as crowhoppin'. A murder (large flock) of crows can ruin a couple acres in no time at all. Farmers have tried many different ways to fight crows out of their cornfields with little success. The most popular, of course, is the scarecrow; another is a black garden hose, representing a snake.

The thing I enjoyed most was cultivating. If you had a well-broken team of horses, about the only thing you had to do was watch the corn pass through under the cultivator. If not, there was a good chance that you could plow out more corn than weeds. Corn was thinned out and suckered one stalk to the hill. A sucker is when there is a strong shoot from the main stalk that will not produce a good ear of corn. The corn should be hilled up, which means to pull the dirt up around the stalk. Corn doesn't have a main root system, but rather many little surface roots. With this horse-drawn cultivator, I could work the corn after it was three feet high. If it bent over going under the cultivator, that was okay because the sun drew it up again in a day or two.

The many varieties of corn included field corn of all types, sugar corn, hominy corn, and broomcorn. My mother told me that Grandpap Cartzendafner put out an acre of broomcorn every year. During the winter he curried out the seeds by laying the head on a wide board and then taking a big comb with lots of steel teeth (known as a rake) to pull the seeds out. From that head, he made brooms of different types to sell. People came from all over to buy brooms—they bought a bunch of them. Later these folks sold the brooms to their friends and neighbors. Every winter they returned for more. If he had a good crop and more broomcorn than he needed, he sold the rest after it was raked. Mom said she helped him until her fingers hurt. The saying goes that a new broom sweeps clean, but in reality a worn broom sweeps better because as you use a cornbroom, the straw wears down to a point, which enables you to sweep in the corners.

Mom made hominy from corn that had dried white or yellow. She used to make her own lye by putting hardwood ashes in a crock, adding water and letting it set a spell. I asked her how many ashes to what amount of water and she told me I would know after making it a few times. I asked her how long do you leave it set, and she said, "Oh, a good while—a few days maybe." Then she poured the water off and there was your lye. In later years she bought it in a box in powder form from the store. After the lye water was ready, she poured the old dried corn in lye water that was strong enough to eat the hull off. The hull is the outside skin of a kernel of corn. She mixed and stirred, and stirred and mixed, until all the hulls were eaten off.

The corn was then washed and put on the stove. It took so long that sometimes it didn't get done in one day. After it was parched, Mom put it in jars and cooked it some more. When it came out of that jar, she put it in a big old cast iron frying pan and it was a real delicacy.

There are many ways of harvesting corn. Each farmer might have a different need. Some farmers pulled the ear off the stalk and put it in a pile and others gathered it up later in a wagon or sled. Some drove along the row with a wagon and threw the corn in as it was pulled. Others cut the stalk and put it in shocks. If the stalk was cut with an ear or two of corn on it and put in large bundles, this was a corn shock. If the ears were pulled off and then the stalks cut, it was called a fodder shock.

Grandpap Cartzendafner had a fodder cutter that was horse-drawn. He stood on a little platform and rode while the fodder was being cut. There was an arm that caught the fodder and put it in little bundles. Then it was carried to the barn and fed to the cows. My father would cut the stalk with a fodder knife, while the corn was still on the stalk. He made corn shocks in rows across the whole field and came back later to husk the corn. Some of the farmers didn't call it huskin' but rather shuckin' corn. If the corn was ready to be shucked, the husk loosened up around the ear and then the ear bent down from the stalk. The corn couldn't have much moisture in it to be kept over winter in the corncribs. Putting it in shocks so it dried out was the best way for a lot of farmers before putting it in the crib.

Huskin' corn was a lot like having a party with all the neighbors coming in to help. Dad said the huskers started early in the morning and worked well into the night. Each husker brought his own lantern so they could see after dark.

In the fall, cider was a popular drink. The longer it sat, the harder it would get before turning into vinegar. Certain people hid a brown jug of cider in a corn shock. It was placed there in plenty of time to turn hard before huskin' time came. Dad said that this was quite a treat for some folks.

Sometimes one or two started tasting cider long before dark. It was easy to tell where the cider was because it took that cider-taster a long time to get his shock shucked out. By late in the evening these guys were laughing and having a grand old time. Sometimes they needed help to get in the spring wagon.

One man was a brassy kind of guy. Dad helped him into his wagon and his horse seemed to know if he'd had too much cider. As soon as this old guy picked up the line to drive his horse home, the horse lunged forward and Mr. Ciderman flipped backwards over his seat and wound up in the back part of his spring wagon. The horse looked around and then started for home. The old horse went home and the next morning he was found standing behind the barn. From there Mr. Ciderman's wife would take over. I asked Dad why his wife didn't get him before morning. He said that as soon as she heard the spring wagon coming down the lane and she could see that he was not sitting up in the seat, she knew he was drunk so she left him there and went on to bed.

Dad told me that he'd leave a fodder shock in the field to store pumpkins in to keep them from freezing. He said he never hid cider like a lot of other people, that he liked his cider before it got hard.

The Bewildered Cow

Medford Jones told me a story about a Jersey cow. He was working on a farm on the lower part of the Eastern Shore. He noticed that when it was her turn to be milked, one of her four teats would be dry. This was most unusual for a cow. He couldn't think of anything except that somebody was milking his cow, but only from that one teat.

For a while he thought it was a local boy playing a trick on him. After a week of this, he thought, "Well, I don't think anybody around here would do that." This one teat was looking a little inflamed. It really got him to scratching his head. He started to keep an eye on his cow. Days passed and it was the same ole thing. By now her left hind teat was starting to swell up. He called the vet in to see if there was something he hadn't thought of. The vet didn't have any particularly good advice. He thought that it was unusual but maybe another cow had stepped on her teat while she was lying down.

Mr. Jones was getting concerned and thought he'd hold her up in the stable. The cow was okay all day long until about three o'clock in the afternoon. She started bawling and pulling on her neck chain trying to get out. Milking time was around 5:30, and this time she had milk in all four quarters of her udder.

Boy, did that cow put up a fit all afternoon. But after milking her, she got better. He turned her out with the rest of the cows after milking. She ran down in the pasture to a certain spot, stopped, and started bawling. Mr. Jones said, "It was like she was looking for a calf." He knew this was impossible.

The next morning she came up to the barn with the rest of the cows; it was the same thing. He couldn't understand what was happening. The next day he did the same thing as the day before: held her up in the stable, let the rest of the cows out. She was fine throughout the day, but by three in the afternoon she started bawling and pulling on her neck chain until it finally broke. He followed her down to the pasture, waited and watched. She went to the same spot and started bawling as usual. Mr. Jones said he'd had made up his mind that if he didn't get another thing done all afternoon, he was going to find out what was wrong with this cow.

He got in a small grove of trees and was hiding behind some bushes waiting to see what the old cow was up to. She continued bawling, but after about fifteen or twenty minutes, the old cow stopped like a clock. He looked and looked and couldn't see a thing. She was standing there as if she was in the stall being milked. He started crawling closer, still couldn't see anything. Finally he stood up and walked to his cow; she didn't move.

He said, "I walked right up to that old cow and was scratching her on the neck, looked down and Lord and behold, there was a snake wrapped around her hind leg with her whole teat in its mouth."

I asked him what he did. He replied, "The first thing I did was jump back. Then, I looked again and yep, I was right, I was not seeing things. That snake was wound around her hind leg, suckin' away." I asked again what he did. He said, "I went to the house, got my shotgun, hurried back and smacked that old cow on the butt. She went running for the barn. The old snake fell off her leg but held on to her teat for 30 feet or more. When that cow got far enough away, I let the snake have it."

For the first few days the cow continued to go to her spot in the meadow and bawl for the snake. Of course, the snake never came. That was one bewildered cow. I asked my father and several other farmers if this could be so and I was told that such had happened before.

Eating Out

While the Jones' were living on Eastern Shore, we went to visit them on weekends. Quite often we ate out at someone's house. During the 1940's I can remember women on the Eastern Shore opening their homes to the public for serving dinners as a way of making money.

This was a common practice for the housewives of the watermen. These hard-worked ladies worked the first part of the week cleaning house and washing windows, and then spent all day Friday and Saturday getting ready for serving meals on Sunday. Lunch or dinner ran from a dollar a head and kids ate free. It was frowned upon and insulting to the ladies if you left a tip. They had a lot of character and were much too proud to accept charity, which they thought tips were. They believed in working for what they got.

Mrs. Jones called around to find a person who was serving dinners on the particular day she wanted to eat out. After she found out which ladies were serving lunch or dinner in their homes, she called several days in advance to make the arrangements. The lady of the house would tell Mrs. Jones what time she had available, depending on the number of people coming. On the Eastern Shore, the number of people in your party was referred to as how many 'head' will be coming rather than the actual number of people. The hostess might not be able to serve a large group.

This was not as simple as it is with restaurants today. After many phone calls back and forth, it would be decided if you'd be dining on the front porch, in the living room, dining room or in the least expensive place, which was on the back porch. The back porch faced the Chester River. Most houses had a working pier out back, which often times resulted in unsightly litter on the water.

While eating lunch or dinner on the back porch, we could look down on the river and see the boats going up and down the river. The lady of the house decided whether you'd be eating lunch or dinner. No options here. These working piers didn't slow down during the crabbing season. Crabbers started to work at 3:00 a.m. They were back in by noon seven days a week, so there wasn't a lot of business going on during the time when lunch and dinner were served.

For most people the back porch, where you could see the water and all the traffic on the river, was the most undesirable place to eat. That's why the back porch had a big cut in the price for dinners. During this time no one ever ate at a table on the lawn. That was something only hoboes did—unless it was a picnic at the beach or some other very informal gathering like a church social.

It was customary for the hostess to ask what it was that we wanted for our main dish. There were a few simple rules. First, everybody ate the same thing. Second, we had a choice of fried chicken, fresh fish (and that was only if her husband had a lucky day, which you wouldn't know until the boat was back by noon), or soft crabs (which were plentiful in season). Everyone who lived along the riverfront had a floating slough-ing crab box full of peelers hanging alongside the pier in the water. It was there by the Chester River that I saw rockfish so large that Mr. Jones had to take a garden hoe to pull the scales off.

In preparation for eating out, we got all dressed up in our Sunday clothes, shined the toes of our shoes, and were firmly reminded of our manners, such as please, thank you and being seen and not heard. All the while, my mother had a habit of kinda licking her fingers, wetting my hair down and pushing it around the way she liked it. While she was doing this, she said, "I don't want no fussin', you hear?" For all the kids, it was "speak only when spoken to." Then we were ready to go.

So the cheap seats on the back porch facing the river and a soft crab platter were the most inexpensive way to go. The vegetables were at the discretion of the cook. The number of soft crabs was up to each person, whatever they could eat at the table. The server kept filling the platter up until you left the table. There were no take-homes. A platter of home-cured and smoked, baked ham, nicely sliced and served cold, was auto-matically served with every meal. During dinner, the main course of conversation among the men was the price of hay and cattle and other farm-related affairs. The ladies talked about how hard it was to raise a bunch of kids that day and age.

When leaving the house, the lady stood near the front door to thank us for coming. The men stopped and picked up their hats, tipping it to the hostess, rubbing their bellies and telling her how full they were and what a good dinner it was. That was the best tip.

On the way to the car, the thanks continued and the lady stood in the middle of the doorway holding the screen door open and waving good-bye, saying, "You're much obliged, come back again sometime." For me, as soon as I reached the car, I shook my head and let my hair fall the way I liked it. Then I was ready to head back to the farm.

"Blessed are they that mourn: for they shall be comforted."
(Matthew 5:4)

There's a long-standing custom on the Eastern Shore of Maryland that I think is charming. When a funeral procession comes down the road, any road, everyone in the oncoming traffic pulls their cars or trucks onto the shoulder of the road and comes to a full stop in respect for the mourners. Dad would pull off his hat and wait for the procession to pass. Then and only then would he proceed down the road.

There were many occasions when I was in the car that we pulled over as the procession was going by. We kids counted the number of cars and made nice remarks about how well-liked that person must have been with the large number of cars following the hearse. If there were only a few cars following, I would make some comment like, "…that poor old guy didn't have very many friends."

This consideration for the mourners didn't matter whether it was a dirt road, an improved road or a big two-lane highway, or who the dead person was. All the people on the Eastern Shore received the same respect.

134

Work and Play

Mrs. Wheelwright was a wealthy widow and the boss of Twiford Farm. Yet, she must have felt wealth was no excuse for her kids to lack knowing the value of hard work. She told my father that while Watty was off from school all summer, he'd have to help on the farm. Watty was a popular figure around the farm. He was a hard worker and everybody enjoyed having him around to help pick up part of the load.

I remember Watty riding the hay baler. It was a wire-tied baler with a seat attached to the side of the baler, which sat just behind the knotters. Every time the plunger pushed more hay into the baler, a large blast of dust poured out. At the same time the baler moved up, the dust settled down all around Watty. This happened about once a minute, depending on how fast the tractor was moving. Watty would be sitting there in all that dust, sticking wire into the knotter for the next bale. He wore a raggedy old straw hat that was torn and full of holes. Baling was a dirty and dangerous job, and many serious accidents occurred while riding balers. By lunchtime you couldn't tell if Watty was white, or a little black boy. He was a good sport and felt that there was no need to complain; he just commented that, "Somebody had to do it."

At the end of the day after getting cleaned up and when supper was over, Watty, Marty and Henry came down to our house. We enjoyed each other's company sitting around on the porch, talking and laughing about the things that had happened during the day. Sometimes if it wasn't real hot, we played football or baseball. Or if Marty or Watty had brought along their croquet or badminton set, we played that. We had a great time until we started to get in an argument over who was winning, and then Mom would come out, and say, "It's

135

starting to get pretty dark, and I think it's time you all go home now." They left: sometimes happy; sometimes yelling to us, "This game is not over yet."

I remember one evening we had some other kids from the farm at our home, and Marty and Watty brought over several watermelons. We cut the melons and everybody ate their fill. Then someone started to spit seeds at someone else. After a while we were all spitting seeds at each other. Before you knew it, we were taking little pieces of watermelon and throwing it at each other. Well, it didn't stop there: The pieces kept getting bigger and bigger until we all were throwing whole rinds at each other. Watty took one piece and hit Marty in the head.

Jimmy, Oliver, and Marvin

The whole side of her head turned red. My mother heard all the commotion and came out to see what was going on. Marty was holding the side of her head but she didn't cry. Mom said, "Watty, you should be ashamed of yourself." Watty said, "Mrs. Fox, you can't hurt her. She's tough." And Marty was tough. Supposedly one time Watty took Marty and tied her to a tree limb on the lawn by her long blond pigtail and just left her there. Nobody ever told me how she got loose.

Another time we were in the backfield getting in corn. Marty and her good friend Gay had to work that day. We were pulling corn off the stalk with a huskin' peg. A huskin' peg is a small half-round piece of metal with leather finger loops. With your left hand you placed a huskin' peg in the palm of your right hand, and then you slipped the leather finger loops though your middle fingers. The peg stuck up about an inch from the back knuckle of your forefinger. You kept your fingers from getting sore by making a fist. This allowed you to easily pull the husk down over the ear of corn by sticking the peg into the top part of the husk, placing your thumb on the outside, then pulling it down and breaking off the ear. When you got to this point, you simply dropped the husk on the ground and threw the ear of corn on the pile closest to you. The finger loops kept you from dropping it in the pile of husks at your feet. It was small and would be hard to find. After we were finished, we drove along with the truck and picked up the piles.

This farm truck had a throttle to control the speed. George Stairs or somebody put it in low gear and pulled out the throttle so it just crept along. Then he stepped on the running board and steered until I was able to climb in behind the wheel. I had a quart-size wooden soda pop box placed behind me on the back of the seat to give me support in case I had to push the clutch in to stop the truck. It was important for me to have something to lean against because my leg was too short to reach the clutch pedal.

I steered the truck through the field in between the corn piles until someone yelled, "Whoa!" Then I grabbed the steering wheel with both hands and stretched my left leg down to the clutch pedal and put my shoulder against the old pop box and stopped the truck until they had all the corn picked up from that pile. Then with a big jerk, I let the clutch back out and moved on to the next pile.

Sometimes we used a fodder (corn) knife (a blade three inches wide and ten inches long with a two-foot handle and a leather or rope strap that hooked over your wrist) to cut the stalk off and put it into shocks to be husked later. Marty was teasing me that day and said she and Gay were good help so that was why they were making ten cents an hour. Then she added that when I grew up, I'd make ten cents an hour, too. We laughed and had lots of fun.

Like any kids, we felt that as the day went on the drive slowed down. After a while we started playing with the corn to see who could make the biggest pile in the shortest time and who could throw an ear of corn the farthest. Then, who was the best dodger from an ear of corn, and who could dodge the most ears at the same time without getting hit.

After a while there was an all-out battle; everybody for himself. When an ear of corn hit the sideboards of the truck, it exploded and all the kernels flew everywhere. If you'd never been hit by one of Marty's overhand throws, you might not know that she didn't throw too accurately, so you couldn't always determine which way to run.

I thought the safest place for me was under the truck. After a short time I realized that was not the best place either and I jumped into the cab. A while later, Dad and George Stairs came up to find out what was going on and they got everybody settled down and back to work. Oh well, it was fun while it lasted!

Watty was a dare-devil. One time I remember our family was sitting on the porch after supper one hot summer evening when we looked up to the silo and spotted Watty balancing himself on the four-inch tiles around the perimeter of the top of the silo some 30 feet above the ground. Mother yelled, "Watty, you get down from there now!" He listened, but not without pretending to trip and fall.

Watty had a motor scooter, which he rode back and forth

between his house and ours and around the farm. He loved to race the incoming cars and delivery trucks like Joe, the iceman. Joe delivered ice to the farm dairy and then to the manor house. If Watty was nearby, there was a race and not always a fair one. Watty took short cuts across the lawn, but I really think Joe let him win because he didn't want to take the chance of running over him. He let us all take turns riding his scooter. As time went on he started driving a car and using the scooter less. One day he decided to give us his scooter. What a nice surprise!

Mrs. Wheelwright often came to visit Mom and Dad. Dad always tipped his hat and "The Madame" nodded her head as if to say thank you to him. She asked how the children were doing. By this question, she was actually asking about each and every child on the farm, including her own. They all had a way of letting us work out any problems that we had. She liked to keep up with what was going on around the farm and the other families living there, always concerned with the welfare of any employee. If she had a problem with one at her house, she still came to Mom.

Carlin's Park

We liked to see Mrs. Wheelwright come for these visits because sometimes there was a treat in it for us, like going to the movies or to Carlin's Park, an amusement park with rides of all kinds. In 1947 Mrs. Wheelwright married Mr. Henry B. Thompson. Even as the new Mrs. Thompson, she continued to be very generous with us. She gave Mom $50.00 to spend at Carlin's Park. That was just about a month's wages for Dad in 1947! She'd say, "The children have been working hard. Will you take the station wagon and take them to the Park?" That was music to our ears. We got cleaned up and ready in no time.

139

We rode one ride after another. Once we each spent the money Mom had passed out among us, we would go back and ask her if there was any more left. It was like having everything you ever wanted—free! We had a wonderful time.

When Watty was riding the roller coaster, he stayed on one time after another for about ten turns, until the man operating told Mom that he thought it was time for him to get off. Mom, in her indignant way, took up for Watty saying, "Well, he is paying for his seat." The operator said, "Yes, but he's not using it; he's standing up and holding both hands straight in the air over his head." My mother said, "Oh my! Watty! Watty!"

One time as we were returning home, coming around Park Circle, the town clock was striking midnight. That was really late for a bunch of little country kids to be out kicking up their heels.

Old Jack

My friends Bobby and Ambler Moss lived on a nearby farm. Marvin and I went to visit them frequently. They had a matched pair of nice black mules, Maude and Jack. Bobby was close to Marvin's age and Ambler was near my age, so to balance the two loads I took Bobby with me and Ambler took Marvin with him, riding the mules through the woods. These mules must have been very old to put up with the nonsense that we put them through.

We played soldiers and tried to hide from each other. I would stop old Jack under a tree limb, stand up on his back, help Bobby get up in the tree and then ride on. When Marvin and Ambler came along looking for us, Bobby tried to scare them by jumping on their mule. Well at least that was the plan. Most of the time Bobby fell out of the tree in front of the mule.

Sometimes we all rode over to our other nearby friends, Bobby and Oliver Perrin's house. They joined us to play in the woods. Those poor mules—now there were three to a mule. That was okay until we got into a trot and somebody always lost their balance and grabbed another until we all fell off. Then we had to lead the mule until we could find a good-sized stump because these mules were so big that without a stump or a tree to shimmy up, then crawl out on a limb and jump down on the mule's back, we weren't able to get on. (I bet those mules hated to see us coming.)

Ambler and Bobby asked their Mom if we could fix up their old chicken house for a meeting house. Mrs. Moss, the nicest lady, said, "Sure, you all clean it up and I'll make some curtains." We all worked and got everything looking nice. She helped hang the curtains and we got wooden orange crates to use for chairs.

Then I asked my mom and dad if we could take their little two-burner wood stove over to our new meeting house. They said, "Yes, but don't burn down their chicken house." Marvin and I took it over on our wagon. Well, we didn't want to cut a hole in the roof so we just ran the stovepipe out the window.

By now, this was a good-looking meeting house. Mrs. Moss said, "I think I have a table and a few things in my basement that you could use." With the permission of our parents, after dinner that evening we all were allowed to spend the night there. The next morning was a special treat! Mrs. Moss came out and cooked breakfast on our little stove. That was the best bacon and pancakes I've ever had. It is the simplest things in life that are worth the time. She gave less then an hour of her time that morning but I have carried this beautiful memory for over fifty years.

Necessity Is The Mother Of Invention— Goat Power

I remember my father trading two pairs of tires with a man named Champ Robinson for a goat. We had this goat and harness (perhaps the harness came with the goat, I don't really know). The goat was a pet, and he went with us everywhere we went. So while I was sliding down the hill, it occurred to me that since the goat liked running after us so much if I put harness on him, he could pull the sleds back up the hill for us. That's what we did and it worked very well for while—until the goat got tired.

Since we were getting tired riding down the hill and walking back up, it was understandable that the goat got tired from running down the hill and pulling the sleds back up. The goat didn't think much of that. Sometimes he only made it up the hill halfway, and I had to walk back down the hill and get my sled, so it only worked out for a while. We had a lot of fun with the old goat anyway.

Moonlight Party

I was about 10-12 years old when my sister Shirley planned a moonlight sledding party. She invited some of her friends. We had a wonderful place to go just behind our house. There was a winding, steep driveway that wasn't used with two large pillars on both sides of the driveway and a chain across the road, so no cars to worry about.

After a couple of hours of sledding, we got chilled and went to the house where we all sat around the old cookstove with the oven door down and our feet propped up. My mother gave us hot chocolate and cookies. I don't remember where my father was, but my guess is he was probably in the living room with his feet propped up on the hassock, looking at a farm magazine, smoking on his Camel cigarettes. He wasn't much for being around a lot of people.

After we got warmed up, we went back out sledding again. We continued sledding for a while. We were all standing around talking and laughing at the bottom of the hill when someone asked, "Where's Ronnie Rosenvier?" We began looking for him and when we couldn't find him, we thought perhaps he was playing a joke on us. But after a while we realized that was not the case. We all started up the hill very concerned, looking and calling for him.

We knew that was a fast ride and sometimes you could roll off your sled if you weren't careful. Sure enough, on about the second turn, there lay Ronnie in the snow. He had stayed on his sled when it left the trail and instead of rolling off, he ran into a tree. After the impact, Ronnie lay there, apparently unconscious, and his sled continued down the hill through the woods off the trail. We tried talking to him and he didn't respond. We thought he was probably dead.

After finding his sled, Bernard Osler (the oldest among us) said, "Let's get him to the house quick." So we put poor ole Ronnie on the sled as fast as we could and started to the house, some pushing, some pulling, and all hurrying as fast as we could. After we got him to the house where it was nice and warm, my mother looked at him and wondered what to do. Then he started to move and at least we knew he wasn't dead. We were still concerned that he could've broken some bones or his neck or something like that, but when he started talking we realized everything was okay.

I guess if that had happened today, they would have taken him to the hospital immediately and had him checked out. But back in those days, as long as you could keep on moving, you were okay. That sort of ended the evening with the sled riding party.

Skiing with Sister Shirley

My sister and I used to do a lot of skiing. We sure had fun. Right behind our house there was a steep pasture field. You could really go down that hill, and we got pretty good at it. We only had these little ole strap-on skis with just a strap that you stuck your foot in. We got so when we put them on tight, we could control them fairly well. After a lot of trips up and down that hill, I thought we could build a little ski jump. The jump was only two to three feet high. Eventually we could go down the hill, cross the jump and keep on going.

Then one day my father came up Greenspring Avenue and saw Shirley and me going down the hill very quickly and then up in the air, having a grand time. He came back to where we were and excitedly asked, "What are you doing?" He was really upset and told us we had to tear down the ski jump right away. I tore down the ski jump, but we continued skiing and sledding on the hill.

Clothesline Tales

My great grandfather, George W. Fox, lived in Baltimore City across the street from the Lexington Market. My family and I visited him occasionally. One time we went for dinner. It must have been a birthday or some special event, for it was on wash-day rather than the usual Sunday visit. Louellen Feeser and her family (my second and third cousins) went also. We all drove to Baltimore in two different cars because there were too many of us to pile into one vehicle.

When we arrived, my cousin Paul was already there, just sitting in the kitchen windowsill twirling a hash knife between his fingers, looking down on the street and laughing. As I looked out the window, I noticed two pulleys with ropes around them. You could pull on the top part of the rope to take the clothes in and out of the window. I'd never seen a clothesline like that before. We were on the second floor and it was a long way down.

My sister was scared that Paul was going to fall so she ran and told his mother. Louellen said, "Oh don't tell me what he's doing, I don't want to know." Well, we all were so surprised and thought for sure Paul would fall, but he didn't. Paul continued to pull and push the clothes in and out the window like it was a new toy.

As I recall Paul was a lot older than I was and he was going to go across the street to the Lexington Market. I asked my father if I could go too. He told me no because there was too much traffic and that I wasn't used to it. I sure had a real yearning to see what that market was all about. I was walking around moaning about having to stay back while the rest went over to investigate all the doin's at the market. My father tried to make me feel better and said, "Oh Chappy (that was another pet name that Dad gave me occasionally), they'll soon be back—don't go frettin' about it." Mom said, "I don't know why they want to be gallivanting around over there anyway." I stayed back and took a seat on the sofa with nothing to do.

As I sat there daydreaming and staring out the window, I saw an old black man down on the street. He was walking alongside a small horse-drawn wagon, with a brown and white spotted pony pulling it. He was calling out in a loud, hollering voice, "Watermelon, fresh strawberries, roe-shad." In Baltimore City, these businessmen were known as Arabs. He stopped to help a customer and then the old man picked up a fish, dropped it on the scales, which were hanging from a hook under the tailgate of the wagon, and continued to take care of the transaction.

His big pony knew his route. Without any commands from his teamster, he automatically pulled in to the curb. He side-stepped so he could jack knife the front wheels and then made a step or two backwards so the front wheel rested on the curb. That way he wouldn't have to stand there and hold the wagon under a strain. The curb acted like a brake, and held the weight of the wagon. After the old man was finished, they both started up the street without a "gitty-up" from the teamster. That pony seemed to know what to do on his own.

I overheard my great-grandfather talking about how one day at Saratoga Street, the painters were working on a swing scaffold when the end of their rope was lying in the street and one of the Arab wagons was passing by. The rope got caught in the wheel and pulled one end of the scaffold up and the painter fell off. I don't recall if anybody got hurt. After all the older kids returned from Lexington Market, we had a nice big dinner together and started back home.

The clothesline had many uses other than for clothes. During spring and fall housecleaning, rugs were thrown over them and then beaten to get the dust out of them. Ray Schaffer, one of the men who worked on the farm, would come in from the field, take his shirt off, and throw it over the clothesline to let it dry until after his dinner. Then he would put it on and go back to the field. Mrs. Schaffer made cheeses of all kinds.

146

After the milk coagulated, it was put in cheesecloth and placed in a stone crock, which had a pie plate inserted in the bottom to catch the whey for the cats. Her clothesline would be full of hanging cheese bags, wrapped in cheesecloth, allowing the cheese to cure.

Mom would leave white clothes out all day, saying that the sun acted like a bleach to whiten them. There was freshness and crispness as well as a pleasant smell about her laundry that had been left out in the fresh air all day. It sure smelled better than today's artificial additives that come with our indoor fancy, filtered dryers.

In 1945 I was a chubby-cheeked, freckled-faced scrawny boy for my eight years. Country living seemed to be a lot of fun with a bunch of horseplay or some kind of entertainment around the farm. My parents weren't always pleased with my sense of humor. Their heartfelt opinion was that I ought to take life more seriously. As hard as I tried not to kid around, I still found amusement in the serious things in life and always had a yearning to tease.

My mother had a wire clothesline instead of a rope, and she would always wash the wire before hanging up the clothes just in case the wire was dirty or rusty. She wrapped a washrag around the line several times and walked it back and forth. That way it would not stain the clothes. Mom mostly had an apron with two big pockets, one of which she carried all but one clothespin. That clothespin she carried in her mouth between her teeth. This one was her emergency pin. We kids had to help with this gruesome chore. With Mom the strange thing was her clothes had to be hung a certain way, not over-lapping too much, using three pins for two shirts and using only one pin in the middle of the sheets. Both sides had to hang evenly to match just perfect. I never thought of that as being very important. My thoughts were: so what if they didn't, they'd all dry just as fast no matter how they hung—even or not, so just through them over the line without using a pin and they'll dry.

Obviously, I needed a lot of instruction on hanging clothes. Even though Mom had that clothespin in between her teeth, she could scold me at the same time! It was pretty funny to hear her trying to talk with her teeth together. I couldn't help but stick a clothespin in my mouth to answer her. She didn't always appreciate my sense of humor.

One time Mom was out washing the line and I went to tell her that the Fuller Brush man was coming. I could see the mixed-up handles of brooms, carpet sweepers, floor mops, feather dusters, and what-have-you's all over the inside of the car. She grabbed me and we hurried into the house. As we passed through the door going into the kitchen, she pulled the shade down and shut the door. We went into the living room, rushed into the closet and pulled the door shut.

I sure thought this was fun. Mom said, "Stop that laughing or I'm gonna smack you." I stopped laughing but asked why we were hiding in the closet. She said, "I don't want to buy anything from him; he's one of those high-pressured salesmen." Every time he tapped on the door, I just couldn't help but snicker a little. After a good while we heard the car start up. Only then did Mom sneak out of the closet and peep out the window to make sure he was gone.

A week later I was feeling pretty spry and got the bright idea to tease Mom about the Fuller Brush salesman. I wanted to see if we were going to go hide in the closet again, so I ran down to the clothesline where she was hanging up our clean duds, acting all excited about the salesman coming again. Mom pulled off her apron with its pocket full of clothespins, dropped it in the laundry basket and hurried into the house like before.

I was really giggling to myself. Everything went as planned. We were standing in the closet but there was never a rap on the door. Mom was getting a little suspicious and after a long time I told her the truth. She didn't say a lot about it, but did say an idle mind is the devil's workshop. I could tell that she was not happy; I said nary a word. As my luck would have it, I heard Dad walking on the porch. Mom said, "You wait here in the kitchen."

Mom walked out on the porch to meet Dad. I saw them through an open window. While I was standing in the kitchen chewing on my fingernails and waiting for the worst and showing all the pangs of fear, they were standing in the middle of the porch with their heads together. I couldn't see any smiles on either face. I'd gotten myself into this predicament and wasn't sure what was going to happen.

Then they came in the kitchen and Dad looked me right in the eye. Dad started off pretty strong and it wasn't exactly clear to me as to what would happen. His retort was that I was a kid acting smart and he felt that I had been joking around a little too much. He wound up his conversation by saying, "If you ever pull a trick like that again, you are going to be in a heap of trouble." I knew he would be true to his word—you-betchum. I straightened up.

Another laundry day was in the dead of winter with a foot of snow on a bitter cold day. The clothes on the line had been frozen stiff as a board. Mom asked me if I would help her bring the clothes into the house. We hurried up, pulled them off the line, threw everything in the basket and rushed into the house. I dropped the basket in the kitchen and pulled the bed-clothes off the top and took them upstairs.

I hung the clothes around the best I could over the edge of the four-legged bathtub and was standing on top of the register, which was directly over the kitchen to warm up a bit. Mom was working on the other clothes in the kitchen where it was nice and warm. She'd pulled down the oven door on the coal-burning stove so the heat could come out, pushed chairs up close to the stove and draped the clothes over them so they would be able to thaw out and finish drying.

All of a sudden I heard this terrible screaming. I came out of the room, raced down the hall and jumped from the top of the steps to the landing that made a sharp turn into the living room with another few steps. When I got to the kitchen, there stood mom standing on one of her bootjack kitchen chairs full of stiff clothes.

A mouse had been under the stove and was getting too hot, so it ran out. The mouse started across the floor, passed over Mom's foot, and she started screaming. The mouse changed its mind, came back and hopped into the coal bucket next to the stove right in front of Mom. She was screaming for everything she was worth.

The poor little mouse was running around in that coal bucket like crazy. Mom said, "Get that darn thing out of here!" By that time it must have gotten dizzy and leaped out of the bucket.

Mom told me to get the broom and pointed behind the door. I grabbed the broom and chased the mouse around the kitchen. After a while I got him trapped in the corner. In no uncertain terms, Mom said, "Take that thing out of here!" I reached down, picked him up by the end of his tail with my thumb and forefinger. Holding it with an extended arm walking past Mom, I made it move like it was still alive and she was thinking it was. She continued to scream wrapping both of her arms around herself and yelling, "Go! Go!"

Mom was terrified of mice, and told me never to tell Watty Wheelwright about this. She worried, "I know Watty. He loves to play jokes! I can just see him catching a mouse and putting it on me. Jimmy, if you ever tell Watty, you are going to catch the dickens, ya' hear?!"

When I was 11 or 12, I had oodles of pleasing recollections of my Grandmother Fox. Monday mornings were wash days for most country ladies. My Grandmother Fox was no exception. Laundry was out on the line before day break. You could see across the fields from one house to the other. The neighbors all knew Grandmother was a widow lady and kept a watchful eye on her. Grandmother was known to be an early starter on her day's work. Once the wash was out of the way, she felt free to start on her farm chores. If her wash was not out on the line, one or more of the neighbors would call on her to see if she was sick.

Some of the visits from these nearby ladies could bring some heavy gossip. There were always plenty of conversations among these modest, dignified women on the subject of politics. My Grandmother Fox was a strong-hearted Democrat and proud of it. She never voted and felt that it was not proper for a woman to vote. That was something only a man should do. She thought that nowadays it was terrible for a woman to run for any kind of public office and any woman who did, well, she was just a hussy.

She felt that you should vote a straight Democratic ticket. Reluctantly, I asked her what if you didn't think that person was the best person for the office? Her response was, "If you're a good Democrat, then you must support your party." Grandmother was dedicated to her party, to her friends, and to her family. It was always clear where you stood with my grandmother. There's a lot to be said for that.

Suppertime

Our evening meal was 6:00 p.m. sharp. Mother would come out the kitchen door about ten minutes before and put her hands on either side of her mouth, lift her voice in a high pitch and call out, "Supper! Suppertime!" She had a set of lungs that wouldn't quit. Her yell for supper could be heard all over the farm. We would all stop what we were doing and get there on the double. Everyone was expected to be there. There usually wasn't any excuse good enough not to be there. Even if you were someplace else off the farm, you'd better be home for supper!

Everyone had to make sure their face and hands were washed and their hair combed, and that they'd put on a clean shirt before coming to the table. In the summertime when it was hot, I might try to sneak to the table without a shirt. Mom would say, "You get in there and put a shirt on." If I was the first to arrive at the table and tried to take the best piece of meat, Mom would say, "Just you wait till everybody else gets here!"

Mom spent a lot of her time at the supper table trying to housebreak us kids. If a plate of fried chicken was being passed around, she would say, "You cannot grab food off the plate with your fingers even if they are clean." Skipping over

152

the person next to you when passing food was forbidden. The only way to keep the grub rolling around the table was to thank the person next to you as they passed it to you. You didn't have to pass it on until the person you were passing it to said "thank you." If you were having a problem with that person, you could always make them say "thank you" a few times by saying, "I didn't hear you."

While we were waiting for everyone to arrive at the supper table, we were allowed to have a drink of iced tea. Mom had a five-gallon pot that she made iced tea in. She'd set it on a stool close to the table. We had iced tea only in the summertime. After Richard was working in the fields all day, he'd really be thirsty and would drink one glass after another. Dad would say, "I think we should run a hose to his glass."

One time during the coldest part of winter while we were still living in the back house at Twiford Farm, Dad asked me to refill the pitcher with more water. Mom had just bought this really nice glass pitcher at the Five & Dime store in Pikesville. It had small red circles and a red rooster painted on it and little ears on either side of the spout. The water pump wasn't too far from the kitchen door so I thought I wouldn't need a coat. I ran outside, set the pitcher down, and grabbed the very end of the pump handle—the place where you get the best leverage. When the pump handle was all the way up, I'd have to stand on my toes to reach it to be able to pull it back down. I'd get the pump going as fast as I could to get a good flow of water, then pick up my pitcher and run around in front of the pump to get some water in it before the flow stopped. I'd come back and pump some more; then grab the pitcher and run to the front again until it got full. It took a while, but I finally made it.

I brought the pitcher in, handed it to Dad and took my seat at

153

the table. Dad began pouring water in his glass and one of the ears fell off. He stopped pouring, looked at me and said, "What is this?" I answered, "Is it ice?" And he replied, "I don't think so!" It was one of the ears off the pitcher, and I guess in my hurrying from behind the pump to the front, I must have bumped it on the pump. The old pump squeaked and shook and made so much noise I didn't hear a thing. I never did get in trouble for that, but I felt bad for Mom and her new pitcher.

Mom and Dad mostly had coffee after they finished supper. Dad would take a slice of bread and spread King Syrup (molasses) on it. Then he folded it over and dunked it in his coffee.

A lot of people poured the coffee or tea out of the cup into the saucer, then pick up the saucer and drink out of it. When asked why they did that, the only answer I ever got was that it was too hot in the cup. I never realized what a hurry coffee drinkers must have been in.

Mom was a firm believer that meat was an important protein for a hardworking family. Sirloin that she had coldpacked in jars was tops. Sweetbreads, which is the pancreas out of a beef, went over big too. Hog brains were fried or mixed in scrambled eggs. Most of the time she had two plates of meat, one at each end of the table. Mother decided what meat she was having and then determined what vegetables went with it. Generally there were certain vegetables that she prepared to accompany specific meats. However, we always had potatoes in one form or another. Of course many of our foods, even vegetables, were prepared by frying them in lard. Her potato soup with rivels (an egg and flour mixture which develops into an unformed noodle) was exceptional—and there's still none that surpasses Mom's potato soup.

Mom canned most all of our vegetables. She also canned or preserved the meat in some way: coldpacked, dry-cured or smoked. Pickling was also a way to preserve. I especially liked the way she stuffed peppers with slaw, and I also enjoyed her pickled tripe. With any kind of coldpacking or preserving, you had to be careful to watch out for botulism. I enjoyed hot slaw. Corn fritters were a specialty. We mostly got them after the corn started to get old in the corn patch. To prepare corn fritters, you pulled the husk, sliced the top end of the kernels with a sharp knife to scrape the milk out, added flour, baking soda, a pinch of salt and maybe some extra milk if the corn kernels were dry. They were great.

I don't remember ever having "bull's-eyes" for supper, but they were popular for breakfast. You put the eggs in a frying pan. Then you take a slice of bread and make a hole in the center large enough so it will fit over top of the yolk. Break the yolk and spread it over the top of the bread. Then place the part of the bread that came out of the hole back into the hole. It will look like a bull's-eye, but yellow with a white center. Fry it on both sides until done. Add catsup and yummy!

Suppertime was an important time for Mom. She told me it was the highlight of her day. She wanted to hear from each one of us. Mom enjoyed being a mother and liked hearing what was happening in school or about our 4-H projects. She felt this was a way to keep on top of everybody's life. We often had family discussions about what we were all doing on Saturday evening and about plans for visiting our grandmother's on Sunday and who wanted to go.

We found out that all this organization was very important. After we kids got older and had our driver's licenses, we realized that. Dad could afford only one car, so we shared it. That meant that if you wanted to use the car, you would have to

155

plan weeks in advance to get your order in to get it. Of course, that didn't mean you'd get to use of the car, only meant that you wanted it. Use of the car was taken in order of priority and priority was set by seniority: first Mom and Dad, then my older brother, then my sister, and then me. So if Dad didn't think it was important enough, you were just scratched. There was no need to complain. You just started over with new plans. These plans were made at the supper table so everyone knew what was going on with the others.

Not only were the good things discussed, but if there was something that wasn't sitting well with someone at the table, you could have a lot of fingers pointing at you from all directions. It could turn into a lecture. If someone was holding out and not doing his fair share or if anybody was too sick to come to the table but didn't have a temperature, it was usually because they knew they were in a heap of trouble.

We hardly ever had dessert unless there was some fruit in season on the farm. But I do remember a dessert that we almost always found at funerals. It was called funeral pie. It was good for the sick soul and good without the grief and so it was known for the balance of all things. Funeral pie was raisin pie.

Beaver Brook Farm

Good Luck Farm

In December 1949, the Thompsons purchased a farm along Ridge Road in the Chestnut Ridge area. Our family began moving and preparing the farm for the Thompsons and our move in early spring. This farm was purchased from the Smithers, but was owned previously by the Harris' and was known then as the Good Luck Farm. Harris had purchased it from the great-grandson of Captain Tipton, who came from Jamaica. In the early 1700's he named the farm "Tipton's Puzzle."  The Thompsons named it "Beaver Brook Farm" after the stream on the property known as Beaver Brook Run.

On June 1, 1950, we moved to Beaver Brook Farm. My mother drove us to school for the next two weeks so we could finish the year out in Pikesville Elementary School. The following September, I started in the fifth grade at Franklin Elementary School. I was doing a little better, but all the teachers thought that if I would repeat the fifth grade, which I had just passed, that it would give me a better start in a new school. This meant that I repeated the first grade, then the second grade and now the fifth, so I was three years behind.

We met the school bus at the corner of Greenspring Avenue and Ridge Road, at Nagel's Store, which was just one mile to the mark from the farm. We walked out to be there by 7:30 a.m. In the afternoon, we got there around 4:00 p.m. I was lucky that there were other kids to walk with: Harold Bebe and his sisters Wanda, Agnes and Martha, along with the Crocker kids, Tisha and Morny, and my younger brother Marvin. Mr. and Mrs. Crocker had some Jersey cows so sometimes Wanda would have to stop by the Crockers to pick up a gallon of milk on the way home, and I would wait for her and help carry the milk to her house.

One day it was raining and my father met us at the store. Wanda said that she wouldn't be able to ride because she had to stop to get the milk. Dad told her that was okay, that it was no trouble for him to stop. Wanda went in and got the milk, came back out, got in the back seat and we started for home. Coming out of Crocker's bumpy driveway, the milk started to spill out of the bucket because Mrs. Crocker didn't have the lid on tight. Wanda was embarrassed but there was nothing she could do. She had the bucket between her feet holding it firmly on the floor of the car. The milk was splashing back and forth in the bucket. She told Dad that she would come over to the farm and wash the car. He said that it was okay—not to worry. What nice neighbors we had!

Description of Beaver Brook Farm

The western edge of Beaver Brook stretched along Ridge Road for less than a mile. Beaver Brook Run flowed through

160

the center of the farm from one end to the other. On the three hundred and forty-five acre estate I got the feeling of having an abundance of elbowroom. There were approximately one hundred and fifty acres of woods and swampland. The farm included fifteen acres around the headquarters of farm buildings, plus a smithy and dairy, a pigeon loft, the manor house and two tenant houses with lawns, small feedlots, and a one-plus acre garden. The rest was in pasture fields and farmland.

There were two major springs. One of them supplied water to the milk house. The whole thing was made with flagstone, including the roof, which was an expanding arched bow with a flashy wooden dome door. The milk house had been built next to the spring with only enough room for horses and wagon to pass through. It was made of clapboard with a six-foot extended roof. The driver could pick up and deliver milk without getting wet. Also, the door could remain open without the sun coming in on the cooling milk. A cement trough was made for milk cans to be placed in for cooling. Water from the spring continually ran into the trough from one end and out the other.

The second spring supplied water to a 2,000-gallon under-ground storage tank for a water reservoir, which provided water to the manor house, barns and tenant houses. The springhouse was made of red clay brick with a flat cement top and a metal door. The forty-gallon per minute spring water was pumped over to the brick pump-house and put in the stor-age tank.

There was a red hay barn with a tin roof and a pale gray sheep barn with forest green trim and a chicken house to match. A two-story slaughterhouse of cement blocks could cool out four beeves at one time, and a turkey house with an aerie, built up off the ground, would house fifty white double-breasted turkeys for Thanksgiving and Christmas dinners. In addition, there was a hen house with a section for pullets. We also had a root cellar for winter storage of vegetables, and a bullpen that held two bulls at one time.

In addition, there was a 180-foot tractor shed with an overhead granary. The boards used for dividers were 24-inch wormy chestnuts from the farm. On the top floor was a grain box where the grain could be fed into the crimper (to crush the grain) and then travel on a conveyor belt to the mixer. From the mixer, the new feed was bagged and then trucked to the different barns.

Back in the days on Twiford Farm, there was a hammer mill in the upper part of the barn. Its power was supplied by an F20 Farmall Tractor, otherwise known as Honeybun. A long wide belt ran from the tractor to a pulley on the hammer mill. Honeybun sat outside the barn, chugging along nice as you please, just purring away. That is, until I tried feeding the mill too fast. Then the governor on the tractor opened up and black smoke poured out of the smokestack. Before you knew it, the belt would fly off.

While working in the barn with the mill running, I had to wear a handkerchief over my face to keep my nose open and to avoid swallowing all the dust. If the belt jumped off once in a while, it gave me a good chance to let the dust settle down. Then I'd go outside to get some fresh air. Anyway, it took time to pull the tractor up, put the belt back on, and then back it up to get the belt tight again.

Once the grain was ground up, it was hand-shoveled into one large pile on the barn floor. Salt, minerals and protein were added on top of the pile and then hand shoveled back and forth until it was all mixed thoroughly. I held the bag while

162

someone else shoveled it in. Then I tied the top shut with a binder's knot (three wraps and pull the bottom end tight).

By 1953 at Beaver Brook, Dad had the mill set up in the feed room. I just walked to the crimper and flicked a switch. The grain got crimped up, and I'd flick another switch to start the conveyor belt, which carried the grain to the mixer. I'd flick another switch for the mixer. After all the grain was in the mixer, I could add salt and the rest of the ingredients. We could hook a feedbag to a chute and fill it without anybody helping. What a change: God blesses America!

The driveway into Beaver Brook Farm was lined with a variety of Mrs. Thompson's favorite trees: oaks, locusts, maples, and Lombardy poplars. A three-hole locust post and chestnut split-rail fence ran along Ridge Road to meet the tree-lined drive-way and continued along the entrance toward the manor house. At the barn area, there were three- and four-plank board fences around the garden, orchard, feedlots and the fac-ing sides of the pasture fields, all painted white. It was a beau-tiful setting for a home as well as a farm.

Below the manor house was a swimming pool, a tennis court, and a heated bathhouse with a living room, bedroom, two bathrooms, and a kitchenette. The siding was cedar shingles, and an American flag flew over a gray slate roof. As you pulled into the parking lot of the manor house, you could see the farm pond and on to a 26-acre rolling meadow. It was a spec-tacular view. Down over the little hill was a place Mrs. Thompson called the Indian Village, where some large machine sheds and the log cabin that Marvin, Henry and I built stood.

The woods included a wide variety of hardwood trees that are native to the beautiful eastern countryside. There were many different kinds of oak, including white, red, black, plus shellbark hickory, maple, gum, poplar, and dogwood around the edges of the woods. Under these beautiful trees were plots of laurel with some shoddy American Holly. Some stands of jack pine had matting of crows-foot that grew under the pines, making it look like wall-to-wall carpet.

Horseback riding on the fire trails in the fall with all those splendid colors was a pleasurable way to spend a Sunday afternoon. It was neat to hear the squawking of the crows as they flew across the trail in front of us, and was fascinating to see them in their artful movement going through the trees as we jogged along.

In the wintertime, with snow on the ground and the sun's rays shooting down and shaking off the trees as we rode over the trails in a one-horse open sleigh, it felt like a token from heaven, a real hand-me-down from the Lord.

The Harris graveyard, the remains of the Harris log cabin, a corncrib, a small barn, a hand-dug well made from fieldstones, and a dried-up spring with a fieldstone foundation were all at the back of the farm. There were lots of Easter flowers everywhere.

Our Colony and Its Pilgrims, 1692-2000

The highest point in Baltimore County, Maryland, is Chestnut Ridge, named for the gigantic native chestnut trees that once stood in the area. With the blight of the early 1930's, all our chestnut trees were swept away. Today only domesticated chestnuts will grow there. Chestnut Ridge is the backbone between Green Spring and Worthington Valleys.

In the middle 1600's Garrison Forest had few white people living in the area, mostly trappers and hunters. The Shawan,

Susquehanna Indians, were not friendly. Fort Garrison was established in 1692 about three miles on the south side of Green Spring Valley as a protection against hostile Indians. It was the headquarters for A Troop of the Baltimore County Mounted Rangers and housed seven Baltimore County Rangers. Captain Oulton was the Garrison Commander. The Mounted Rangers busily patrolled the wilderness paths over Chestnut Ridge and its valleys below.

Fort Garrison was the first outpost of its kind to be built in the United States. The chimney was built inside the fort rather than on an outside wall so the Indians wouldn't be able to climb up to enter through the roof. There were no windows, just long narrow portholes to shoot from and two doors all on the same side. It was my thought that the Indians would have to be in front of them to shoot. The fort was made of stone so the Indians couldn't burn them out or burn it down. After many attacks this charming old fort is still standing and looks as good as new.

Soldiers Delight was close by and named for its good hunting grounds at Fort Garrison. As the years passed, it finally had enough people to get a post office. The government didn't take the full name. They just called it "Delight."

A good friend of mine, Mr. Joe White who lived in Shawan, Maryland in Worthington Valley, knew a lot about the area and spent many Sunday afternoons digging around the larger springs in the pasture fields. He had quite a collection of artifacts he'd found, mostly stone tools. I found a stone head of an axe.

Lord Baltimore did not give out a lot of large land grants for Chestnut Ridge until the middle 1700's. It's only my wild guess that the Ridge was left for the "potato people." The fertile valleys below were of far greater value. Chestnut Ridge is only five-and-a-half miles long and a little over six miles wide. The area equals approximately 30 square miles, not much land to start a fight on. This measurement is all judged on the accuracy of the odometer on my mother-in-law's Cadillac.

As explained in the *Baltimore County Historical Society Diary of 1864*, the south side of the Ridge through Green Spring Valley to Pikesville was one of the largest pro-Confederate territories of Baltimore County. At the start of the Civil War, Baltimore County landholders willingly freed 29,911 slaves. Some owners were still credited with holding 5,400 slaves. Baltimore County never formally seceded from the Union. I'm opposed to slavery; however, I do appreciate some of the old traditional ways of the South. There is nothing wrong with a man trying to be a gentleman, or a woman to be a lady.

As stated in *The Jeffersonian* in 1864, the top of Chestnut Ridge became Yankee grounds. Chestnut Ridge was only a speck in the county that stood with the northern Union in this part of the country. To stand up for Blue Coat opinions and be so awake, surely must have had a strong grip on their values. Then to be completely surrounded by Confederates meant they were definitely living on the edge.

It was rumored that the Southern army would eventually come, but nobody knew when. In the early morning hours of July 10, 1864, Major Henry Gilmor, a dashing idol of many Baltimore "blue-blood" ladies, with his brigade of soldiers and the First Maryland Cavalry attached, marched through Green Spring Valley and up Green Spring Avenue onto Chestnut Ridge.

166

A Bit of History: Lies or Legends

As reported in *The Jeffersonian* in 1864, the teacher for Kelly's one-room schoolhouse on Chestnut Ridge was tough; the students studied hard and discipline was strict. A hickory rod was used to uphold law and order. (Although the log house has been covered over by brick, it still stands today as a cozy home known as "Valley Hi" belonging to Mr. and Mrs. Howard Miller. My landscaping company kept his pasture fields manicured for a number of years.) The teacher had the kids drive nails around the wooden flagpole so the Confederates couldn't chop it down. All the nails would surely ruin an ax. The students argued convincingly to keep their flag, but the plan didn't work out as hoped, for the leading officer demanded that they themselves take the flag down. Eventually, with wholesome fear, they submissively lowered the flag.

Mr. William J. Harris, a third grader at the time, remembered the soldiers taking his mother's best driving horse and as much booty as they could manage plus all the meat from the smoke house. Little Billy recalled his mother chasing after the looters for a few miles trying to get her horse back. Later the same day, General Johnson with his brigade of soldiers passed through the Ridge on their way to Cockeysville with orders to destroy railroad bridges and later returned the same day. No harm came to the Ridge that day to speak of.

I have a Yankee neighbor, Vance Kopp III, who told me a story about a Confederate soldier: He was kind of a sorry soul, driving a horse and cart—just a single horse—and got too close to the edge of a ditch and the cart upset. Vance's great-great-grandfather had just sat down for his noonday meal and heard a commotion out in front of his house. When Grandpa

167

went outside to see what had happened, he helped the old soldier out of his tangled-up mess. The soldier had been wounded and was drunk. Come to find out, he had fought at the Battle of Gettysburg and was traveling about trying to find his way home.

Vance's great-great-grandfather took him inside, cleaned him up, fed him real good, and then took him over to the county seat. Back in those days, they were giving a silver dollar for every prisoner who was captured, so he took the poor troubled guy over to the Towson Courthouse to collect his silver dollar. Long before he got there, the county ran out of reward money. Since there wasn't any money available, they asked if he would take the horse and cart for payment rather than the silver dollar. He said he'd be obliged to do that so he brought the horse and cart back home. Being feeding time when they arrived home, he put his new horse in a tie-stall in the stable and fed him. Then the next morning, he went out and walked in behind the horse. The horse kicked the old man in the head as he walked by and killed him. Vance said, "Darn Confederates! Ha! That rebel got in the last kick again."

In the 1960's part of the barn burned down. They simply threw that nice Confederate harness with bridles, single trees, and other horse-related regalia in there and then put a cement top on it. I thought to myself that it was a real waste.

Vance Kopp III also told me about Jonze Uhler and his brother William Henry, who were from Chestnut Ridge and had been raised in the same house as Vance's family. They both went off to fight in the Civil War. William Henry became a Union Sergeant and on May 23, 1863 in Front Royal, Virginia, Stonewall Jackson came storming down out of the mountains and caught a regiment of Yankees sitting on their thumbs. William Henry got shot in his right leg during the battle and was later discharged.

168

Jonze was a good teamster but wasn't sure of his given name; he thought sure it was just Jonze. He didn't know how to read or write. Jonze was transferred from one unit to another and never signed his name the same way twice. After the war, he went West and became a scout for the Cavalry.

About once every couple of years, Jonze would try to get home. He wore the typical homemade rawhide buckskin clothing that scouts wore in those days. On one of his train rides back to the Ridge, people started complaining about how bad he smelled. The farther east he came to sophisticated people, the more appalling Jonze became. The whole pullman car reeked of his odor. The smell finally got so bad they stopped the train and put him off, and he had to walk the last thirty-plus miles to get home.

Jonze was pretty typical of many army scouts back in those days. There was a persistent problem with ticks and lice. At this time, the best-known cure was to comb rancid bear fat or the like in your hair. Usually the hair was worn well below the shoulders.

A scout dared not cut his hair because that was the only way he had of keeping track of time by how long his hair had grown. And all that hair kept his ears warm while sleeping on frozen ground with the wind howling all around. Otherwise, he could lose his hearing. The next problem was with lice and ticks in long, dirty hair. The rancid fat took care of that. The smell was so bad that it kept the mosquitoes, ticks, deer flies and gnats away in the summer time. So scouts had long hair, no bugs, and the good will of only their own kind. It is my personal belief that Jonze must have smelled pretty bad.

The remnants of an old log cabin that was half-burned down was next to the graveyard on Beaver Brook Farm. After Jonze was mustered out of the Cavalry, it's believed that he moved into what was remaining of the cabin. According to an old tax map, many of these boys lived well, worked hard, died poor, and left only a whiff of a memory to be passed on.

A few slave owners in the valleys below held onto their slaves throughout the war. As far as I know, there were no fights or altercations on Chestnut Ridge or in the surrounding valleys. Most surely the Ridge must have shaken from the cannons during Pickett's Charge, which was the loudest noise on the North American continent. It was reported that those cannons were heard all the way from Gettysburg to Pittsburgh.

The call of peace came so high that when the smoke cleared, undoubtedly, the mountains must have bowed down with shame to witness such a terrible sight. On April 9, 1865, "Bobby Lee" surrendered the Army of the Confederacy to the Union. The love and loss of battle, hopes and dreams of war that fed the faith for so many had ended. Today we're still selling their experiences from both the winner and the loser.

Chestnut Ridge is very American. Some of the most colorful characters in the country lived on Chestnut Ridge. Only a few were "spotlighted" nationally or globally. However, they're all walled in my mind together forever.

On a hill across the way to the south side of the Ridge, Samuel M. Shoemaker lived on his large dairy farm, named Burnside Farm for the two streams that divided the stunning property. Mr. Shoemaker was a potent Republican and strong supporter of Lincoln and the Union causes. He was a close friend of General Ulysses S. Grant, who frequented Burnside and became President of the United States on February 21, 1873. In the 1890's Sammy Shoemaker had the first telephone in the area. A husband and wife team operated the Lutherville

170

exchange. People on the exchange soon learned what time they were in church on Sunday and what time they were in for their evening meal. On a good hay day, they both might be in the field at the same time. So for the most part the telephone wasn't operational. It was great to have a phone but had much to do with nothing. It was called "The Useless Line" and eventually taken down.

Sam Shoemaker created many firsts for his time. For example, he worked with the doctors at The Johns Hopkins Hospital in Baltimore and was the first to serve pasteurized milk commercially. Sammy's wife Augusta was a very religious person, and a wonderful story still lingers after her. She faithfully served the church on numerous committees. However, she liked to arrive at church late on Sunday mornings and slowly walk to the front pew. One Sunday they held up the service while she scrubbed the money that she planned to put in the collection plate. She had to wait for it to dry; it would be disrespectful to put in dirty money.

Before the days of postal service, residents dropped letters off at the church, hoping that someone passing through would stop at church, pick up the mail and carry it to Owings Mills to the tavern. There the proprietor would ask anyone traveling by horseback or wagon to carry it in the proper direction; only in trust would it reach its destination. This became known as "Flea Bag Mail" after the horses and mules that carried it.

Once Augusta was at the market and saw a nice-looking colored woman. Immediately she began talking to her like she did with everyone. She asked, "Haven't I seen you before?" The young woman smiled and said, "Yes ma'am, Mrs. Shoemaker. I've worked for you going on three years now." There were so many employees in the house and on the farm she didn't remember her. This estate looked like a small village then and even today. As a young man I had a career that led me through many parts of this 45-room house and around the farm that few ever got to see. It was unfortunate that the beautiful mansard roof had to be replaced with a gable.

Major General Douglas MacArthur lived directly east of Burnside, facing Green Spring Valley. He named it Rainbow Hill in honor of the Rainbow Division he led during World War I. Among the many famous sayings of MacArthur is my favorite: "Success is not what you are, but what you become."

In 1964, the 36-room marble and stucco home with its 10-car garage was sold to the Baptist Home of Maryland, Incorporated. I had a contract with them to remove snow from the roadways and parking areas. The view from Rainbow Hill was spectacular; in one good look, you could see clear across the valley at all the large estates.

Brigadier General James P. Devereux lived in Stevenson. A World War II prisoner of war, he owned and operated the Eli O'Carroll Farm. I used to help with harvesting hay and picking corn along with his sons Pete and Sugar, Pete's little brother. I remember Rachael, his lovely wife, a delightful heavy-set lady who was known for miles around for her cooking ability. Whenever I came within hearing distance from her kitchen window, she yelled, "Come on in Jimmy, I got something for you." There were always baskets of homemade cookies, cakes, pies and candies. Lots of times I made a special trip over there to get her wonderful sweets.

Our little laid-back community was laced together with yeomen and large estates and a few snug merchants. Shortie Tillman's store had the necessary commodities of a mercantile. Herbie Harr's Feed Store carried chicken, turkey and cow feeds, wire and fencing materials. Mr. Nagel turned his living room in the front of his house into a grocery store. It was a buy-now and pay-later kinda store. Mr. Jim Hoffmeister's gas station had a single pump sitting in the middle of his front yard. He served one grade of gas. The grass was all run down in his front yard. His pin name was "Jim's Pump," and he wore it with pride. If you needed gas you walked up on his porch, yelled through the screen door, "Jim, keep your seat, I'm getting gas." If he wasn't home, you got your gas and paid later.

There were a couple of "shade-tree mechanics," covered with grease from head to toe from fixing puddle-jumpers, but only for the Ridge-Runners—that's what the locals were commonly called.

We had two active sawmill operators in our part of the country: Wilbur Baublitz and Raymond Whitcomb. Anything that was needed from a log, these guys knew how to saw it out. And we had a private airport without a hangar. Before takeoff you had to run the cows out of the field and before landing, you had to radio ahead to get a cow-count to make sure they were all clear. Chestnut Ridge used to boast about having its own post office in Henry Cronhardt's house. There isn't a post office any longer. In the early fifties we got a homemade fire truck, made from an old three-quarter-ton army truck, engineered by Morris Long and Son. The only available water came from a stream.

The Boys Race

Cross country horse races are popular and have set a tradition in Maryland. The steeples on churches were used as landmarks to guide horse and rider from one point to another. This race became known as "steeplechase" or "point to point." In my day in Green Spring Valley, it was known as "The Boys Race."

173

The battling four-mile race had all natural fencing: five-foot-high post and rail or white-board fence. The race was to show physical stamina for both horse and rider. Many a good horse has plowed through the solid fence and if his mind ceased all operation, then he was shot. The humane decisions were respected by all.

There was a fee for each vehicle to enter the race grounds regardless of the number of passengers. In 1954 one of the young men of the neighborhood got the bright idea of hooking a hay wagon to the farm tractor. On race day we all met at his farm. He had already placed bales of hay on the wagon for the small kids and ladies to sit on. The hayride was on the way.

We arrived at the gate laughing and having a fine old time. At this point it probably wouldn't have made much difference if we got in or not. We stopped in line like all the rest of the cars. The young attendant at the gate collecting the parking fee didn't know what to do. He spoke with his fellow workers and together they decided it might be best to pull over and wait for his boss. His boss came, looked us over good, scratched his head and said since we were not breaking the law it would be okay to come in on the usual fee of $1.00. The following year a large sign was placed over the entrance to the race grounds weeks in advance, stating "No hay wagons, farm trucks, or carriages of any kind permitted."

In the early spring on the first full moon, as few as two and as many as nine upright members of the Green Spring Hounds dressed in white night garb and rode the two-mile course on the hill in front of the woods. Their white pajamas and long nightcaps made them visible in the far distance from the road. These guys were the scary ghost riders of the valley. There was no great secret about it and a small crowd gathered to watch. It was unfortunate that by the late 1940's, the pure nature of

174

such a chase had become inappropriate for the changing times. Without anybody ever telling me, I suspect there must have been complaints that they resembled the Ku Klux Klan.

Wild Dogs

My grandfather-in-law Johnny Raver and I had an old-fashioned friendship. He was born in a log house along Ridge Road in 1894. He told me some neat stories before he died in 1974. Parts of Ridge Road continually washed out in the spring of the year. The farmers living along the road placed logs longways across the road to keep gullies from washing the middle of the road out. Then with their horses and dump carts, they filled in-between the logs with rocks and dirt, and dragged it smooth. Log roads like this were called "corduroy roads."

Johnny told me about taking a load of loose hay to Baltimore with his father in 1904. Four horses were hooked to the hay wagon and when they got to the top of Red Hill on Caves Road to give the horses a break, a pack of wild dogs came out of the woods and attacked them. "Grandpa," then just a young boy, grabbed one of the two pitchforks and was ready to jump down off the wagon to help the bucking, stomping horses that were getting torn up by the dogs.

The dogs were trying to climb up onto the wagon of loose hay to get at him. Dry hay is very slippery and the dogs couldn't grip enough to get up to him. His father was scared that

Johnny was going to slip off the wagon and fearfully yelled, "Stay where you are, boy." As the dogs made attempts to get at them one at a time, they got a good stab with the fork. After so many wounds, the dogs left, and Johnny and his father got down to take a look at the horses in the pale moonlight. Johnny said that they left the farm at 4 a.m. and had not traveled much more than a mile or two before the attack. The lead horse had his hocks torn up so badly they had to return to the farm. Then they had to borrow a neighbor horse for the trip to Baltimore. By the time they got to Baltimore with their hay and unloaded it, it was well past midnight.

Suitcase Farmers

We had a fair number of farm owners who lived in some far-off land like New York City. We called them "suitcase farmers." Ordinarily their "farm houses" were old mansions with domestic architecture on large estates that came with a full-run of household help the year 'round. The wealthy owners only came several times a year to visit their farms. Chauffeurs trucked the suitcases and satchels in and out for the week. Mr. Alfred Vanderbilt, the owner of a famous racehorse farm, "Sagamore Farm," hired a lot of farm help. These wealthy "country nuggets" were a pleasure to have around, especially since they created a lot of work for the neighborhood, in spite of the fact that it was a rare privilege to see them. For many of the "old money" well-to-do-ers in the valley, to be poor was only a curiosity. My mother said many times, "We are far happier than many of the very wealthy." Great wealth and contentment seldom live together. Actually, happiness is the "weigh-station" between having too much and having too little.

Roger and the Runaway Mule

One of my best friends was Roger Howard, a neighbor and good friend, more like a begetter. If you have one true friend, then you have more than your share. Roger was a true friend indeed. He had his own morals and a code of ethics he lived by. We lived on the Worthington Hill side of Chestnut Ridge. It was a common practice to hire day help for a large farm. Roger didn't live on the farm where he was employed but lived in the heart of farming country. Back in the '60's, Roger worked for Alfred Vanderbilt on his farm—during the days when we got an egg from a chicken and milk from a cow. Our biggest pollution came from horses or a tractor towing a trail of dust across the field.

After his ten-hour day on the farm, Roger worked in his garden at home. He was not a physically big man but he was as tough as a pine knot. Once a tree fell on his right foot and broke it. It never healed properly, and after that he took slow steady steps with his foot flatly turned outward. Many people whistle or sing to themselves while they work. Roger hummed. I have stopped by to visit Roger at his garden as he knelt on one knee pulling weeds from around young plants, just humming away to himself—a very self-contented person. He had the neatest little piles of weeds all in a trail in a perfectly straight row. As he made a leap forward, another little pile was started. These little mounds of weeds were not moved until the last weed was out and placed on the pile. Even if it took several evenings to do it, they were all gathered up at the same time.

I helped Roger move piles of topsoil many times; he never dug a hole in the side or got a shovel-full off the top. He kept moving around the pile and the pile just seemed to be melting down until gone. Patience was true to his virtue. Roger's gardening ability was exceptional: what he didn't grow wasn't needed. His garden was neat and manicured at all times. He continually rotated his crops; every little space was used, and each plant was just the right distance apart from the other. Roger worked in his garden the year-around, having a winter garden as well as spring, summer and fall.

I had a white Chinese goose with the typical orange bill and topknot. Her name was Madeline. Madeline was a free-ranger in the neighborhood and spent many hours helping Roger in his garden. Yes, geese will eat only weeds, not the strawberries—no joke! However, Roger said, "Wash the berries good before you eat them, or they will taste like goose poop." The Howards ate an early supper in the summertime. Madeline would smell dinner on the table and stand outside the kitchen door pecking and honking until Mrs. Howard threw something out to her.

Roger's winter garden was mostly in hotbeds; however, he dumped leaves on some areas to keep them from freezing. Turnips, parsley, winter squash and such could be harvested by raking off the snow. Just before the ground froze in the fall, it was time to plant peas. Peas were not covered with leaves but planted extra deep, and they were up in the spring before the grass turned green.

During dry weather when weeds were not growing, Roger continued to cultivate his garden regularly. He claimed he had to work the dew into the ground to keep his plants growing. It must have worked, for he had a fine garden.

Unquestionably Roger must have carried a "golden hoe": Everything he grew was a winner, and he had a horn of plenty. Roger and Beulah had their back porch lined up with comfortable rockin'-chairs—cushions and all. There were enough to go around no matter who came. Pull one up and prop your feet up on the baluster. There weren't many evenings they didn't have pie and ice cream before going to bed. One evening we were sitting on Roger's porch eating up the last of Beulah's gooseberry and rhubarb pie. (In our neighborhood rhubarb was known as "pie plant.") I was listening to Roger's stories, watching Madeline pecking grubs out of a dead tree stump in the backyard. As Roger lit up his corncob pipe he said, "Did I ever tell you about Ches Reter's old mule?"

Roger told me lots of neat stories. There was never the slightest doubt about Roger's stories: they were as straight-forward as a wagon tongue and embellished with plenty of cussing which only added to the exciting story. His delightful theatrical mannerism was a bit of a rib-tickler. Roger's yesterday's spoken rubbish is my today's golden memory; but the details must be censored due to respect for my young readers.

Ches Reter owned and operated a dairy farm not more than a half-mile away. There were but few dry farmers (a farmer without cows) in the area at the time. It was customary for farmers to hire out their dray stock to off-farm residents in the community to work their gardens.

It was nearing the beginning of late summer when Roger walked over to Ches' farm and harnessed a mule and rode him back to his garden. It's an ill-founded belief that mules are lazy, stubborn and ornery. I personally have found mules to be heart-warming animals that are willing to please. Roger had the mule hooked to a three-legged cultivator and was working the potato patch. The mule was a slow mover, something that was a credit. He was able to work the ground adjacent to the plants and not plow them out. The day had been long and bone-tiring; now it was past sundown. The sky turned black, and Roger was hurrying, for as much as Roger ever hurried, to get done before it rained. There appeared to be some heat lightning off in the distance.

By jiggers, all of a sudden from out of the calm and stillness came a mighty clap of thunder. Three seconds later the lightning stabbed a nearby tree at the edge of the garden. The tree-top limbs came crashing to the ground within 50 feet. Telling me the story as it happened, Roger acted out each movement, waving his hands and showing expressions. His good humor came out with a bounce. As Roger explained that that so-and-so mule dropped to the ground, he put his hands to the ground, Roger then smacked his hands together and came up off the chair with a few new words I'd never heard before.

As Roger told it, the quivering mule sprang up with a pair of double kickers that could have knocked your hat off. He was a big strong mule that was built to do whatever he liked. After his feet hit the ground, the only view seen was from his south-end. His tail curled over his back and he brayed a few times, taking off with the cultivator behind him. Oh yes, he was faster than a New York banker with your money.

The hee-hawing and the excitement with the jingling of chains brought the hounds out from under the porch where they were hiding from the storm. The pack ran full speed to the garden. The roar and the echo of the thunder continued. The old mule wouldn't whoa; he plowed out a triple row of potatoes as he went.

Roger paused in his story and taking the backside of his hand, wiped the tobacco juice from the corner of his mouth. He

180

gathered his wits and then the cussin' began. Yes, Roger chewed and smoked a corncob pipe at the same time.

Then he continued telling me that in no time the mule was out of sight. The triumph of the hounds was close at hand. That dang blame "jackass" kicked up a storm all of his own. Sometimes the pleasures in life are hard to find, but Roger managed to find one. He told me later that those three rows were the hardest to hoe anyway; a mule is a good animal in the field but don't let him get loose in the garden.

As the mule rounded the turn to the main road, the cultivator struck broadside against a large sycamore tree, the yapping hounds hanging close to his heels. Roger, galloping along as fast as he could, tried to keep up but just couldn't do it. The old term for farmer, plow chaser, certainly applied to Roger that day. He got to the tree, picked up the mangled pieces of the cultivator, and placed them up tight against the tree out of the way of any traffic. For a moment Roger had to do some sleuthing to see what direction the mule had taken.

By now the wind had hit and the sky opened up like a blue porcelain teakettle. It rained so hard the road suddenly sprang into a rivulet, a real "gooser." Without rain gear, Roger in his lumbering steps plowed his way back to Ches' farm. All the way back to the barn, Roger picked up bits and pieces of harness. He found the crupper hanging on some brush along the road. The only complete parts that hadn't been torn up were the single tree and the bridle.

Being late in the evening, it was milking time when Ches heard a clamor at the barn door. He looked up and saw his mule cutting the corner coming into the barn. The mule fell sideways from the cowslip on the smooth cement floor. Then he jumped up, shook himself off and walked to his stall to get fed. Ches said, "Why the old mule didn't walk in like he was supposed to, I don't know." Pretty soon, Roger got to the barn, tediously carrying as much of the miscellaneous harness as he could manage.

Roger didn't see hide nor hair of that mule until he laid eyes on him at the barn—the ole bucker standing in his stall "peacock-proud" without any giddy-up. The lather was still dropping off as he stood there resting on three legs. Ches spoke to Roger about the efficiency of his mule. He came through the door crisscrossed and mopped up the floor as he came.

Roger told Ches about what had happened, and Ches said, "What did you do?" Roger, a little provoked at that but with his typical shrewdness, said, "I didn't have no more than a thimble full of choices." Ches replied, "Nevertheless, it's a rare day you'll see my mule run away. Well that's okay. You can straighten out the cultivator parts and make new handles. Don't worry yourself about the old harness; I have more. That will be a dollar for the use of my mule." The usual price was two dollars for a full day; most of the time just for a few hours in the evening, it was free.

Roger chided, "I only got a couple of rows worked up and he plowed out three of them!" Ches said, "Since the mule run home like that, he lost some fat, so that will be a dollar." Roger didn't want to impinge on Ches' rights any farther, so he let it go. "Tight money" was no stranger in our neighborhood. Times were lean for nearly all; everybody needed that dollar.

Roger, with a wrinkled face, made an impressive spit in just the right spot over the railing. It would have been hard not to notice him as he fumed to me, rekindling that old flame. "I could have bought them blankety-blank potatoes for all that. Furthermore, Ches has more trouble with that dag-blame mule than you can shake a stick at. He just won't admit it." I have a notion that Roger had a "craw" full of Ches' mule that day. Needless to say when a nine-hundred-pound mule makes a snap decision to head for the barn, you can't hold him. Roger is still complaining about Ches' mule and having to pay that dollar. It's unfortunate that sometimes healing old wrongs moves slowly.

That same mule is the one Ches used in his own potato patch, which was close to where Roger lived. One morning Ches hooked his mule to the spring wagon and drove to the patch. There he unhooked the mule, did his cultivating, then hooked him back to the spring wagon ready to go home. Still having time before the noon hour, Ches picked up his hoe and did some finish-up work closer to the potato plants that he'd missed. For some unknown reason, Ches had to babysit his young son Lawrence. Lawrence was only a few years old and got tired of following his father around in the potato patch, so he climbed in the back of the spring wagon and went fast to sleep. Twelve noon was feeding time and the old mule knew it. Without Ches knowing it, the mule turned around and walked home. When Ches got there the mule had walked into the barn as far as possible with the spring wagon stuck in the door and couldn't go any farther. The mule was happier than wise. Roger told me "darn good thing there wasn't a storm come up that morning or little Lawrence would have had a heckava ride to the barn." Roger carried his sense of humor on the end of his tongue regardless of whose taste.

The Sport of Cock Fighting

Cock Fighting has been a big sport around our part of the country for many years. It was done on a large scale, first one weekend here and then another one there. Huge tents were erected with stadium-like seats, a little ring for the chickens and big bucks on the fight. My good friend Bruce Stallard had a friend who had some fighting cocks that he claimed never lost a fight. Bruce said the secret was a jalapeno seed. On the upper end of a bird bill is a small hole on either side of the beak, which is the nostril. His friend would place a half-jalapeno seed in each nostril. Yes sir, that baby came out fighting mad.

The gamblers place both sporting bets and high-stakes gambling bets. A sporting bet is only a few dollars for fun; whereas, a gambling bet is for making big bucks off the gambler's favorite entry. Both types of bets are placed on fighting cocks. The entries are matched within ounces of each other and have to be the same age. Metal spurs of the same length are attached to each bird.

The birds are placed on the diagonal at the corners of the pit. Each pitter releases his stag (year old bird) or cock (older bird), which then runs to the center of the ring like a boxer and begins to fight. Feathers will fly until one bird is no longer able to fight. Or, they may run, and one will jump on the other's back, and with a peck on the top of the other's head, he's dead.

Harry Keller was a friend of mine who used to fight birds. He offered to take me with him when I was thirteen and Mother told him, "No, absolutely not!" Mom told Harry that it was against the law and only bad people do those kinds of things. Harry asked, "Mary, you go to church, don't you?" And of course Mom quickly replied, "Why yes I do!" Harry proceeded to tell Mom that they have bad people in church too. Mom wouldn't accept that as a reason and told Harry, "He is not going and that is final!" I never did go to a fight, but did see the tent and the after-effects of the event. I knew and talked to a lot of people who were there.

Each entry chose his own pitter and the most popular of all pitters was Ole Frank Watts, the local barber in Reisterstown—he won religiously. He could revive a half-dead bird by putting his head in his mouth, sucking the blood off his eyes, running him up and down a short fencing board held between his hands to get his bounce back and then putting him back in the ring all pumped for another win.

Many a story was told about these contests. It was said that one night a gentleman in attendance had a heart attack and died. He was gently placed behind the bleachers, the ambulance was called and the fight continued. The ambulance and police arrived, picked up the poor ole fellow, brushed off the feathers and took him away. No questions were asked and the fights never missed a beat. This story was verified by Marie Forbes in her book, <u>Speaking of Our Past: A Narrative History of Owings Mills, Maryland</u>.

There was enough political power behind cock fighting in Green Spring and Worthington Valleys that there was little fear of a raid; however, that didn't hold true for some of the smaller fights in the outlying areas. In well-hidden pasture fields, out of sight from the public view, the cockfights continued to take place on most Saturday nights until early in the morning, each weekend in a different location, and running from December to July, due to the chickens' molting season.

Sometime in the beginning of late fall nearing the end of the 1970's, "a party-man" called me presenting himself by saying that he had found me through a mutual friend. I told him I didn't know that I was lost. He gave a quick approving chuckle and said he'd been trying to find me for a while. He kinda' took the long way 'round the barn before introducing himself. You know how a lawyer can talk a long time and not say nothing.

185

It turned out that he was a popular figure and the owner of a well-to-do plantation on the far side of the valley. He had earned the respect of his neighbors and they held him in high regards for his expert horsemanship and his ability in fox hunting. On one occasion he won first place in our cross-country horserace. I heard he had a great fancy for some feathery sports and it wasn't all bird hunting. In fear that his reputation might precede him, he asked if I was the same Jimmy Fox from over at Beaver Brook Farm. Once he was satisfied that I was and the formalities were out of the way, he became much more sociable. I will say that some of these "old money boys" are the most down to earth persons you will ever meet. We became friends right off.

He asked if I had time to put up a temporary fence like a snow fence around a portion of his pasture to hold his cattle up for a few days because he was going to have a party. From the description of where he lived in the valley, I got a mental image of the area for the fence and suggested to him that an electric fence would be faster and cheaper. As long as there was good grass to graze and access to water, his cattle would be content for a while. Without any dickerin' to barter, he asked if I could meet him at his horse barn around six or a little after in the morning. I suggested the little after would be just fine.

The horse barn had a number of stalls full of fighting cocks—all in little transport cages and crowing up a storm. Mr. Partyman apologized for the short notice as he hopped in the truck and drove to a catawampus spot in the field he wished to block off for his cows. The weather was peaceful and cold and his Black Angus cattle were covered with a silver frost. As we passed the large white tent in the first section of the field, he asked if I knew what that was? I said, "Why yes, that's the tent where you're going to be holding the party. And if I'm not

186

mistaken, I think the chicks are going to be invited." I turned his party invitation down, and told him I would be back up Monday morning to remove the fence.

One day as I sat on Roger's porch, he told me about one of the heavy creamers in Worthington Valley. Mr. Harry Parr came over to Sagamore Farm and asked if anybody would care for his prized fighting cocks while he toured Europe for six weeks. This is Roger's story and I don't claim it to be Gospel. Roger carried no blame but each adventure promised enlightenment. He never considered outside opinion above his own.

It seems Roger volunteered to feed and water Harry's chickens while he toured Europe. Harry got back from his vacation and never said anything to Roger about the chicken feeding, no pay and no thank you. I mentioned to Roger that a lot of these wealthy people living here in the valley are big business guys and he, with almost certainty, just forgot. When Roger got rubbed the wrong way, he could get rough, tough, and as hard as any stubborn hangnail I've ever seen. He said, "Well that's your opinion; it's an insulting way to treat your help. Politeness to your neighbor is like warmth to wax. While he was busy with his leisure, I was taking care of his birds."

The following year Harry decided to go on another six-week vacation. He came back to the farm and asked Roger if he was the same man that fed his fighting cocks last year. Roger told him he was. Harry said, "Well this year while I am gone will you feed my birds for me again?" Roger, with a knotted forehead and a squalling tone, said, "H--l no! You didn't pay me for last year, so this year, you can take your darn chickens with you!" Sometimes Roger's boldness could make you crouch like a quail.

I asked Roger what Harry had to say about that. Roger

187

lingered a bit then said, "Well Jimmy, I rightly don't know. His English was so perfect I didn't understand a thing he said." Injustices done to an individual are sometimes of service to the public. After that I never heard of any more chicken feeders that ever "forgot" to get paid.

There was a strain against my heart the day Roger died. Birth and death are the kings of all mile markers in life. Death gives the worth to life. I'm sure the grass will never stop waving over Roger's grave. To live long is almost everyone's wish but to live well is the ambition of few. Roger did both. I don't believe he'd content to re-cradle life for a second time.

As the years advanced into the 1960's, a heavy influx of new residents was apparent on Chestnut Ridge. With this influx, the increase of land value soared, and farms declined in number. A new era of builders and roofers gave birth to new beginnings. By the year 2000 the farms had made a noticeable change from wheat fields and cows, to houses, swimming pools and golf courses. I don't know what will happen in 2060, but I'm nearly positive that there won't be any runaway mules.

Barky

During the whelping days at the launch of my landscaping career, I had a customer who was a wonderful older gentleman. Mr. Bernard Barksdale Thompson came to Baltimore from Thomas, West Virginia. Thomas is a small mining and logging town. There the wind and times change thinly and unchecked over wild and beautiful dish mountains. After all, West Virginia was our first "real west." What more could we expect than the rustic beauty it offers? I always referred to Mr. Thompson as Mr. T. Mr. T was better known as Barky to his friends. He was called Barky after his family surname.

188

His lovely wife, Mrs. T, came from Davis, West Virginia, just two short country miles down the road. She spoke often of Davis with great delight. One of the most striking features, and recognized both far and wide, is the stunning Canaan Valley. The 14-mile-long valley is known as "The High Valley" with up to 200 inches of snow in a season. Davis claims the title for being the highest incorporated town east of the Mississippi at a lofty height of 3,200 feet.

Mr. T, a soft-mannered person who was born in the early 1900s, had spent much of his time with his grandmother. She lived only a few miles away in the little town of Leadmine. The love for his grandmother was unconditional; she was the glue that molded a great deal of his future. His grandmother was a meager mountain woman whose modest ambitions were best known to herself. He spoke of her often and only with the kindest of affection.

Mr. T recalled that, at the age of nine, before the rooster finished crowing one morning, he pulled himself out of a comfortable crouch that comes only with a rope bed. Barky hurried down the stairs to gulp down his breakfast. Then in lively steps he set course on a short cut through the mountain to visit his grandmother on her farmstead. The early spring sun was shining warmly; it was a fine morning to travel through the woods. He had gone but a short distance when he discovered a bear's "stomping path." There were claw marks and freshly open bark on a scab tree. He followed the bear's tracks for a piece; then it became clear they were very fresh tracks, and so he curiously trailed on.

Presently three little honey bears sprang up, no larger than the size of a half-grown housecat. They bounced out of a small laurel thicket where they'd been playing. The old mother bear was out feeding on acorns and had left her babies at the entrance of her den to wait for her until she returned for them. The youngsters instinctively stopped to look, listen and search for any danger, but didn't see Barky. The bears were attracted to the noise of the many squirrels scampering through the dry leaves, and unbeknownst to the bears, Barky was able to creep closer. He continued to follow them and watch them roll over and over each other and scuffle around trees—a scene not often witnessed.

Barky stood as still as a stump. Finally, one little bear ran up a tree about two feet off the ground and looked around. He caught the playful little guy with the greatest of ease, and as he cuddled him in his arms, the bear started making a kind of contenting purring sound. Then Barky carried the cub off to his grandmother's farm. He played with it for a while, then put him in the old corncrib for "safe keeping." Needless to say, this was back in his young and ignorant days about bears.

By late morning the momma bear had trailed the scent of her baby bear back to the corncrib. Barky's grandmother heard all the commotion outside between mother bear and baby bear. Honey bears are not spiteful unless provoked. Grandmother was concerned that the momma bear might become a bad customer, so she sent Barky outside to release the little baby bear. With a long stick he flipped the latch on the corncrib door and freed the frightened little bear. The mother bear took a few good whiffs from her baby, gave a snort and ran off into the woods with the rest of her little family.

His grandmother said, "Now Barky, why don't you go down to the falls and get us some fish for supper." Eagerly he took off at a tolerable gait for the river. Along Blackwater Falls, life was in full swing with birds singing and whistling happy notes. Down at the bottom of the falls, Barky snuck along a large pool of water that was only half-a-leg deep. He found just the right spot and rested on a fallen tree. He spent the afternoon down by the falls, fishing in the tea-colored water with his homemade fishing line. There, rainbow trout got as fat as any good well-to-do trout can here.

On the way back home, he stopped in at the Leadmine General Store, the local one-room store. The store was a small simple one with a lengthy porch made of a wide-split puncheon board. As usual for the area, the screen door was lined with houseflies. Looking through the screen door, he was greeted by cheerful and lively chatter as he opened the door. Two men were sitting on nail kegs talking to the storekeeper. The smell of hot coffee came from the potbelly stove in the corner. Along with groceries and hardware, was hunting and fishing equipment; harness and logging tools lined the wall.

Barky noticed these two strangers were gaping wide at his fish. The one to the left kept his seat and asked if he would like to sell his fish. The reply was, "No sir, these fish are for my grandmother; they are not for sale." That seemed like an unusual question. He never knew of anybody around Blackwater Falls, who wanted to buy fish. If you needed fish, you just went down to the river, threw your line in and pulled out whatever you wanted.

Thomas Edison, the man who lit up all the cities across America with his invention of "the great white light bulb" and his close friend Henry Ford, the inventor of the Model T Ford car, affectionately called the "Tin Lizzie," were the two men in the store. Both Edison and Ford had been the top seeds of the invention world for many years. Not only well-heeled businessmen of the past and future, they were also prized customers of a happy storekeeper.

Edison stood up, walked a little closer to get a better look at

Barky's fish, "That's a nice string of plump fish, young man." With that, he again asked to buy the fish. Barky didn't care to give up his fish to a stranger; however, he didn't think it would be proper not to answer politely. So he replied again, "No sir, they are not for sale. These fish are for my grandmother and she wants them for our supper." Without any hesitation he had been guided by his internal code of ethics and wholehearted love for his grandmother.

The mere presence of Edison and Ford in the neighborhood created quite a stir for a small village. That is, with the exception of Barky. They often came to Blackwater Falls to go camping and fishing. For Edison and Ford it had been a wearing day. It was getting late, they had to make camp, and it would be nice to have fish in the pan for dinner. Then they could just enjoy the quiet and peace of the fullness of their evening by the falls as they had on many other occasions.

Edison, seeing that he had run Barky as far as he could with this conversation, reined back a bit and brushed off his "no's" as though he thought it was best to change the subject to get to know the young lad a little better. Then Mr. Storekeeper set his cup of coffee down and introduced Mr. Edison and Mr. Ford to Barky and said, "This is young Barky Thompson. He lives over in Thomas." Mr. Edison asked young Barky what he did for excitement in Thomas. His reply was, "In Thomas, we don't get excited." Edison laughed at that and realized the ice was breaking. Then he leisurely pursued to clinch the deal, as the bartering continued, "What if I give you this new shiny silver dollar. How about that?"

Edison and Ford had already attained much distinction for themselves, and the storekeeper was well aware of it and enjoyed the frequent business from such fine distinguished gentlemen. However that was of small concern to a country boy. Mr. Storekeeper took a puff of his pipe and convincingly continued to thaw Barky further by saying, "I don't think your grandmother will really mind if you trade off your fish for a shiny silver dollar like that one," as Mr. Edison held it up high for him to see. Barky, remaining polite but starchy, kept his feet planted and said, "Well I don't know."

In a calming tone Edison said, "Barky, I'll throw in a good old fishing rod of mine for you." With the thought of that brand new silver dollar and a promise of a fishing rod, Barky lost his taste for trout that day. Dumbfounded and befuddled with the thought of anybody making such a trade, he took the silver dollar along with the fishing rod and thought he was quite well off. As meek as a fawn, he happily handed over his fish. The deal raised some friendly laughter, and together the men trooped across the road to their campground. The handsome fly rod bore the name 'Thomas Edison' inscribed on a silver plate by the handle. The fishing rod brought about new charm for Barky's fishing in Blackwater Falls. It would be difficult to find a boy living in the mountains with less trouble and enjoying more pleasure than Barky at the time.

Today there stands a plaque that marks the spot for the campground of Edison and Ford. Henry Ford had brought on faster transportation, while Tommy Edison gave us light. Both of these boys made life easier than ever. To know that I had a friend who knew Thomas Edison and Henry Ford seems almost unreal.

The nicest compliment anyone could ever receive from his wife came from Mrs. T, when I asked her if she thought this story about Edison was true. She replied with serious concern, "I sure don't believe Barky would ever tell a lie!" Many times I have taken my family to enjoy the beauty at Blackwater Falls. I thought of Barky every time.

Life at Beaver Brook Farm

My Little Brown Dog—My Ole Friend

When I was in elementary school in Pikesville, at the end of the school year, I got a little brown dog. I named him Rusty. I carried him home in my lunch bag. The bus driver thought it was pretty funny seeing a little dog in a lunch bag. He told me right to my face, "Dumbest thing I've ever seen." Well, I didn't tell him because I thought I'd get in trouble, but I thought he was probably the dumbest bus driver I'd ever seen. So, what he said didn't really bother me too much.

I brought this little dog home and with the approval of my mother and father, I was able to keep this little half-Bulldog and half-whatever else. (I don't really know what it was). It turned out that he was pretty smart.

Anyway, I started training him right away—the very first day I got him. I thought, "Well, he might learn, he might not." Not realizing how young he was, I felt that he really started doing pretty well in the following years at Beaver Brook Farm.

I would take him out groundhog hunting because he loved being with me all the time. Rusty and I would sneak up over the hill and I would crawl up in the pond field. On one side right above the pond, there was a valley close to the hedgerow where there were groundhogs everywhere. I would sic Rusty on the groundhogs. Then I would go to one hill and lie there and watch him run down in the valley and up to the other side to get to the groundhogs. He learned to crawl on his belly, just like I would do. I was real proud of him. I started calling him my Army dog. I remembered seeing in the movies where the dogs would crawl around on the ground like that.

Let's face it, Rusty was a pretty talented dog. We used to milk the cows by hand and I would take him down behind the cow I was milking and tell him to sit there. I would squirt a long stream of milk from the cow's teat and it would hit him right in the mouth. He would lick it right up. He got pretty good at that.

Rusty went to Eastern Shore for a while because Mr. Jones needed him there to serve as a guard dog. Rusty's stay was short-lived, I think because he began catching chickens and sucking eggs. He was a good hunter. I was glad to have him back home.

Besides groundhog hunting, I would also take Rusty squirrel hunting. We would sneak through the woods real quiet until one of us saw or heard a squirrel. Then Rusty was off running through the woods barking like crazy to get that squirrel. Curiosity killed the cat, but in this case it was the squirrel. The squirrel was so curious that it had to stop to see what all the barking was about. The squirrel would stop, turn around and come down the tree headfirst, chattering and barking back at Rusty. Rusty would stay there and keep barking with cat-like movements, while I would sneak cautiously to a spot where I could get a good shot. At other times I would find a hickory nut or shell bark tree and get a nice comfortable seat and wait for Mr. Squirrel to come to me. Rusty would make a seat next to me and remain just as quiet as he could be. With the slightest noise or rustling of the leaves, his ears would perk up, but he wouldn't move until I gave him the command.

Because of school I did more hunting in the late evening than morning. My father would still be finishing up in the barn when I'd be coming in from the woods. He was never too busy to tease me. His first question would be, "Do you have anything for the pot?" If I said, "Yes, I have two," he'd say, "I heard three shots. What happened to the third squirrel?" Then he'd laugh. He always knew where I was in the woods and counted the number of shots. It was hard to pull one over on him.

There was a butcher-block that I kept in the dairy to dress out squirrels, rabbits, wild game, and fish. After the game was cleaned out and dressed to my satisfaction, I placed it in heavy salt water for 24 hours, changing the bloody water periodically to fresh water.

I also raised rabbits and sold them for meat. Mom was my best customer. Rusty was very athletic. As the rabbits lay motionless in line while waiting for the butcher block, he would sneak around, grab one, throw it up in the air and run around with it. I had to call Rusty back, take it from him, and send him back to the house to stay on the porch. He always obeyed.

Mom sure knew how to make good rabbit and squirrel potpie. If the rabbits or squirrels were young ones, more then likely she would fry them; that was even better.

During the 1950's, Mrs. Thompson hired a colored man name Herbert as her cook. He asked me if I ever went groundhog hunting. I told him I did. He asked if my family ate them and I said, "No, but since they're grassers I'd think that they'd be good to eat." He said, "A young groundhog is more than just good; it's delicious. The next time you go and get a young one, bring it to me and I'll fix you up something you'll think was the best fried chicken you ever had."

So I made a point to go hunting for a nice young groundhog. I came across a den of four or five that were munching on some grass in the pasture close to the woods. I got one and sent Rusty to fetch it. I waited for the others to calm down and come back out; then I got a second. I took these two young groundhogs and gave them to Herbert. Herbert said he'd clean them and soak them in salt water, and he'd let me know when I should bring my younger brother Marvin for a feast of good eating.

Two days later when Herbert saw me working on the farm, he said, "Stop down for dinner this evening." Marvin and I went down, tapped on the back door to the kitchen. Herbert let us in and we went straight to the help's table. The table had been set and everything was in place. I was ready for some fried groundhog. Marvin and I each sat in a chair and pulled it up close to the table. Herbert was right. It was great ground-hog—fried up like Mom's fried chicken. It was delicious! From that day on, I took all the young groundhogs to Herbert, and he gave them to some of his people who lived in the city. His family was glad for the fresh meat.

Turtle Soup

One late spring when Rusty and I were out groundhog hunting, we were crawling up the hill to the pond. I spotted something small over on the next hill. For a long time it didn't move. Rusty saw it too. He stayed down but was excited about whatever it was. What little it moved was in the direction towards me. I eyeballed the spot where this thing had stayed for such a long time and got some good landmarks in my mind, so I'd be able to find its location if I decided to walk over to where this thing was.

As it moved into the valley between us, we moved onto the top of the hill. As I was trying to get a closer look, it crawled up the other side in front of me. I could see it was a snapping turtle from out of the pond, and it was working its way back. I wondered what the turtle was doing way over there. I let it pass by without any trouble. It was of noticeable size, but not a bragger for one of Mom's big soup pots. I was puzzled as to why it was over there on the next hill so far away from the pond.

Groundhog hunting was out of my mind for now. Mr. Thompson gave me a quarter for every groundhog I shot, and I could use the pocket money. Only being able to jingle 40 cents in my pocket, I still passed it up. I had to see what that turtle was up to. I got up and walked over to the next hill, keeping my landmarks in mind so I'd be close to where the turtle had stayed for so long. When I got there, I looked around and soon discovered the exact spot where it had been. I couldn't see anything but a little pile of fresh dirt. Using a small rock, I pulled the fresh dirt away from the pile. Looking around, I couldn't find that snapper or any of his cronies close by. Everything seemed okay, so I continued digging and didn't have to go too far before I found some small, white, rubbery eggs.

So that's what the turtle was doing. I put everything back where it was and thought I'd keep an eye on them. Rusty was ready to dig them out and eat them. I thought after they hatched out, I'd catch them and have me some snapping turtle pets. I watched and watched that same spot for weeks, but never saw them hatch. They must have hatched out overnight and left early in the morning for the pond, because one day I found their empty shells.

On another day that spring, my father was going to town to the lumber company and asked if I'd like to ride along. I asked Dad if Rusty could go too. I knew Dad was not one to be willing to haul a dog around in the truck, but to my surprise his answer was "yes." We made it to the lumber company and on our way home, as we passed Foster's Farm, which had a large pond, a huge snapping turtle crossed the road in front of us. I asked Dad if he'd like some snapping turtle soup.

He said, "Sure" and stopped the truck. I jumped out and Rusty ran right behind me. On the way out Dad said, "Don't let that turtle get a hold of you." I told him, "Don't worry, he won't." Attracting him with a fair-sized stick, I let him snap onto it. Rusty continued running around barking at him. With the turtle still hanging on to the stick, I picked him up and flung him into the back of the truck. We took off for home.

While pulling into the driveway, Dad asked me how my turtle was doing. I looked in the back of the truck and didn't see him. I thought he must have been hiding under some boards. We pulled in front of the shop; I jumped out looking for the turtle and couldn't find him. We unloaded the truck and there was still no turtle. That dog-gone turtle was not there; he must have jumped out on the way home. Our best guess was that he climbed on the boards to the top edge of the truck and jumped. I said, "Maybe he committed suicide jumping out of the back of the truck like that." Rusty and I walked back an entire mile—as far as Greenspring Avenue—and saw no signs of a turtle.

One day Rusty and I went fishing at the pond. It was like any other typical farm pond. I had my favorite luxury fishing spot in the shade of a white oak tree that hung out over the water. It was one of those listless days. I was fishing and having pretty good luck. Then I hooked on to a big snapping turtle. It took a while but I finally got him to the surface. Often times a snapper will snap on your fishing hook, but won't swallow it. You pull him in nice and slow but by the time he gets to the surface of the water where he can see, he'll let go and sink back to the bottom. That's what this snapper did, so I got a bright Sunday afternoon idea that I would go to the house to see what I could find. Something like a chicken neck or anything that Mom might have lying around for supper, something that a turtle would want to hold on to and not be willing to give up.

I was in the kitchen scrounging around to see what was there, when I spotted some of Dad's home-cured country ham that was left over from yesterday. I was cutting a piece of the rind off, when I heard Mom in a good clear voice say. "What are you doing here?" I loved teasing my mother and, without being a smart-aleck, I replied, "I live here." She got a chuckle out of that and said, "I know you do." I explained the urgency with the turtle and what I was up to. She said, "Okay, but only take enough to catch the turtle. I need that rind to season my string beans for tonight's supper." When she saw how I was cutting off the rind and making a mess on the counter with the grease, Mom said, "Don't be so hoodley." (This was a word that I often heard in my growing up years. It was German gibberish dialect from the Cartzendafner branch of the family, the translation meaning disarrayed or haphazard. From my own barnyard lingo, it meant I was making a holy mess.)

I got back to the pond and started all over. The turtle liked the ham rind and as planned, I got the turtle on the bank. Then with a branch off the white oak tree, I smacked him one time on the end of his nose. Whoo! That got him mad. Then I put the stick in front of him, and he snapped onto it. Every time he'd let go, I'd take the stick and smack him on the nose again until I pulled him to the house. This was the mildest tempered turtle I'd ever seen. Most turtles snap on and won't let go.

201

Mom asked me if I'd dragged the turtle all the way up the hill from the pond to the house. "Yep, I sure did!" Mom said, "My gosh, that's a big turtle!" Mom was surprised and well pleased with the size of the turtle. I asked her if I could borrow her washtub and dropped the tub over him so he couldn't run off while I cleaned my fish. I started to leave and noticed the tub was moving to one side. The turtle was lifting the tub up off the ground. I thought, I'll fix him. I put a big heavy rock on the top of the washtub and thought to myself, "Mr. Turtle is here to stay!"

I was just finishing up with cleaning the fish when I heard Rusty bark and Dad yell to me, "There goes your turtle." I said, "That gentleman is next." After I got him cleaned, Mom made a big pot full of turtle soup. A turtle has seven different flavors of meat and they are all delicious: that turtle made wonderful soup. My father got a lot of laughs out of the turtle and all my troubles. He enjoyed telling people about the turtle, and making up his own descriptions of the adventure, and always ended up by saying, "By-golly, Jimmy sure must love turtle soup."

Helping Hands

Medford Jones was a very knowing gardener who once had worked on Twiford Farm in Stevenson, Maryland. He was a small, sandy-haired man with a slouching gait nearing the upper end of middle age. He was as plain and wonderful as the weathered side of an old rail fence. Our family became very fond of the Joneses.

It was unfortunate that Mr. Jones' arthritis prevented him from doing what was considered his fair share of work on the farm. They stayed there only a short time, and then found a job on the Eastern Shore, where he attempted to work on a farm along the Chester River. He couldn't collect any disability income until the beginning of the next year, so I volunteered to stay with them for the summer after school closed and help with the farm duties. Mr. Jones' employer, Mr. Jimmy Hayes, Sr., told him if he could get someone to help him with his farm chores, they would continue to pay him a full salary, as modest as it was.

So one Monday morning when the fog hung heavily over the terminals for docking many large ships, Mom and I went directly to the terminal for the Old Bay Lines and found the "SS Bay Bell," one of several passenger ferries that catered to the lower shore. She dropped me off and we said our good-byes. With much excitement I took off, scurrying wide-eyed from deck to deck until it was my turn to disembark.

I got off the ferryboat and walked down the long narrow, free-swinging gangplank over the open water with a country boy beam. I was fourteen years old by the calendar; however with my farm responsibilities lying ahead, I felt a great deal older.

Mr. Jones' 1951 forest green pick-up truck was easy to spot; in fact, it was the only vehicle sitting in the middle of a gravel parking lot. Since I was the only person that got off the "Bay Bell," we soon found each other. After I safely reached the ground, the Captain gave a little all clear toot from the foghorn and I passed him a wave of thank you and good bye.

We did our "howdies" and soon we were on the gravel road rattling along toward the farm. We slowed down to a near crawl as we passed a dangerous intersection where five roads came together. The five points were known as "Cats Corner." At this junction was the only store in the area for miles around and, yep, the storekeeper loved cats. Everybody knew it: if someone had a she-cat and they didn't want her litter, they dropped the kittens off at five points, sometimes even in the middle of the night, without any doubt they would be cared for.

We stopped by and did a little farm shopping, picked up a dozen bags of cow feed and a salt block. Then we continued down first one dusty road, then another. The dirt-packed roads were swept clean by our breeze as we passed row after row of tasseled cornfields. The tall corn flowers were girdled by a pine forest. It was an easy morning's ride from the ferry to the farm.

The Joneses lived in a well-aged cottage on a lonely little farm along the Chester River. To the side of the house stood a tall wavy pine. In the orchard a covey of bobwhites picked on fallen fruit. Every boy should have the opportunity to hide from a bobwhite, then call to him in his own whistle and have the reward of the bird's coming to find him. A blue jay that gave scolding shrieks to all that came near his feeding ground was hunkered in an attempt to fight anybody that tried to come close. In the full flush of summer, for a quiet little farm, it was a busy time. This was a good feeling and it felt like home.

Fate had it we arrived just in the nick of time for the noonday meal. I followed the wonderful smell of crab cakes to the stove and picked up the lid for a better whiff when Mrs. Jones walked in and with a greeting smile, said "Get out of there!"

Like most "small-fisted farmers" on the Eastern Shore, Mr. Jones wrestled with the blights and bloom that flow with the coming tide of farming. The 40's and 50's were thought to have been the glory days for farming. Horses were once used in front of the plow; now they were left standing back in the barn.

I worked hard, but enjoyed my summer stay with them. I did

the milking in the morning and in the evening, and also helped with the fieldwork. Mrs. Jones fed the hay crew with a groaning meal that stuck to the backbone. Southern fried chicken and cornbread were mainstays here and on most Eastern Shore farms. Her table was small for the crowd that had gathered. To make room enough she had placed our "eating-irons" (knife, fork, spoon) in tumblers and then the tumbler sat squarely in the center of each plate. She was a first-rate cook and had earned herself a positive reputation on how to make do in a pinch. Kids were invited to come along for dinner but she insisted on good "stable manners"—no reaching, grabbing or pushing while at the table.

In addition to all the dinner fixings, Mrs. Jones worked in the garden and took care of the chickens and cleaned out the pigpens. All this heavy hard work was considered "woman's work." Mrs. Jones was a liberated woman and didn't even know it. She didn't burn her bra, but I'll bet the women's lib of today would have a hard time measuring up to her stature, even if they were willing to scrape off the soles of their boots.

The nicest sound heard in the summer was the slamming of the screen door. I knew right off it was Mrs. Jones bringing lemonade out on the porch where Mr. Jones and I sat talking, looking and listening to all the happenings of the boats running up and down the river. Their back porch was roomy and a wonderful place to take shelter from the summer heat. The hunched shoulders of the shoreline brought a simple mix of shade and breeze when you were looking for comfort. We could sit there and watch traffic leisurely moving up and down the river.

Large ships sent high rolling waves slapping the shoreline. Mr. Jones talked about the differences among the boats, and he carried a mark for these details. A flat-bottom boat, which has a large crane with a big scoop that looks like a basket, is for raking out oysters and is commonly called a "dredge-boat." One that carried square wire baskets on one end of 18-22 foot scissor-like poles is called a "tongue-boat."

Mr. Jones knew all sorts of classical legends about the backwaters of the Chesapeake Bay, and he always held my attention. There were gun battles from moonlighters as they trolled over illegal oyster beds; it was "blood on the half shell." It was Maryland Oystermen firing on Virginians: I could almost smell the gunpowder. I shouldered up plenty of enthusiasm when he spoke of the watermen and how they lived by their wits during the days of the "Oyster War." There was still plenty of gunplay on the Potomac River up until the 1970's. I knew he was not a man to indulge in fiction; it was, "speak the truth and shame the devil." I loved learning of the gunplay that sounded across the Bay. His rich river stories were new to me, and I could hardly wait to hear about the chase and the excitement of thundering guns exchanging fire.

One Friday evening a crabbing vessel came floating down the river out of the channel with a young fellow balancing himself on the side rail yelling something. Mr. Jones said he recognized the boat as belonging to an old friend of his in Rock Hall. He told me that during plump times Captain Mocks brought in as many as fifty bushel of crabs a day from out of the Chester River. That was the full strength of an average catch in the '40's and '50's. Captain Mocks was a typical Eastern Shore captain who understood the waterways and knew how to catch crabs, and without hesitation had a passion for wayward language.

Ducky was the young man who was balancing on the side rail. He was helping his father run a trout line on the Chester. To work a trout line is quite a task. The rawness of a hard life on the water made these young boys grow old fast into "hard-wearing" men. Ducky called a while later that evening and said he was yelling for Jimmy to be ready on Saturday night, and he'd be over to take me to the movies.

Ducky wasn't old enough to drive a car—at least legally. So he picked me up in his father's boat and we followed the water-ways through Fly Creek back to where Ducky lived with his family. Rock Hall is a fishing village that hadn't gravitated with the times. You couldn't throw a stone without hitting some-body who made a living from the water in one way, shape or form.

Rock Hall was filled with crab pickers, packing houses and an assortment of wholesale seafood suppliers. The smell of salt air from the water and fish guts tingled your nostrils. Rusty oyster sheds and mountains of oyster shells piled sky high spotted the landscape. Oyster shells were so plentiful that the county used them to repair the backcountry roads in place of stone, and the farmers used them as fertilizer. Everyone did anything they could to help to melt the giant piles of oyster shells.

The boats that provided the fresh fish supply houses were known as "gravy-boats" on the Chesapeake Bay. Oyster boats were known as "back-breakers." Roustabouts dredge or tongue for oysters, performing long, hard, vigorous winter-time work. Many oystermen trove oyster beds along the Chester River from daylight till dark. Oyster hunting is a busi-ness of endurance; the tossing water and slippery decks can soon become icy in freezing weather and have caused frequent drowning. Hurricanes and storms can bring on shipwrecks, which encourage the Bay's hungry appetite; it can flip you overboard and eat you up in one almighty gulp. Many a person has learned the cruel way from the hardships that nature has provided on the water.

The movie house was just a plain old Victorian house that sat on Main Street. The front living room served as the theater. The screen stood on a tripod, with steel folding chairs sitting one row in front of the other. There were five or six rows and no aisles. No neon signs or flashing lights. No pictures or advertisements. The name of the show and what it was about was passed around by word of mouth.

Ducky and I met some of his friends in front of the movie house. I was completely out of my element and they weren't sure of me. Most Eastern Shore people meet strangers with reluctance. So there I stood, a Western Shore country boy face to face with several Eastern Shore fishing boys, just standing around grinning at each other without knowing what to say. These young fishermen were from a long line of breeding stock that strongly straddled their heritage. Their young roots grew from out of the water and to them this was the only way of life. There was nothing to excite ambition for a formal education, and there was little pressure for the necessity of it. Time and nature had been left unchanged for generations. The new century did little to dim old ways; young and reckless for the future, they lived for the moment.

Finally the owner and operator opened the door and in a bold voice he yelled out, "Show time! Well, are you boys coming in or not?" We filed in one at a time and took our seats. Time was ample: I guess he wanted to get us inside before we stared each other down. During the show, every once in a while, the boys took turns craning their necks to see if I was enjoying myself.

After the show, we all met outside and got better acquainted. We watched a young fisherman come out of the Pint & Pitcher Tavern, better known as Rooster's Bar. With a sailor's consumption, he swaggered across the street. I thought he just

208

couldn't decide what side of the street he wanted to go on. Scathingly, some of the boys bellowed out catcalls to the poor soul. Back in my part of the country where social skills were a little bit fussier, most would take a dim view of such actions. As far as my knowledge went, that sort of behavior didn't exist; but here on Saturday night the rules were quite different. Nevertheless, that difference didn't constitute a fair hearing from my mother, for she was a severe judge of such action and she'd say, "The idea of anyone carrying on the practice of such a stunt!" My mother held a low opinion of any person who had more than one drink. There was never any allowance for gray with Mom; it was either black or white.

We loafed together in town for a while; then Ducky and I drifted down to the wharf to look through the crab sheds. A crabbing shed is only a rusty tin roof without any sides, just supporting poles. I've never seen one that wasn't in bad need of paint.

Commercial crabbers have long strings of wire boxes called sloughing boxes, all tied together with rope or light chain, hanging in the water. It is important to keep shade over the peeler's flimsy little body until they are fully hard again and safe from the hot sun. Blue crabs molt several times a year. I had the privilege of watching this process while they were in a sloughing box.

A hard shell crab that is ready to slough puffs itself up to break out of its shell, then gradually pulls itself out over a period of a few hours. To pick one up, be careful; it could easily become disjointed. To eat the jelly-like body of a newly sloughed crab, it's mushy and almost tasteless, watery and weak in flavor. A new soft-shell crab is very defenseless for the first three days and will be eaten by the hard crabs. Before long he's a paperback; then within a few more days the shell will turn hard, and he is on the prowl to eat anything dead or alive.

I got to go out on the river many times and made lots of new friends. The people who owned the farm had a son and daughter, Jimmy and Mary Kendal Hayes. Jimmy was about two years older and Mary Kendal about four years older than me. Jimmy had a speedboat he would take me in and Mary Kendal had a large sailboat that slept eight or nine people. She'd have parties on this boat with her friends and I was always invited to go with them. We'd go way out in the Bay and watch sailboat races on Sunday afternoons. I became somewhat skilled at sailing and studying the weather. We swam off the back of her boat, and I learned real quick that you look before you leap. One time I dove straight into a nest of sea nettles and came up with some bad stings. It was my foolish pride that hurt the most.

The tail of summer came. Mr. Jones drove me to Port Claiborne and raised the flag on the wharf. This signaled to the S.S. Bay Bell and other passing ferries that there were either passengers or cargo for them to pick up. The Bay Bell stopped to pick me up, and I paid the seventy cents haulage. Then we stopped at Betterton and on to Tolchester to pick up and drop off other passengers.

The sun was burning gold as I rode the ferry on to Baltimore. I noticed some thick clouds that hung around for an afternoon storm. The seagulls were flying head-on in the high wind far above the water. Mothers were sitting on long benches with picnic baskets near their feet. Kids were laughing and hanging over the side rail of the boat watching water pass by—all in all, it was a peaceful and calm ride.

We were paddling along at a pretty lively clip, more so than usual I thought, when the sky turned gray and within twenty minutes a wild, eerie darkness rumbled toward us. As the wind picked up and the Bay foamed and roared, a broadcaster from

210

the crew cleared each deck, telling everyone to go below and stand in the center of the boat under the overhead life rafts. The big bay windows were closed and the curtains pulled down and tied tight. Still the rain poured and the wind screamed; wooden folding chairs slid back and forth, newspapers flew in the air. The supplies for the snack bar that so neatly lined the shelves behind the concession stand came violently crashing to the floor with a thump. The scuttle, sometimes called a hatch door, to the engine room was closed to keep debris from falling on the giant motor. High spirits of laughter had diminished. People were holding on to whomever and whatever they could to keep from falling down. Little toddlers were crying and screaming while moms and dads with frightened looks were snatching them up with bulldog grips.

In the pandemonium, we slowed down to a near idle. Treading and awash in treacherous waters, we faced the windward side, taking our poundings. The waves heaved up mountains of water lifting the stern up and then down with an almighty smack. The old lady of the sea was strong, steady and sound. For many of the land-minded travelers, the rock and roll brought on the chew and choke. The storm ebbed; lightning struck continuously, rattling the passing buoys. Rising waves broke in half, creating white caps with wailing sounds of bottomless water. The winds chased a driving rain through broken panes, lashing at the curtains and ripping some to threads, while the crew struggled to hold them together. After more than an hour of rocking, rolling and bobbing, the storm began to dissipate.

The calamity over the water continued to rumble. Aboard, there was a silence that followed; we waited for what was going to happen next. Then the old lady of the sea started off with a mighty groan, and we slowly paddled our way on to Baltimore. Coming into port, the last of our troubles on the water was behind us as our tow swept a smooth wake. Without any bragging, our keen-eyed captain brought his hostages of the sea home safe and sound. He received few thanks for the gallantry of his day's work. There were a few complaints of such a bumpy ride, but then some people would complain even if they were hung with a new rope.

My mom was the 'HEN' in a hypHENated mother, separating herself from other mothers and always watching after her clutch. She had already learned of the severity of the storm and was mighty put out. Mom rode herd on her brood and brought along the rest of the litter to make sure none of them got blown away in the squall. She wanted to know where each and every one was. They'd all been worried sick about me and then came the reassuring feeling when I stepped onto the ground alive and well.

I had to squeeze my mouth shut real tight to keep from laughing when I realized how worried they were about me. I guess it was that prideful care that I didn't know they had for me that made it so funny. After that I couldn't help but add a little color to the event to get a few more "oooh-mys" out of them. The day had been beat and the people had been more afraid than hurt. I must have been a better swimmer back then, for I thought it was exciting and fun. I guess "every jackass thinks he has good horse sense."

This drifting mist in time seems so long ago; it's almost ancient. I don't believe I could enjoy the same bumpy ride today. I'm ever thankful for my days spent on the Eastern Shore. Yep, the "good old days." All days when old are good. It was on the Sunday just before my birthday that the Joneses came to visit us. Mr. Jones brought his double barrel 12-gauge shotgun. He told me his father had purchased it in the 1890's from a hardware store in Chestertown for one silver dollar and his gold pocket watch. He was sorry he couldn't pay me anything for all the work I had done on the farm for him. Mr. Jones had wanted to give me his gun when I worked for him, but it was his only family heirloom, and I thought it should go to a family member. However, he insisted that I should have it. I did very much appreciate his generosity.

We were sitting around the table talking about my new gun while Mom put on the last few remains of vittles for supper … excuse me, I mean dinner. Nowadays, Mom serves "dinner" at "suppertime." Finally she set down a big plate of fried oysters almost in front of me. I learned to love oysters and the Chincoteague Oysters are the best, nicest, plumpest, meatiest and saltiest with the most delightful flavor of any oyster there is in the world! They are by far one of the most valuable commodities of the Atlantic shores, and they're in great demand around the globe. The Joneses had generously brought our family a gallon of fresh-shucked Bay oysters from an oyster-peddler in Rock Hall. What a treat!

Have you ever said something for the sake of being polite? I have, and I have always had a knack for saying the wrong thing at the wrong time. I spoke up and said, "Oh, I just love oysters." Then I bit into one and said, "Why these ain't Chincoteague oysters; these are Bay oysters." Then from under the table Mom started kicking me on the shin. To make up for all my ignorance, I said, "They aren't bad for Bay oysters." The shin kicking kept up. Yes, I guess I have done some shameful things in my time.

The Lord came to my rescue when there was a knock on the door. I jumped up from the table to answer it. It was Miss Busymouth (I never knew her correct name). She came occasionally to get a pound of our homemade butter. Miss Busymouth lived outside the neighborhood, but was one who knew everybody's business except her own. She started telling Mom that she'd heard that Watty Wheelwright had a lot of shenanigans going on in the neighborhood; and furthermore, he was one of those boys that was just plain mule-headed and nobody was going to tell him what to do. Well, that threw the fat in the fire and by now Mom had stood up from the table and said, "Just hold on there now! Maybe you don't know it, but I love those Wheelwright children just like they're my very own. They work right here on the farm, and they work hard; their mother sees to it that they go to Sunday School, and they often come here and have supper with us, and I have never had o-n-e minute's trouble out of them."

Well, Miss Busymouth never came back any more after that. Mom said she must have gotten a little too much salt in that last pound of butter. Mom's loyal convictions to her family and friends were strong and everyone knew where they stood. If anybody was on the wrong side of her, she let them have it with both barrels; otherwise she was as sweet as honey.

Amazing Faith

Mary and Medford Jones were righteous people and their religious insight was straightforward. It was amazing faith. It was strong, it was bold, and it was clear. Their gentle homespun hearts were tied together with an easy thread.

For many years, Medford trawled from doctor to doctor, seeking help for his arthritic pain. Mr. Jones became the doctors' best contradiction as his health spiraled downwards. The agonizing pain increased and the years passed to the point that finally one day, the doctors asked him to stay in bed. The days drifted into months and the months passed into years. The years grew and time marched on. I judge it must have been around seventeen years that he lived in bed. I know it was a long time. He surely must have been on the rage against death. It was easy to see his future was a blank. He lay flat on his back day in and day out, his condition so bad that if he held his hands up his fingers fell back against the back part of his hand. Yet, even without the pleasures of air conditioning against summer heat, Mr. Jones never had a bedsore.

Medford was in need of constant nursing and attention; however, love and care had not been his cure. Mrs. Jones' nurturing had only geared herself up for gray hairs. Her worries carried a high mortgage; love is a great pleasure in life that brings jolts of pain without any rules. Sometimes it's warm and sometimes it's burning, one never knows what is in store.

As a little tyke I didn't understand why Medford had to suffer so. Not all could weather up to such a storm and remain so cheerful. My father said many times that Medford had racked up a fine crop of bills and that his vision never grew dim until that last dime was paid. Through the years, they learned to do much with little. Even through all this, he would lie in bed and whistle one happy tune after another. There was no television back then, and he couldn't hold a newspaper or sit up very well in bed. He was so cheerful and loved to tell jokes—he was as happy as any farmer in tall corn. When the wind blows up the wrongs in life, it takes a strong person to whistle a merry tune. Whenever he had to call Mrs. Jones in for something, he would say, "Oh, Mary dear, " and for Mr. Jones the bedroom to the kitchen was a world apart. He personified an everlasting impression of strength to all who knew him.

During the 1950's, it was unheard of for a working class woman to go to a hair salon to get her hair washed and set. However, this was one of the few luxuries that Mrs. Jones had. She always took great pride in her appearance. As a kid, I heard some unnecessary and hurtful comments from other ladies about how this was too extravagant. There were many quick judgments and whispers that were carried behind closed doors. I believe some of these same women would eat their young if they had half a chance. They say a jealous woman will set her own house on fire, but I can't vouch for that. However, I was greatly impressed that Mrs. Jones took a little time out for herself.

By the time Mr. Jones' condition had deteriorated and he could no longer work on the farm at all, Mrs. Jones had taken a job as a housekeeper so she could take care of Mr. Jones at the same time. The love and loss of a spouse is not always pleasant—sometimes darkness is felt. But when he died, she was not the weeping widow one might expect. She hid in complete composure and a practiced smile. She had survived the last seventeen years of their turmoil to his ravishing death. With a passing shiver, I agreed it was a grateful death. It was a good end; he left a good impression and made many folks smile. Even the strongest of men are pulled to the ground when their time comes.

After Mr. Jones died, Mrs. Jones stayed on where she had been employed as a housekeeper. That only lasted a short while because her employer had a heart attack and died, so she was left with no husband, no job and no place to live. Mrs. Jones came to visit our family and explained to Mom that she was going to have to move. Mother said, "Mary, what on earth are you going to do?" Characteristically, with folded arms and after a long second thought, she leaned back in the wingback chair in our living room and said, "The Lord has helped me through unbelievable times, rough times in my life, and I am sure He will open up doors again!"

She returned to where she had been staying, and knowing she

only had a week remaining to live there, she began packing up all of her possessions in preparation of moving, but didn't know where she would be going. An old acquaintance of hers had passed the word around. Her situation was a simple one— she needed work and a place to live. Then the phone rang and there was Mr. Jum Wilson calling to see if he could talk her into keeping house for him. Her honest reply was that she didn't approve of drinking, smoking or foul language. He said that he didn't do those things and would pay her generously. What dignity and powerful faith this lady had! Here she had no place to go and no income, but she had her values and integrity and she wouldn't give those up for anything! She stood strong and solid as Fort Knox.

She worked for Mr. Jum Wilson for less than a year when he asked her if she would accompany him on a visit to Florida for a week. Mrs. Jones' apt reply was, "Why certainly not! It would not be decent for me to travel like that with a man and not be married." Mr. Wilson, a well-to-do gentleman, immediately asked for her hand in marriage. She graciously accepted and they went off to Florida. Mr. and Mrs. Wilson had a happy marriage together for a number of years. He cared deeply for her and always respected her as a real lady. The Lord had indeed provided for her. The trudge in life had cut off her youth after all those years with her nose to the grindstone, but The Lord had made sure she was going to have golden years. How incredible to have such amazing faith!

The Best Lesson

It was the dark part of winter in 1950. I was a tall, thin, carefree 13-year-old country boy. I was old enough to know better; in spite of that, I was too young to care. The shivering walk had been one full dragging mile from the farm to the store. Mr. Nagel, a gentleman with brittle gray hair; was the nicest

217

person around. He would open his one-room country store door at 6:45 in the morning just to let us kids in out of the weather. Then he circled back to his living quarters to eat his breakfast. On this one particular blustering day, it was cold, dark and gloomy, and we were waiting quietly inside. We all were lined up, standing next to the candy counter. Some kids were saying softly, "Look here at all that candy." The canisters had been freshly stocked, and the eyes of desire peered from jar to jar.

Then they started teasing me, saying that I couldn't fetch up enough nerve to take a piece of bubble gum out of the large blue jar. Together we hit on a plan: grab it and then jump on the bus when it comes. Nobody will ever know. Well, after a lot of teasing and betting, I started to think only of the gum. Every little while I looked around to see if I should do it or not. Secretly, they each nodded their heads, saying "yes" in low whispers so as not to let Mr. Nagel know what we were up to. The bus arrived on time; lo and behold, with trembling fingers I reached into the enticing jar and clenched one piece. The devil sure must have been on the job. After that I shot onto the bus as fast as my legs would carry me. The bus driver hollered out at me, "Hold on there now. Stop all that foolishness. Lands alive, can't you wait until you get to school?"

I took a seat in the middle of the bus and started chewing and acting frisky like a colt, as if the gum were some of the better frills of high living. After all, it was only the kids in town who could afford to buy chewing gum. I was thinking that I really had gotten away with something and was blowing and popping bubbles all the way to school. My schoolmates were

218

laughing at me as though they were proud of the disgraceful action. They laughed even harder the next day, and were glad they hadn't enjoyed the same "wicked good time."

That same evening, we were all getting ready for supper when I noticed that Mom and Dad were having a lot of private chit-chat in one corner of the kitchen. I didn't know it at that time, but someone had very well informed them of the early morning bubble gum snitching. Dad and Mom kept eyeing me up while we were seated at the supper table.

Dad gave me a smoldering look over his eyeglasses with an expression that I didn't like. He said, "I heard that someone took some gum from out at the store." Staring straight at me, he asked if I knew anything about it. I dropped pretty flat and started to stutter, twitch and turn in my chair when he said, "Don't schmooze me, boy. If you know anything about it, speak up." The hot glow of his words stung as they rang in my ear. Mom's startling reply came: "Good gracious, child, whatever was you thinking of? You've got me plumb scared to death doin' things like that!" Her usual smile grew into a bewildering face of fear. The near choke of speculation was final: There was no cause for pride; I wasn't going to fib. Without question, my unanticipated change of color told it all. I was feeling perfectly awful; my dreadful secret was out. With absolutely no defense for new wrinkles, I knew I was going to be in a heap of trouble. I said, "Yes, Sir, I took some gum."

Dad raked me over the coals pretty good for a while, then asked how much it cost. In my early formative years I learned that the best way of getting out of answering any question is by asking another question, but this time, knowing full well there wasn't any room for argument, I told him two for a penny. Then he asked how many I took and I told him one. Dad handed me a penny and told me in a saucy tone to stop eating and take it to Mr. Nagel—pronto! It was cold, wet, about half-raining and freezing. At six o'clock in the winter-time at our house, it was plenty dark. On this particular evening it got so dark that when the black clouds rattled, you needed both hands to find your nose. The pressure grew. I put on my hat and coat and started for the door. I thought to myself, "This is my own dratted fault." Dad looked up from his plate and said, "Now mind you, just to make sure, I will be out to pick you up at the store and ask Mr. Nagel if you gave him the penny." In a muddle of the hard-earned qualities of endurance, I turned up my collar against the swarming wind. I didn't relish what lay ahead.

By the time I arrived at the store, I was in a frigid, worrisome sweat. Mr. Nagel was sitting on a stool looking out the window. I suppose he was hoping for a paying customer. As I walked in he remained seated and said, "Jimmy, what are you doing out trompin' about in the dark?" Briefly I sputtered, and the words wouldn't come. Then I began to scratch my shoulder, cleared my throat and took a deep breath. I told him the reason for my visit and was very apologetic; I mentioned how miserable and worthless I was feeling. Mr. Nagel was a soft-hearted man. He put his hand on my shoulder, saying that it was okay, but "We won't let it happen again, right?"

My family had a strict set of rules to go by, and I wasn't doing any credit to the family name. Dad kept his word and came to the store. He told me to wait by the car. After a while he came out. I was seated all comfortable in the car, trying to let on like nothing was wrong. I had the radio turned on and was tapping my foot to Elvis Presley. In a surly pitch Dad said, "What in the Sam Hill is going on? What did I tell you to do?" I said, "Wait in the car." He said, "No, BY the car, not IN the car! Now you can just march yourself right back home. I've never seen the likes of anything like you in all my life. You are going to learn to behave better than you naturally want to, whether you like it or not." I wheeled toward home, thinking that inside the store I had been forgiven, but not outside.

By now the weather had not improved; in fact, it had worsened into a drenching rain. With thundering steps, I went into full power going uphill and then sloshing down. A quarter of a mile into my walk, a red fox crossed the road carrying a young rabbit tight in his mouth. Like the spokes of a wagon wheel, he placed one foot directly in front of the other, first with one forepaw then with one of his afters, the rain washing his muddy prints dead flat as fast as his trot. He disappeared into the underbrush and would not let himself be seen again.

In the hollow, the feud and war of the wind howled a high note, throwing the tops of the rocking trees. Furious bolts of white lightning struck close by as I continued to follow the darkness. I passed through a little stream of trickling water where loneliness continued to flow. Indeed it was a time of dim darkness. Darkness doesn't kill people. It wasn't the storm that needed to be cleared from the sky but the storm of forgiveness towards my peace of mind that needed to be cleared.

Drawing near the lane to the house, I was cold, wet and hungry and feeling rough as a corncob, as streaks of light fell from the window. I couldn't see the curl of smoke from the chimney, but the fallen weather had brought the smell of burning oak to the ground. I was pretty near glad to see the light but wasn't sure what was in store. I walked into the house and slammed the door shut to keep out the blast of cold air. From the living room my siblings necked around the corner to get a clear view to see if I was all right. No one was fighting over using my shoes today.

The fire felt good. I pulled off my hat and coat and dropped

221

them on the floor. From out of the corner of my eye, I spotted Mom standing at the kitchen sink doing the supper dishes with a colorful tee-towel flung over her shoulder. She turned and produced a forgiving smile and quite sweetly asked if I was hungry. With a nod she beckoned for me to sit down at the table. I took a chair at the head of the table and hopped it up as close as I could get. Then she handed me a hot plate of food all fixed up with our own country ham, fried potatoes, string beans and corn. It all went together like honey and a bee; I was ready to eat.

Dad came to the table and said, "I guess you think I was a tad hard on you. I will tell you here and now that a father will do whatever it takes to protect his son from confounding ways and it is not done out of mean-ness." With that a wave of emotions flew over me with a bonding flood. I almost whispered when I realized how much of me was him, "Can I follow his logic and remain rigid with my children with such fine examples at his age in my after-years? I guess the up-to-date age has its growth; most surely I will jell in due time."

Dad was an enthusiastic disciplinarian and was pinned to his beliefs. He worked and he labored and advised me how to make wise decisions. He didn't merely instruct me; he modeled his belief and he lived it, and it was either black or white—with no allowances for gray.

My father never told me he loved me, but I know he did. I won't sit here and tell you that's why I stole the gum. I'll say,

"Today I'm a grandfather and I have three full-grown sons that I hug and kiss and tell them that I love 'um and I had a loving dad to thank for that."

My father was a wonderful man!—He was kind!—He was honest!—He was steady!—And he practiced what he preached. It will take a lot for anyone to stand up to that. It was not over, though. I had to speak to my mother about the black blemish that struck the zest of my soul as I ate. Mom told me, "Jimmy, tough times bring great rewards. There is a devil at every turn in life, this is just one more behind you." I was awful glad to have happiness again and to throw away the nightmare. The house was warm and happiness was born once more. I sat beside the fireplace that evening and watched the blaze from the last little flame to the flicker of totter before its death.

Looking back at the occurrence of the morning, my heart grew cold as I traced the path of my day. It happened that I traded the wrong for the right and good fortune smiled on me. It was only this morning that the devil sparked a flame that grew out of control; then, like the little flame, my troubles were gone. It came at a tremendous cost; it's not easy to repair such mistakes. I learned a lot about swiping gum, and the sun never shone that day; the devil almost got his way. That was "The Best Lesson." Thank you, Dad.

The rustic rules for country boys are frequently cultivated from firm roots. My folks wanted to make sure their offspring didn't fall short to sorrowing ways. Never fly so high you can't come home to roost.

Wheeler-Dealer

The first few years at Beaver Brook were busy ones. There was a road crew working on the driveway and putting down a hard-top road and parking lots. Carpenters, painters, electricians and plumbers were all working at different places. Towson Nursery had a party of workmen at different places on the farm planting shrubs and trees. People of all sorts were working on the Fox house adding a nice large country kitchen. The bull pen was also being renovated.

The new buildings included a four-car garage, the first addition to the Manor House, the shop, a dairy, a hog pen, a sheep barn, a chicken house, machine sheds and a bathhouse. Workers were also busy digging the new swimming pool and farm pond, as well as preparing for the new tennis court. Some days there must have been upwards of twenty workmen on the farm. This was a fun time with so many people to visit with.

I liked socializing with the men mostly during their lunch break. One day I was walking around eating a homemade Popsicle and one of the carpenters asked if I had an extra one. I said, "I think so." I got him one and he insisted that he pay me a nickel for two Popsicles. In 1950, that was a lot of money. Every penny was needed, and I couldn't afford not to take advantage of the situation.

This was one of those hot, humid Baltimore summers. It didn't take me long to realize that I could make a little extra money out of all this new action on the farm. I started selling Mom's iced tea and lemonade and Beaver Brook Farm's fresh spring water, as well as carrying two flavors of Popsicles, orange and grape. These were my favorites, just in case they didn't sell. Yes, this turned into a good business. For one thing, it was hot; for another, there wasn't any competition.

The "Jimmy Fox Popsicle" was born, and every day at lunchtime I would have a bunch of Popsicles ready for sale. Then I realized I could sell again around three in the afternoon. Business was booming. I was thinking about retiring from farming and being a Popsicle baron.

After a week or two, Dad found out about my new business and made me give it up with no ifs, ands, or buts about it. After that, everything was free—even my service for delivering their goods. The wheeler-dealer was put out of business.

I was telling Martha Wheelwright about my excellent venture. Martha and her friends usually called me Jim-Bo; that was their nickname for me. She suggested, "Jim-Bo, come to my house and we'll all make lemonade. Then take it out to the intersection of Ridge and Falls Roads to sell it there." So my brother Marvin, Henry, Martha and I made our lemonade. Martha had a dark blue 1949 Ford convertible.

She put the top down and we all sat around inside the car. We propped a "Lemonade for Sale" sign in front of the car. Business was good, but I wasn't sure if it was good because of the taste of the lemonade or because all these young fellows just liked stopping and talking to a nice, good-looking blonde teenage girl. We had a cigar box that we kept our money in and after our lemonade ran out, Martha divided the money just three ways—not keeping any for herself. That was the end of our lemonade business.

Dad's Idea of Air Conditioning

With all this activity at the farm going on at one time, my father had his hands full. A line of contractors was always around asking Dad questions and wanting an answer for some problems they were having.

One day Mrs. Thompson came up to the barn, walked to the front of the line and said, "Fox, you certainly have your hands full." He tipped his hat and said, "I hope you are pleased with the progress." This was the hottest part of summer, and was back in the days when air conditioning was just a breeze under a shaded tree. She asked my father if he knew of any possible way of cooling down her bedroom. The newly planted trees weren't yet large enough to shade that portion of the house.

He suggested that Richard and Jimmy go to Mel Burnham's Ice Plant and get a 100-pound block of ice. He said that we could set the ice in a washtub and place a fan behind it. Then Mrs. Thompson could sit in front and have the cool air blow over her. She told Dad, "That would be simply divine!" Dad, pulling out his pocket watch, saw that it was a couple minutes 'til twelve, which indicated that it was lunchtime, and said, "I'll have them get it first thing after lunch." But Mrs. Thompson responded, "Oh, heavens, Fox, I think the sooner the better." Dad told her then that he'd have them leave right away, and she replied, "Oh, that would be marvelous!"

At first I was grumbling about going to get ice on my lunch hour and Dad said, "Hush up, and do as you are told." We brought the ice back and carried it to the front door. Irene Taylor, Mrs. Thompson's personal maid of many years, who was British and with a good humor, met us at the door with a smile. She held the door open wide, and we brushed off our feet one at a time on the large welcome mat. As we passed through the door, I pulled off my engineer's cap, rolled it up and stuck it in my hip pocket. We hauled that 100-pound block of ice back to Mrs. Thompson's bedroom.

Irene told us where to put the tub of ice. Gertrude Jones, another maid, was a small, slender lady who was thoughtful and always running while she worked. Here she came running down the hallway with both hands full, a fan in one hand and a mop in the other. She set the fan on a small stool and turned it on. I pushed Mrs. Thompson's fully-stuffed boudoir chair in front of the block of ice. Mrs. Thompson picked up a book, sat down in her chair very ladylike and courtly, looked out the window overlooking her swimming pool and onto a 90-acre pasture. There she could see her fifty purebred Black Aberdeen Angus cattle with their calves grazing on the next hillside. She said, "That's a beautiful sight." I stood there waiting to see if there would be anything further. Then she said, "That will be all." She added, "Oh, this is for you." She handed me a dollar (that was half a day's wages) and I said, "Thank you!" and walked out.

On the way to my house for lunch, I heard the screen door slam shut. I knew I would be meeting Dad about half-way on the path to the barn. As I approached him coming, I said, "Look!" holding my hand out, palm open. "Now, I've got some folding money." Dad said, "See, Jumpie (that was a pet name Dad had for me), never bite the hand that feeds ya." He had a kinda joshing smile and said, "I got a notion that you might have learned something today. You'd better be holdin' on to that foldin' money."

I went into the house to get my lunch. Mom mostly had a large pot of soup on the back of the stove. In the summer, it was usually vegetable soup from fresh vegetables out of our garden, whatever was in season at the time the soup was being made. In winter, it could be some sort of dried bean soup (lima, navy, split pea) made with a hambone.

We seldom ever bought lunchmeat. Sandwiches were made of home-cured smoked ham or a cold pork, or a beef roast sliced thin and served cold. In the summertime, as long as tomatoes were in, it could be tomato and onion with lettuce sandwiches.

One of my favorites was cold-packed fried down sausage that

Mom had jarred during butchering time. The sausage was just a little larger than a hot dog that was heated. I rolled it up in a slice of bread with sliced onions and some mustard. Scrapple sandwiches were popular in the winter. Served hot or cold, they were good. I carried a many of them for school lunches.

Mom and Dad had learned to adapt to the leaner times during the Great Depression. They were survivors of the bitterest of the harshest of times. Always, they worked diligently to be prepared for the worst. Their slogan was, "Hope for the best, get ready for the worst and take it as God gives it to us."

Pies and Fun

It was in the fall of the year and the apple trees had been full. My father adored apple dumplings and apple pie. At dinner he asked Mother if it was possible for her to make some dumplings or pies. She said, "I have so much to do now." Dad said. "What if Jimmy helped you tomorrow?" After a lot of "yeah's" from the rest of the clan, she said okay.

The next morning I got a bucket and started for the orchard. Dad stopped me and said, "I think you should get a bigger bucket." I said, "Oh yes, I will!" I realized then that he wanted a lot of pies. I got the biggest bucket I could find and filled it with the best apples in the orchard.

Mom said, "Do you want to peel all those apples?" I peeled them, but what a surprise I had when she took most all my apples and turned them into applesauce. I was sure I had enough for at least a dozen or more pies. Mom asked me to start mixing up the pie dough. We never measured anything. I started by pouring the flour into a large wash pan that was sitting on my lap. Mom looked over and said, "That's enough."

I'd made piecrusts many times, but Mom felt it necessary to keep an eye on me. Next to me was a full 50-pound can of lard. Dad had planted the seed—so I took the ladle and started dipping the lard and putting it on top of the flour. I knew what the texture should be but when Mom wasn't looking I started mixing and dipping. Mom soon realized what I was doing. She said, "You know better than to put that much lard in the flour." I was sure that she wouldn't want to throw all that dough out. Well after I got a good scolding, she calmed down.

I said, "Do you want me to go get some more apples?" To which she replied, "We don't want to eat nothing but apple pie all the time!" And I said, "Why not?" She told me to go down to the cellar and bring up six jars of those cherries that she'd canned last year. And I said, "Yes ma'am!"

It had been a good day: five apple pies and six cherry pies and then that applesauce. That evening at supper, Mother was telling Dad about what had happened. He said, "What a shame," looked at me and winked. They were some tasty pies.

My mother insisted on teaching her kids how to cook and clean. We all had turns working in the kitchen, making beds with hospital corners, tucking everything in just right, helping with the laundry, ironing, sewing and even making tea towels. On Sundays, Mom and Dad would go to visit my grandparents in Carroll County. We kids stayed home and cooked fried chicken dinners with all the trimmings. We invited the neighbor kids in and had memorable times.

The Big Purchase

One time Marvin, Richard and I put all our money together to buy a horse. After a diligent search throughout Baltimore and Carroll Counties, we finally found a nice black one, which seemed to be the best buy. We bought the horse from an old guy, a horse dealer, up the road in Westminster. He told us this was such a nice horse and that he gave him two or three quarts of oats a week. He went on and on about how the horse really liked his oats. Well, by the skinny shape of King, we understood why he really went after the oats! By golly, he was hungry! So we got a big chuckle out of hearing that man tell us how King would really go after his oats.

On the way home, we thought we'd swing by Reisterstown Veterinarian Center and get Dr. Frock to come out and check our new horse over for us to see what he thought of it and what kind of health he thought King might be in. He checked the horse out and said he thought it was a pretty nice horse. "Well, Doc, how old do you think this horse might be?" He replied, "I don't rightly know his age but I"ll tell you this much, he's been  voting for a while." I really thought that was kind of funny. After bringing the horse home, we hooked him up to the buggy. What a wonderful time we had. It didn't matter how old that horse was.

One time I was helping my father when he was clearing the

woods in the pond area. He was making his pasture larger, so he wanted to get all the logs pulled out that he had cut down, and I suggested using the horse. He said, "Well sure." That was a good idea, but what I didn't know about King was that he had a fast gait. When he was pulling a log, you had to darn near run to keep alongside him, so it didn't take me too long to get tired of pulling logs, and by lunchtime, I was pretty much wiped out. My father just really found it funny that King wore me out that fast. He said it was a good thing I didn't have a 12-hour day to work because I wouldn't have made it through. Anyway, we hooked old King up to use him with the buggy to take the trash out. You didn't mind going around gathering up trash when you had your horse and buggy. It seemed like a lot of fun.

I remember on Sundays taking my Grandmother Fox for buggy rides. We went around through all the logging trails in the woods. She told me that that really brought back a lot of good memories for her and she enjoyed it very much. We even went back to George Fox's house, visited a while and then turned around at Mrs. Wadsworth's, coming back home through the woods, having a grand time.

Off to the Beach

After Mrs. Wheelwright married Mr. Thompson, she gave Mom and Dad money to take us kids to their house in Rehoboth Beach in Delaware. After Labor Day, we would leave on a Thursday and come back on Monday or Tuesday. There was enough room that Mom invited other couples to come with us. Sometimes there were two or three carloads of us.

We swam in the ocean and played in the sand. But after dinner, we would go down to the boardwalk and sit and listen to the waves, sometimes staying as late as 10 or 11 o'clock.

Shirley and I enjoyed getting up early, renting bikes and riding on the boardwalk in the early morning. Then we slowly rode up and down Main Street in town and looked in the store windows. We finished up by riding around the duck pond and then back home. What fun we had.

I heard Mom and Dad talking about going out for dinner on Saturday night. On our bike ride, Shirley and I had seen a restaurant. I'd had enough dinners with Henry to know that any time you had a fine linen napkin to wipe your chin on, that had to be a good place to eat—not just a "sit and pitch." Mom just thanked me for my knowledge on etiquette and told me to go for another ride. She didn't take my advice but instead went to the edge of town to a little '50's-type diner. Dad was telling Mom that the fried chicken was not nearly as good as hers. We had a wonderful little vacation.

Black Ball with a Tail

One hot, humid, sweltering summer evening my father and I got some easy chairs and pushed them up in the shade of a large maple tree in the front of our house. We were there drinkin' up some of mom's iced tea and talking about the day's work. Mom was still in the house finishing up the supper dishes when she looked out the window and saw a large black ball with a tail about ten feet off the ground flying toward us. She rushed out the house and hollered to Dad as she pointed over to the hay field, "What is that?" Dad was looking around still in his chair, stretching his neck as far as he could. She said, "Stand up and look over there." As she pointed again, "There across the road in the hayfield."

By now it was in good sight. Dad said right off, "Why that's a swarm of honeybees." We stayed there and watched them. They lit on a lower limb on the tree next to us not more than 50 feet away. This swarm was larger then a basketball.

Mom asked what he was going to do about them. Dad said that the bees would not hurt you so just stay calm. "I'll call Mr. Robert Stallard, Sr. to see if he would like them. I know he has some hives." Mr. Stallard lived on a farm down off of Greenspring Avenue not far away. Mr. Stallard said he had an empty hive, would very much appreciate it if he could have them, and he'd be up a little closer to dark. We kept waiting and watching the sun go down and wondering how Mr. Stallard was going to move those bees without getting stung. It took a long time for that sun to go down.

Then the dog ran past us barking with the hair standing up on his back, lookin' all bad. I said, "Here he comes," Dad called the dog and sent him back on the porch. Mr. Stallard was in his station wagon. Dad and I met him as soon as he stopped. He was a nice kinda country gentleman. We let him get out of his wagon. Then we showed him the swarm. He said that he was pleased that they were still there and they were such a nice large swarm.

He looked everything over closely and said, "I think we'll wait a little longer." I pulled up another chair and Dad said, "Get Mr.

Stallard a glass of tea." He said, "That sounds great. It's really been hot and sultry today." We all sat around visiting and Mr. Stallard was telling us about the bees and how the queen was born in the hive she just left. That there is only one queen to the hive and after she was born and big enough to have her own hive, she had to leave and part of the worker bees left with her. She was in the middle of that swarm and the other bees were protecting her. Wherever she went, the others surrounding her would go too.

After it was good and dark, he stood up, walked over to his wagon and got out a white bed sheet. He brought it back, laid it on the ground under the bees, pulled out a pair of clippers from his pocket and snipped off the limb with his right hand. He held the limb in his left hand and gently laid the bees on the sheet. He said that the bees could see the white sheet and would stay on it, so he hoped. He pulled the tailgate of his wagon down, walked back over to the bees, and with his right hand picked up two corners of the sheet. With his left hand, he got the other two corners, then walked back to the wagon, and laid them in. He said, "I think I'll leave the tailgate down in case they decide they want to start movin' again."

Dad said, "Good idea, don't forget to take your bees out of the bedsheet before you go to sleep." Mr. Stallard hollered and laughed hard with his mouth wide open to where you could see that gold tooth inside. He left and headed home with a wagon full of bees.

Watty in the Korean War

One day, Mrs. Thompson came to visit my mother by herself. Mom said to her, "What a beautiful day." Mrs. Thompson spoke softly, "Maybe so, but there's a dark cloud over my head." She asked if she might come in. As she sat in the middle of the sofa, she said, "I have some bad news." Then she asked if I might be excused. So I politely pardoned myself and went back to my chores.

My mother told me that she came right to the point and said, "Last night during our party, someone from the Air Force came to the door and asked for Mr. Thompson. I wasn't aware of this until after breakfast this morning when Hank told me that Watty is missing in action." Mrs. Thompson, being a strong lady, tried not to show her emotions. After talking about Watty for only a short time, the tears began and Mrs. Thompson left the house. Our family was very upset about this tragic news. My parents thought of all of the Wheelwright children as their own and to learn that Watty was missing in action in the Korean War was devastating.

Watty was a unique individual and everybody loved him for what he was. He chose to serve as a tail-gunner in the US Air Force during the war. Watty was always adventuresome and my understanding was that he volunteered for this most dangerous job. Mom wrote to him often and sent him his favorite chocolate chip cookies. He wrote to us regularly. I remember Mom telling us when we had a letter from Watty, and we all sat around the table and listened while she read his letter to us.

He always remembered each of us in his letters and especially liked to tease Mom and end his letters by saying, "Well, tell the brood I said, 'Hello!'" In the last letter we received from Watty, he said, "Last night I blew up a locomotive. It did something to me. I just don't think I will be driving so fast any more when I return to the states." To read this letter, it was clear what he was feeling.

After the days and weeks passed without further news on

Watty, Mrs. Thompson told us that she and Mr. Thompson were going abroad for six weeks. She said, "I feel a need to get away for a while." She asked if it would be possible for Henry to stay with us. We all were delighted to have him. Marvin and I helped Henry move in.

I particularly remember Henry at this time because he was living with us. The tragedy of war hit us all hard. I knew other people serving in Korea. This was a most difficult time for Henry. He was young and still in school. His father had died shortly after he was born, and now his older brother was missing in action. His mother had remarried and was going abroad for six weeks. He must have felt all alone. I knew no one in my family could take the place of his brother, but I also knew we all must try to make him feel at home.

Henry was a good guy and easy to please. When it came to his brother he was very brave. Then the day came that we heard that some of the POW's were going to be released. Television was the most modernistic device of its time and we felt blessed to have it. We heard there would be a special broadcast, listing the names and addresses of those prisoners of war who were going to be released. Henry went to my mother and asked, "Oh please, Mrs. Fox, may I stay up this evening to see if Watty's name comes on the television?" My mother, knowing how little Henry was feeling, put her arms around him and said, "Yes dear, you may. Tomorrow is Saturday and you can sleep as long as you like." When I looked, the tears were falling from both of them. I can still see her holding Henry, in the middle of the doorway to his room, sobbing.

Not all the POW's were released at one time. Every few days they would release some more. We were always looking for Watty's name to come across the television set. So the agony dragged on and on. Every night we would sit in front of the television looking for Watty's name. Bedtime would come and we would ask to stay up later. Henry would say, "Mrs. Fox, if you see Watty's name, would you please call me so I can see it too?" Mom would say, "Yes dear, I will." First thing in the morning he would say, "Did you see Watty's name last night?" She would answer with tears, "No, not last night, but I feel certain we will." But the weeks went by, and we never saw his name.

I always felt we lost a lot in that war, but we hadn't been put through anything like what Mr. and Mrs. Thompson, Martha and Henry had been put through. I still had my brothers and father living with me. On occasion Mrs. Thompson would say, "Mrs. Fox, I realize that you don't have lots of money, but you do have four beautiful jewels." After first hearing this about myself, I was puzzled. Me a jewel? Well maybe so. I guess we all are, although when I was young, sometimes I wasn't sure about Richard, Shirley and Marvin.

Watty meant a great deal to me and my family. A little part of all of us died during that war.

The Indian Village

One of the first things I did after we moved with Marvin and Henry Wheelwright was to build a log cabin. This is one of my fondest memories. We spent weeks building this wonderful cabin. It was a one-room, two-story log house with a lean-to for outside supplies. After trapping some groundhogs, we tacked their skins up against the side of the cabin. It looked real cool.

Henry Wheelwright had a horse named Ginger, which we used to haul walnuts that we gathered in the pond field for the squirrels back at the cabin. We even built a corral for Ginger to stay in. My father showed me how to make a cookstove out of a five-gallon bucket. Sometimes we would spend the night, sleep upstairs in the cabin and use the homemade cookstove to cook our meals.

The first Christmas the cabin was built, we put up a tree decorated with paper chains and pinecones. My mother  gave us presents with cookies to put under our Christmas tree. It was just great! Henry was still believing in Santa Claus so I left a note saying, "Santa stops at little houses as well as big houses." Mrs. Thompson referred to our cabin as "The Indian Village." She even took some pictures of it and gave one to me. There was a trail that ran from the cabin to the pond field. There we had a log raft we used to play on and fish from. We had great times with our cabin.

Foxes and Guineas and Chickens, Oh My!

One time I got my father to take me to Howard Miller's farm, Valley Hi, on Greenspring Avenue, to purchase twenty-five guinea eggs for hatching. I had found a setting hen when I was taking care of the chickens for my mother. I thought this hen looked like a perfect mother for my little guineas. Well, there were so many eggs she was unable to cover them all. My thought was that if she were to rotate them she would be able to hatch them all out, but she had a different plan! She decided to pick out the eggs she liked and discard the remainder.

Twenty-eight days later, approximately 18 guineas hatched out. I took good care of them for about a month. Then Dad said he thought I should turn them loose. I felt certain the dogs and foxes would catch my babies and kill them, but my father assured me that since they were wild, everything would be okay; that they would fly up and hide in trees. But, by the next day they began to disappear.

My father didn't understand why. He said that guineas don't usually get caught by other animals. Then he told me, "I guess your guineas are just too tame. You should catch them and try to put them back in the hen-house." I tried, but they were too fast for this fox! Within two weeks, they had all disappeared. (I hope those foxes enjoyed the open buffet while it lasted!)

Taking care of the chickens and turkeys was my job. I can't remember when I didn't do it. I know it began when I was five or six, maybe. When I got older, the job broadened into helping pick the chickens. At Twiford Farm, we did it in the brooder house. Dad mostly used the electric picker. One of the other men did the scalding and I handpicked whatever was missed by the electric machine. My mother and other ladies would draw (remove the intestines) and package. The smell was unbelievable, with chicken "guts" everywhere!

When I gained more experience at picking chickens, I was given the task of scalding in addition to helping out with all aspects of this fun job. Marvin helped Mother draw, handpick, and package. To this day, I am still raising chickens, guineas and turkeys. The largest turkey I ever raised was 49 pounds, and I sold him to George Shaneybrook. He had to cut off the neck and the tail to get it in the oven. Then his wife said the oven was way too full, so they cooked it in the oven at the Chestnut Ridge Fire Department.

Flabbergasted

I was sixteen and in dire need of some pocket money even though I was already working on the farm during the day. Mr. Thompson had a friend who lived on the edge of Green Spring Valley by the name of Hamilton.

The Hamiltons lived on a large estate in a big, yellow brick, two-story house that needed the windows washed. I settled for the job without asking what all I was to do. I didn't know how much it paid and didn't even care. I was glad to have the extra money whatever it might be.

I asked if it would be possible to do the job in the evening and on the weekend. Yes, that was possible. Since food was not important to me, I never thought of eating as fun or an enjoyable thing to do. I skipped supper after my day's work on the farm and went right to work on my new job.

Up to this time I had not met Mr. or Mrs. Hamilton, but got my strict orders from their black kitchen maid. She was one nice lady with excellent eyesight—she could detect the smallest speck in a piece of glass! I arrived at the Hamilton's house in the evening, prepared to tackle this window-washing profession all by myself. I was told where the 38-foot extension ladder was kept in the garage. I was to start on all the top windows first. I was to do one window on the outside, come down the ladder, go into the house and do that same window on the inside.

Then, I was to go back outside, move the ladder and do the

next window. I asked Mrs. Kitchen-lady if I couldn't do all the outsides of the whole row of windows on the top. Then I wouldn't have to be running up and down the ladder. The answer was, "You do as I tell ya!" I suggested that it would be faster to do it my way. I realized later the reason was that she wanted to inspect each window as it was done—one at a time.

Doing all the running up and down the ladder and steps as I was told, after a few evenings I got the top windows done. I started on the bottom windows. There were gigantic box-woods around the house, which I crawled under, while dragging a six-foot stepladder in after me.

I was told to do the kitchen windows last and that was okay with me. Once in a while I saw a tiny pie pan with milk in it. On occasion, I'd hear this kitchen maid come out, take a wooden spoon and tap it on the back of the pie pan and say, "Here, Blackie, here Blackie!" Then she poured the milk. I didn't think anything about it. Most everybody had a bunch of cats around.

I reported for work the next day and the maid met me at the door. I was supposed to check in with her each time I did a new window. Finally it came time to do the kitchen windows. The kitchen maid said, "Don't you go back in them boxes until I tell you." This was in the hot part of summer and it was nice and cool there. I was looking forward to being in a cool spot. She went in the house, came out with her spoon and milk, picked up the pan and started tapping and calling.

I was a little puzzled and then she said, "There you are, come on." I looked, but didn't see anything. I asked, "Where?" She said, "There coming up from the springhouse." Again I looked and looked. By this time, I saw something in the grass. It was the head of the largest black snake that I had ever seen in my

241

life. I was flabbergasted! To me that thing looked like a stovepipe moving in the grass.

I said, "I quit! You can get somebody else to do those two windows back there." She said, "Oh now, he won't hurt you. If he comes up here, I'll put him in the cellar way and close the door." I said, "There might be more like him under them boxwoods." I didn't want to look like a sissy, so I hurried in there and did the windows in no time flat. She said, "You're done already?" I told her, "Yes ma'am, and I won't be back! You tell Mrs. Hamilton to give any money that I have coming to me to Mr. or Mrs. Thompson and I'll pick it up from them."

Mr. Thompson paid me and said that Mrs. Hamilton told him that I did a really fine job. He asked me if I thought it would be a good idea if we got some black snakes on the farm to keep the mice down. I replied that I thought we had enough cats and that we were getting along just fine the way we were.

Back To School

My brother Marvin was a little less than three years younger than I. So now that I was repeating the fifth grade, we were in the same class. He understood that I had a problem and never made me feel like I was stupid or half-baked or anything dumb. I think what helped Marvin to understand me was when he was small he spoke "Dutch"—words like milk, he pronounced "nilk" and so forth; and I did the interpreting for those who didn't know what he was saying. Then when Marvin realized that I had a problem, he was willing to help me. I guess that might be one reason Marvin and I were so close.

My schoolwork was improving because I was learning to compensate for my reversal reading. I still felt awkward, having a terrible time reading. I had to work a lot harder than anyone else. If I had to read one chapter that took another kid one hour, it would take four hours for me. But I was lucky that after I read it, I was able to retain it because I kept going over it and over it, to get the words I read in the chapter turned around in my mind. Although I had a serious reading problem, my classmates would ask me what the assignment was about.

I passed the fifth grade with ease and sixth grade proved to be better. I started junior high and was doing okay and started to take a liking to sports. In the winter I was doing well in basketball. By the end of the season, I was called in front of our school assembly and given a Franklin Letter for doing an outstanding job in basketball.

In the springtime, I'd be sitting in school and if the windows were open, I'd hear Raymond Thuma, better known as Bumblebee, walking up the street singing and humming to himself, sounding just like a bumblebee. He mumbled, "I don't wear no underwear" over and over, the same ole thing. He never worked that I knew of. Some say that he was a former patient at Rosewood Hospital, a local state mental institution. He always seemed happy, had a remarkable memory, and never forgot a person's name. He could tell you where everyone lived and all about them. He never caused anyone harm.

Raymond always carried a brown paper shopping bag—I think everything he owned was in that shopping bag. He was a real hobo and liked by a lot of people. I was told that he had a sister who lived in Taneytown. I could be with my family in Taneytown and see Bumblebee hitchhiking down the road towards Reisterstown. If a car passed him by, he put his thumb to his nose and gave them a wave. We could pass him by, but when we arrived at Reisterstown, he was already there, getting out of a car in front of us. He sure got around.

Bumblebee made it to all the local carnivals, horse races in the valley or any kind of public affairs. He could be seen traipsing all over the country. He could take a newspaper, fold it up and take a pair of scissors, put both hands over his head, and cut out a horse jumping over a plank board fence. It turned out perfect every time. Of course, there was a small charge for this to the recipient. Then there were the five-cent Hershey candy bars that he carried inside his coat pocket, which he sold for twenty-five cents. He knew how to make money, that's for sure.

The eighth and ninth grades went fairly well, although I still had to keep working harder than anyone else. I was doing better in sports all the time, which helped me to gain popularity among my classmates.

I started to major in agriculture and earned straight A's all the way though. English was my hardest subject, as you have already learned. I always just made it. History I loved, but had to work really hard to get a C or an occasional B. Agriculture was lots of fun. We raised pigs in a hog-pen for butchering, which we did behind the schoolhouse. We asked local farmers if we could pick up corn in their fields after the corn picker was finished. That's how we got the feed for our pigs. We also raised chickens and dressed them for market. Every week we purchased another brood of chicks to replace the dressed ones we sold. The town boys took turns feeding the stock on weekends. At Christmastime, we made fresh wreaths of evergreens, crowsfoot and pinecones to sell.

Every year our agriculture class used the profits to take a trip to some place like New York City, where we visited Radio City Music Hall, Ellis Island and the Statue of Liberty, and took a boat ride around Staten Island, the World Trade Center, and the Empire State Building. Once we even took a trip to Niagara Falls. Sox Seabold, our teacher, must have been crazy to take all us kids to a place like New York City, but we loved him. One time we met at the Pennsylvania Railroad Station and another time at the Camden Yards Station for the B&O Railroad. We always had dinner in the dining car soon after leaving Baltimore. We had great times on these class trips— something we all will never forget.

One day I was walking over from the main school building to the Agriculture (Ag) Building with Sox Seabold after our lunch break, and there was a cloud of dust. It was brother Marvin, rolling around on the ground with an unpopular classmate. It wasn't long before Sox and I realized who was fighting. Sox said, "This is too good—I won't stop it as long as Marvin is on top." I said, "Don't worry about it. Marvin will be all right." Sox turned and went the other way. As I walked up, Marvin's opponent was saying, "All right, all right." Marvin let him go, got up, brushed himself off and offered this kid his hand, asking if he was okay. The kid said, "Yeah, I'm okay, but don't do it again." Marvin has a unique way with people and didn't carry a grudge; all was forgiven.

I asked Marvin what had happened. My best understanding was that this new kid came up to him said, "My name is Pigg, P-I-G-G, Pigg, and I'm from North Carolina." Marvin held up his hand Indian style and said, "Hi Pigg," with a guffaw. For no apparent cause, Marvin's greeting didn't suit Pigg, so he pushed at Marvin and Marvin didn't move. This new kid didn't realize Marvin was stocky and solid. That's all it took for Marvin to defend himself and take him down.

Marvin had a temperament like Dad's. He never threatened anybody, but without warning, he just put his fist alongside their nose. He never carried tales or said anything bad about anybody that I know of, but don't make him mad. Marvin had our Grandmother Fox's habit when starting to get mad, he would stomp with his right foot, then next was his fist. So when I saw this foot stomping, I was ready to duck; other opponents didn't always know this.

One time when Marvin was in the 9th grade or so, we got off the school bus, and Morny Crocker, a senior about three heads taller and a lot heavier than Marvin, made a remark—I'm not certain about the particulars. I saw this foot stomping, Marvin dropping his books, tearing into Morny. The first thing Morny knew, he was on the ground and I was pulling Marvin off. Morny's remark was "That boy's a hurricane."

There was an old colored gentleman we saw as we were working around the school. He had a pair of black mules, Madam and Queen. In the spring, he plowed our neighbors' gardens. After seeing him for a number of years using two mules, I noticed that this spring he was using only one mule hooked to his spring wagon. He came down past the school and stopped to plow Mr. Schaeffer's garden. After being unhooked from the spring wagon, the mule walked into the garden by himself and stood there. The old gent unloaded the plow out of the spring wagon.

While I was staring at him; he pulled the plow inside the garden gate, hooked up his mule and gave me a friendly wave before starting to plow. A friend of mine told me that the old man was retired from Sagamore Farm, and that the owner of the farm, Mr. Vanderbilt, had given the mules to this old man for his retirement, along with a truckload of hay each year; one of the mules died, so now he was down to one mule for working.

One time I went with my father to Sagamore Farm, the famous racehorse farm, to see about some hay deal for their horses. We were standing in the entryway in the hay-barn and I noticed a pair of beautiful Belgian gelding workhorses. Their names were Amos and Andy. They used them for mowing in the pasture fields and hauling manure.

Years later our school bus traveled through the road at Sagamore Farm. My friend, Wanda Beebe, would point out Native Dancer in the field. Native Dancer was the famous gray racehorse of the year. He was the prizewinning racehorse for Sagamore in 1954. I would tease Wanda and say, "No, it isn't! That's not Native Dancer, that's a mule that works on the farm." She would smack me on the head with her heaviest book and say, "It is too!" I sure had a fine time teasing her.

Her Prom Night

I made it to the tenth grade and was having fun. One day a senior asked me if I would escort her to her senior prom. I knew this young gal and considered her a friend. She told me that everybody she asked said that they were going to the prom with somebody else. I figured she must have been getting pretty desperate to be asking a sophomore to her prom.

I went through all the proper procedures of attaining permission to use the family car before saying "yes." My reservations were far enough in advance that unless I did something out of line, it was okay.

I didn't own a suit, so I asked Mom what I should do. She told me that Dad had his wedding suit, and that she kept letting the inseam out for him as he grew over the years. When my older brother got big enough, she pulled the waist in for him and as he got older she would let it out again and now it was out as far as it would go. She said, "I'll ask him if it still fits." He told her, "No, it's way too small."

247

So Dad's 1930's wedding suit was going to have to do, regardless of style. Mom was pulling the waistband up again when she said, "As many times as I have done this, I should have put a zipper on the dagblame waistband." After it was finished, the trousers fit just right, but the jacket sleeves were way too short. Richard was short and more buttery than I was. Mom said, "Now that's okay, Jimmy, just keep your arms pulled up and take the coat off whenever you get a chance. Nobody'll see the difference." Mom brushed it off, pressed it and told me how nice it looked.

It was too hot to be wearing a wool suit (Mom and Dad were married in February when wool was quite appropriate.), but since it was the only thing I had, it would have to do. You should have seen me walking around in that black wool suit with my long arms pulled up in the sleeves and Mom trying to make me feel good, saying, "Oh don't you look swell!"

There was no romance, just taking a friend to her last high-school prom. Mom told me it was the proper thing for me to get her a corsage. I called a florist and told them I would pick it up on my way to Reisterstown.

I lollygagged my way up the walk to her front door and rang the bell. Her father answered the door. He was a short, stubby guy with a red, meaty face and bullish eyes—kind of a townie person. He said, "So you're the rooster who wants to take my daughter out." And I told him that I was Jimmy Fox. He said, "Well, come on in Mr. Jimmy Fox." I could detect a tone of sarcasm in his voice and as near as I could understand, he'd been misled as to why I was there. He'd been reading the paper and it was still in his hand. Without shaking hands or introducing himself, he went back to his chair and started reading the paper again. I thought that this was all the formalities that I'd get if I'd been a stray cat that came to his house.

I hadn't been asked to have a seat so I stood by the front door and shifted from one foot to the other. I was bouncing a box of flowers with my arms pulled up in my jacket and trying to scratch first one leg, then the other—that wool suit was making me itch. I caught him peering around his newspaper giving me the once over. I tried to ask him something conversational like how was your day. He grunted and made some noise so my best guess was that his day wasn't too good.

Then from behind the paper he asked, "Are you one of those big wheels from out there in the valley?" I was never deliberately rude, but I had a notion that he knew I wasn't a big wheel, so just answered, "Nope!" His reply, continuing his sarcastic manner, was, "Is that right?" I sharply replied "Yep!" I think my short, curt answers threw him back on his heels a bit. With that he removed the paper in front of him, got a big smile on his red face, and said, "Hmm." Then he beckoned with his hand for me to come over and sit down.

I took a seat not too close to him. He started asking a lot of none-of-your-business questions like who I worked for, where they lived, what did I do, how well did they pay? I told him I lived on Beaver Brook Farm on Chestnut Ridge, that I knew most of the people in both Green Spring and Worthington Valleys and had worked for most all of them at one time or the other, doing something. I had helped out on their farms doing painting and handyman jobs and never met one I didn't like, that they all treated me great. I thought that ought to cover it.

By now my date and her mother were coming down from upstairs. I tried to be a gentleman, stood up and said all my howdies and handed my date the box of flowers as graciously as I could from across the room without my arm popping out of my sleeve on the jacket. When I gave them to her, she told me, "These aren't the right color," and that I should have

249

asked her what colors to get. Her mother, a delightful lady and well-spoken, interrupted and said, "The flowers will be fine." Then she took some pictures and complimented us on being such a nice looking couple. I think this was probably my friend's first date and I was new at it myself.

I walked my friend out to the car and tried to be as polite as I knew how, opening the car door while she took forever to get in. I closed the door on about a foot of her long white prom dress which was hanging out the door. So I reopened the door and with my best barn-side manners, I gave her my full sincere apologies and with my most sorrowful look, tucked her dress inside the door.

By nature I'm an easy-going person and find too much humor in life, according to some friends. While she was bawling me out and giving me a disgusted look about my carelessness, my smile slipped back. I didn't think it was worth that much fuss. Hearing the town clock strike eight, I realized that the dance was starting. (That's assuming Jimmy Eline, the clock keeper, had set the clock on time). I was beginning to be a little remorseful about this dating business, but I continued to be courteous and mannerly. By the time we got to her shindig, she was seeing what a nice time her friends were having buzzing around and talking to everyone. Then she started to be pretty forgiving.

This was on a Friday evening, and I had to work on the farm the next day. I didn't know about an all-night party that she had accepted an invitation to. Well, that evening I guess I stepped on one too many toes. I had just spent $2.50 on flowers and knew that after the prom I was to treat her to a snack and coke. This was my first half-day's wages. I boldly said, "No" and made it clear that I wasn't going to a party. By 1 a.m. Dad's car would be home in the shed like I promised him and by 1:15 a.m., I'd be in bed. She was totally surprised (and probably thought that dating a farm boy wasn't all that much fun), but still thought it would be nice if we could hold hands like the other couples were as they walked around engaging in idle conversation. I thought that wasn't in our deal. One more thing about me that she didn't like.

After the dance we stopped at the Dippsy Doodle, a little hamburger place, with her closest friends. We had placed our order and were waiting for it to arrive when she asked me if I'd play A1 on the jukebox. It was her favorite song, Fats Domino singing "Blueberry Hill." I only had one nickel which I'd been carrying around for a while and kinda didn't want to part with it. That was the only thing I had in both front pockets. Of course, these britches weren't used to carrying change around anyway. I had $3.00 in my wallet, hoping that would cover the bill. If not, I was going to be in a heap of trouble. But I didn't want to look cheap, so I said, "Oh, sure" like I had plenty of money.

There was enough money left to take care of the bill and still leave a nice tip for the waitress. I took her home, walked her to the front door, trying to smile pleasantly, and bid her good night. I made it home on time.

Our school had a weekly newspaper, and the kids would write letters and comments on different things. When the paper came out, there was an article stating that my friend was very disappointed with her date and her best advice was never to ask a sophomore to a senior prom.

This piece of news hit the hallways several days after our prom date. I was the only sophomore male there so it was common knowledge that I was the sophomore. I was asked to respond to these accusations many times. I was cordial, and said, "Oh,

251

it's better left alone!" I could take a little ribbing; it didn't bother me. Again I replied that I understood the situation, and that I realized my social skills weren't the best. For the most part I wasn't overly concerned with what other people thought; I knew I'd done my best to help a friend out in a time of need.

This wasn't good enough. Finally the editor of the school paper asked for a comment. Oh, okay, I'd do it. My answer to the letter was "If a senior can't get a date for her prom, it would be better to go alone." My friend came to me and apologized for putting that in the school paper. I responded, "It's nice to be able to help somebody out, and it's nice when they remember, but too many people too often forget."

No More Ferry Tales

For many years the car ferry was a valuable source of transportation. From Sandy Point in Baltimore to the fairway crossing to Stevensville took about 30 minutes. It depended on the tide, the weather, and the captain's ability to moor his ferry. To park any large ship takes tedious skill.

During the duration of my rooster years, I remember my father behind the wheel of our shiny new 1946 blue DeSoto family car hurrying down the road to meet the ferry, only to be greeted with a long line of cars and trucks waiting to cross the Chesapeake Bay. The ferry only ran from sunup to a little past sundown, one load every

hour. Sometimes it took hours before it got to be our turn. The cars were loaded into the bow of the boat, staying in one single line, The line of cars moved up, only to stop and wait another hour for the ferry to return. Thank God for all the farmers and their cornfields, which provided a convenient area to visit during the long wait. Our trips were so frequent it seemed as though I knew every cow by her maiden name.

Lots of times Mom would break out the lunch basket and tell us, "Only one piece of fried chicken per person until we get to the other side." The sun was hot and it seemed everybody had the car doors open. The roadway wasn't lined with traffic cops as might be expected today. Most of the road was entirely bordered by trees. While waiting, we were allowed to get out of the car and pick a good shade tree. We lie around on the grass, loafing and laughing and eating chicken until it was time to move up. That was as long as there was no fighting.

To a country boy, all days were the same, only separated by assorted names, except Sunday—then it was time for some fun if we were going on the ferry. Every once in a while some kid on the "peck" would wing a stick at another one to test his grit. Guess it came from boredom. The young sprouts didn't know what to do with themselves during the long wait.

In more recent years, there were two ferries running at the same time, passing in the middle of the Bay. After we boarded the "easterner" and all the cars were fitly parked, the deafening sound of a diesel engine roared as it dropped into gear, a steady stream of black smoke poured out of the smokestack (known as the funnel), and the motor hammered and labored to get us into a drudging sail. The trail of our wake sent waves lapping to the shore. When we reached the end of the jetty, the captain did a little "scud"—a fancy side-wheeling maneuver like a crab—that got us pointed in the right direction. It was then we took off in a trot. Then I'd get out of the car, find a good spot on the bow to get a breeze, and wave to the kids on the passing ferry.

The beauty of the water was intriguing; looking overboard down the stern I could see the churn of sudsy chug water in tow. It was hypnotizing to peer into the water for a long time. On the sly I watched other boys spitting in the water. I spit a spat on a smooth wave only to see it get washed away with a sweeping wind. It doesn't take much entertainment for a country boy to be contented. I turned on my heels, back to the water, resting my elbows on the side railing. I took an easy look up on the bridge to get a gander at the captain, to see how he was getting along. He was holding the wheel steady, with a corncob pipe clenched tight between his teeth, a typical "Captain Hook" kinda guy.

On top of the "binnacle," the case that houses the ship's compass, lay a distinguished coal-black tomcat. He wore an identifiable gentleman's type of snow-white tie that ran from under the chin to the deep of his chest, and he carried a snip of white on his swatting paw. His fur looked soft as goose down.

I'm not sure what a sleeping cat dreams about. I suppose a fat rat. Well, it didn't make much difference; he stood up, arched his back and jumped out the window. Sure footed, he made his way down the monkey rail that ran along the steps, bounced across the deck and hopped onto the top of the side railing with little concern. Without any fear of falling overboard into fifteen feet of rushing water, he moved slowly towards me. Just short of being touched, he stopped out of my possession —about two lengths of a hounddog.

I kind o' promised myself after the first glance I was going to catch that cat. I sneakily moved up ever' little bit and tried to touch him; he scurried a few feet, then stopped. I tripped along over the anchor chains and port-ropes that were all strewn around in the hustled disarray of a busy ship. I followed him circuitously about the boat, and I still had no cat to hold. He was so "scatty," I suspect he was raised on sour milk. Then the most dreadful thing happened.

A little girl came from out of nowhere hollering and screaming, "Don't hurt that cat!" Old Cap looked up with a fretful glare, took a half turn, and his hind feet slipped off the railing; it was sure to be a gamble with sudden death. Unsteadily and simultaneously, his front paw claw-nails clinched in on the wooden pommel part of the handrail, while his hind legs went into a pendulum swing. He was fearfully holding on with his forepaws and trying to catch a spinning grip with his trailers. The longer his turmoil, the more furious the dither; with a frightful meow, he gave into a final squeeze, drawing himself to the top. Feeling perfectly awful, the little girl gaped at the sight of what was happening. With Cap's survival off the hook, he regained his usual self and made a go for the monkey rail.

Cap hit the top rail in a scat that seemed to show confidence. He went up the rail waving his tail high in the air with a fanning twitch and leaped back through the window. The ferry captain looked down at the three of us. He pulled his curved corncob pipe, which had been resting on his chin, out of his mouth and broke into a full laugh.

Unbeknownst to me, a group of older men, wearing big straw hats, stood on the starboard side. They'd been watching me trying to catch the cat. A gust of laughter rose from the small crowd. I was a grateful loser so lingered a moment, waved with a stiff smile, and turned my attention back to the water.

Dad saw what was going on. He called to me to get in the car and rest myself. I wasn't tired but knew that I wasn't hankerin' for any ear and tail marks. I wasn't privileged to speak freely; therefore it was best not to speak at all. But first I had to take another look at the picnickers on the gritty pebble beach, passing speedboats, sailing vessels and fishing boats. There was a lot for a country boy to see, a tide of joy with all the sparkle.

The first scent I noticed from the Eastern Shore was the smell of salty water and seaweed in the air, a smell I'm not likely to forget. A steady stream of seagulls was crossing the sky, squawking on land and bumping around on top of twisted waves.

Coming into port, we slowed down to a crawl, hit the much-battered pier with a thud. Crushing heavyweight truck tires hung along the onward side of the wharf to cushion our blow. When we stopped, a lanky young sailor unwound the rope from around the camels, the large stump on the bottom deck of the ferry that the tie-lines are fastened to. With a struggle he fetched it to a waiting shoreman who dallied it around the hitching post. In less than no time, he had her tied up. Soon afterward the stern gangplank was lowered and the batten settled in place. The cars inched forward, and with a loud rumble over the bump, we were off. It took us over a little gut creek with a rickety bridge chopped from the homeliest of logs and onto solid ground.

The Eastern Shore was low, flat and laid back. There was a wide spread of homegrown scenery, with watermelon, sweet corn, and grazing dairy herds. Not only the watermen but also the farmers that were able to outlast the hard times caught hold of the newer ways and flourished in the good times. Some folks worked hard to get rich, other folks worked hard to "get" poor. In the country, many folks were working hard to earn enough money to live on; in the city it seems like they were all trying to take it away from each other.

256

One thing I can vouch for: the land of plenty had plenty of mosquitoes and a flood of gnats. We did our picnicking, bug-swattin' and shooing the bees away from the "Honey Drummer," an Eastern Shore honey raisin bread. Then we played and visited with our friends. Mom made sure to have us all gathered up and in the car by early afternoon so we could be among those waiting in line for the ferry; it was first-come, first-served. The only other option was to drive north two and a half hours to cross at the headwater of the Bay in Havre de Grace over the Susquehanna River Bridge. That was a pretty good throw back in those days.

Dad mostly made it in time, although there were times we were hitting it close. Mom would be getting worried and say, "Russell, do you think we're going to make it?" By the time we got aboard the ferry, it was late. The ferry left the harbor, steadily made its turn into the channel, then at full speed headed west straight into the setting sun, leaving the land of sand and pine behind.

The dewy fresh fog was just starting to drift across the water as we returned to Sandy Point Port. The cool moist wind called for a waistcoat. The clanging sound of buoy bells brought a bit of mystery out of the settling clouds, the far-off ships giving way with their gentle toots from the fog horn— they could send a little ripple up the spine. The peacefulness was uniquely different from that on the farm. By the time we arrived at home, the darkness was starting to fall and the shadow of light was gone. Lightning bugs and fireflies were flashing a soft glow. Tucked away in bed that evening, I soaked up the best parts of the day. I relived my land of make-believe with wonderful dreams.

Eastern Shore-ers always felt apart from the rest of the state of Maryland and thought they should become their own state.

They tried several times but it never happened. Their strong beliefs were as southern as if they were in the heart of Dixie. Some of these old boys talk so slow, it's as if they were dragging anchor. Some things didn't end with the Civil War or lessen their differences.

The armchair bureaucrats of Baltimore and Washington thought it was high time to put a bridge across the Bay. The more larded families had enough money to chase all sorts of fantasies, with vacation homes up and down the sandy ocean beach. But for myself, if I were to harbor a stately winter home in the city and possess a homely summer cabin on the shore, I think I'd spend all my winters in my summer home.

If my memory hasn't failed me, on the day of election, the people voted not to have a bridge across the Bay. To my surprise and with a great throb of emotion, the headlines blared out that they were searching for a place to build a bridge across the Bay, and it was coming about pretty quick. The surveyors had picked the spot! They were ready to cast the first stone, and the rewards would be great. The big daddy in Washington was going to send a fat check to help pay for it. I'd heard about the George Washington Bridge in New York City and the Golden Gate Bridge in California. In a wondrous world of tomorrows, it was going to be one more wonder on the Chesapeake.

It would be historically incorrect to imagine there were not serious conflicts over the building of the Chesapeake Bay Bridge. With mild profanity Eastern Shore people thought, "Ha, the plan's just too dumb for words." The Western Shore legislature broached the subject by convincing the Eastern Shore that this bridge-building would help with their economic troubles, promising jobs on the bridge. Time altered the plan, and the promised prosperity didn't happen.

258

The only jobs passed out to the shoremen for bridgework was sandhog-in' (shoveling sand into a cement mixer), the lowest paying job. The bridge bosses bussed most of their laborers in from faraway New York City and Boston. Hostile feelings exploded; the new imports from the north referred to their southern friends as "Rebel-hicks." Several times it got a bit hectic with fights. The employment office on the Eastern Shore side was burned down. That threw a little excitement back over on the Western Shore, giving them city folks something to howl about. The tried and true Eastern Shore-ers were not going down without a fight. It turned out to be a splendid little war. It was talked about in the paper, on the news and among friends. There was plenty of fresh gossip as news about the bridge flowed.

There was an unconfirmed report that a sporting lady, working in a millinery shop by day and traveling the lower shore by night, was accused of the arson at the unemployment office. Rumors pointed to her. If the young men on the shore were hired, it was theorized she'd have an increase in her nightly profession. This was big time news that went around back then for us fifteen-year-olds.

It would've been fun for my friends and me to work on the bridge one summer. But my father thought it was more important for me to help with "buck-in" hay and cutting wheat and oats than to be putting up a bridge. I was told, "Besides that, you don't have a place to stay." I enlightened him by saying we could camp out along the water and hitchhike home on the weekends. With a deep eye and taking no pains to look pleasant, Dad politely told me I didn't have to bother because I wasn't going anyplace. For sure my eyes must have dropped and my heart sank on the tactless words. Way back then, it was hard to understand the pain and fret that comes with love and care.

I had several close friends, including Ducky (which was a good name for a nice Eastern Shore boy), who lived in Rock Hall on the lower shore. Ducky was about my age give or take a year or two. He kept me informed on the latest happenings on his side of the shore, and I let him know about mine.

One Friday evening, instead of staying at the Teen Center Dance like we ought to have done, three other boys and I decided to take my friend Fred's 1947 Henry J and breeze our way down the road to see how the Chesapeake Bay Bridge was coming along and what more was going on that we should know about. We drove to the bridge and stopped the car. With a daredevil attitude, we asked if we could walk out on the bridge, and the person we spoke to told us that it was okay with him.

We walked out about a mile to where they were working. Feeling a little cocky, as we passed the men working, we'd tell them that we were the new bridge inspectors. Then a foreman and heavyweight man carrying his hardhat under one arm happened to overhear us. He came fluttering up to us, ranting and raving, squealing like a pine knot in a sawmill, asking about us being on the bridge. "What are you boys doing here?" Our testy reply was, "The guard said it was okay." "Oh no, dagummit, that guard had no business letting you out here! Get out of here before somebody gets hurt or falls off." Actually, the way he spoke at us, it was right down plumb insulting with no doubt about it. I had a hunch we shouldn't have said we were bridge inspectors.

This was good-bye to the old ferries that so faithfully had bobbed the commute to and from the Eastern Shore for many years. The birth of a new bridge would surely bring the death of the old ferry. This bridge was going to change the lifestyle of the people on the shore forever; we thought we were really making history. Just think, Jimmy Fox and friends out on that bridge before any cars, almost within jumping distances of the Eastern Shore. If my father knew about this, I'd be history! The arrival of a new-fashion bridge was a warm welcome. The old commute of Mom and Dad in the front seat with four kids in the back seat, sailing down the road to meet the ferry—and wait and wait—was over none too soon.

The four-and-a half-mile bridge was completed in 1952, giving the upper shore plenty to purr about. The opening of the new bridge was quite a "coming out party." For the travelers those were exciting times, and the vehicles kept moving in both directions. Without fanfare, the ferry was shoved aside, steadily slipping away into history. The old ferry didn't seem to threaten the purity of southern fashion to my knowledge. For some of us, old ways change hard.

Travel "learns" us many customs, not always accepted or appreciated, but it did seem to me most all excursions were greeted with a gracious smile. For my friends, courtesy was always expected and is still in place. However, with best intentions, all the cars, trucks and "Tin Can Tourists" brought on complications with the "Sand Cutters," farmers dragging farm machinery down the road behind big tractors. This was something the city racers were not accustomed to in their travels, and the farmers were not accustomed to picking up debris in their tractor tires.

In 1964 the 23-mile Chesapeake Bay Bridge Tunnel opened; by now the traffic was snarling. The Eastern Shore people were cussing the people crossing their land and the people crossing it were cussing the traffic. There were consequences and repercussions. In 1980 a second Chesapeake Bay Bridge running parallel with the first was built; it split the traffic. Now it's no longer called the "Bay Bridge" but was renamed the

'William P. Lane Jr. Memorial Bridge'—an enormous mouthful. Regardless of the name, there was a tangled mass of astonishing handiwork that hung high over the Bay.

On the eastern seashore side, dusty pathways turned into stone-throwing gravel roads, then into sticky tar-and-chip, single-lane country roads. Then they turned into smooth asphalt dual lane highways whose summer name was "Swimmers Highway," then into a deluxe divided superhighway known as "Ocean Highway." The road map soon became a spider web of red and blue lines. I suppose the high-rise apartment city folks, who are known to a country boy as cliff dwellers, felt a need to escape their cave-life on weekends, and this was the route to take. My Eastern Shore friend told me the upper shore had got in the last scratch one more time.

Having friends living in each location, I got the opportunity to experience the harmony on both sides. It was awful nice not to have that dreadful wait in the heated lines for the ferry. Yet it's mighty sad to see so many people crossing over the lower shore and bringing grief. The true grace of the passing ferry had aged, but it still stirs energy in an old traveler's soul.

Study Time at Franklin High School

It was in 1955 that I learned some new words in the current-events part of my history class—things I had never heard about before. Rosa Parks, a black seamstress, was riding a city bus in Montgomery, Alabama. The law required that black people ride in the rear of a public bus. She was seated toward the rear of an overcrowded bus, and she refused to give up her seat to a white man. Mrs. Parks was arrested and given a fine. After a year-long battle, the Supreme Court made it legal for blacks to sit wherever they liked on a public bus. This was the first time I ever heard of anything about any kind of national

262

racial affairs with blacks. There were all kinds of supporters and detractors on the issue. I didn't know it, but history was being made as we were discussing the event in a divided classroom. This was roughly ninety years after the Civil War.

I became the President of Future Farmers of America (FFA) and was elected to represent Maryland at the FFA National Congress in Kansas City. Only one representative from each state got to vote on the upcoming election for new officers and on new bills. The Lions Club and the Kiwanis Club paid my expenses for the trip to Kansas City for a week. On my return I was invited to be a guest speaker at their dinner meeting to tell of my experience. Then I was invited to different schools to share what was happening in the FFA Club. One meeting was held at a college in Hagerstown, Maryland, as a central location for members in western Maryland to come hear about what had happened at the national level of FFA. This meeting saved me from traveling to individual schools throughout western Maryland. My agriculture teacher, Sox Seabold, drove me all around.

FRANKLIN GAZETTE

Jimmy Fox

Among the famous people Jimmy saw were the Governor, Mayor, and a sight which would have interested most any teenager, or movie star lover, Annie Oakley and Gene Autry. His greatest disappointment was in the famous Mississippi river. Jimmy says, "It was just an ordianary muddy river; the way people talked about it, I had expected much more. I think the Missouri had it beat without trying".

On account of the old attraction boys have for girls, these boys almost missed thier train home. It seems the directions that were given to the boys in finding the girls' houses were right but the bus they caught wasn't, and after a few hours' ride they decided they were lost and started for home. Having been in formed to be back at 4:00, they were still trying to find their way around at 3:00. But it was pretty obvious the train was caught and the boys were safely on their way home, for Jimmy is back, and I don't think that gleam in his eye was cuased by overwork.

It was nice of Sox to take his time for me. The fall is a lovely time of the year to take a ride in Carroll County and the western Maryland counties. Sox and I had a great deal to talk about. On the sharp turns along the winding roads there was always another farm that looked even more beautiful than the last. Our conversations were, "Oh, look at that field of corn! Look there, do you think that's winter oats he is planting?"

Sox was busy explaining how much different it was to farm in this part of the country compared to Baltimore County. He said that he'd driven this road many times taking Mrs. Seabold for Sunday drives just to see the country. He was familiar with this area of Carroll Country and was pointing out various farms and highlighting the different things around the farm and the buildings—how old they were and how elegantly they were built long before the Civil War and so on.

Sox slowed down to a drag as we rounded the next turn, "Jimmy, I want you to take a good look at this farm. It is one of the finest farms I have ever seen. This guy is a real farmer. He really knows how to farm." We made the turn and stopped on the edge of the road and looked down into the deep valley below with an old time hefty fieldstone house and a well-built hay barn with a mighty big straw stack in the middle of the barnyard. There in a small meadow stood an old log smoke house and off to one side of it, a tiny little sheep barn. Sheep were grazing on the lawn.

"Isn't that a picture to behold, and look at that contour farming. See how they plow around those steep hills to keep the soil from washing way? I don't know who lives there, but he surely knows his stuff about farming." I said. " Mr. Seabold, that's not a man's farm, that's a woman's farm!" He asked, "How do you know that?" I told him that I know the lady who owns it. "Well, who owns it?" I told him, "It belongs to Sally Cartzendafner." Sox said, "Jimmy, how would you know that?" "Mr. Seabold, that's my Grandmother's farm." He laughed, "I think I know somebody who just flunked their Agriculture Class this semester!"

We passed a large herd of 50-60 Holstein dairy cows waiting for milking time—another beautiful place, all white buildings trimmed in forest green. Not thinking that I would know, Sox asked, "Who lives here?" I told him, "My Uncle Carroll Fritz." With a smile, he replied with a hum. I confessed that a lot of the people living in the area were either friends or relatives of some sort. My grandmother had seven or eight siblings and most of them had large families and still live close by. I was happy to point out who lived where and naturally a little bit of the history on the neighborhood. He thanked me for my knowledge and teased me for the rest of our trip on how I'd be repeating his class next year.

I was a "wannabe" farmer, and thought this was what I wanted to do for a living. Three of my friends and I hooked school one day and went to the Harrisburg Farm Show in Pennsylvania. It was spitting snow on this cold January day, and we thought school might close early. Like most teenage boys, I never thought about getting stuck in the snow. We didn't think about our parents worrying about us if we didn't come home after school.

In the morning when it was snowing as we left school, we went across the street to Schaeffer's store, where we purchased Prince Albert Smoking Tobacco and cigarette paper (for rolling our own cigarettes). After all, we were the Future Farmers of America; you'd have thought we each had our own plantation! We came back to school, got in my friend's 1946 Buick with fluid drive—a car that you could change gears in without pushing in the clutch. We each rolled our own cigarette and smoked away. Rolling them was the most fun. We kept smoking so we could get a chance to roll more. We were trying to see who was the best roller, rolling a cigarette in one hand like the cowboys do, and pulling the string of the cloth tobacco pouch shut with our teeth.

Because of the cold weather and the lack of a good heater, we didn't have our windows down, so before long, we had to stop to get out and catch our breath. You see, we didn't usually smoke, and we were all feeling pretty bad by now. After putting those cigarettes out and walking around for a while, we started back up the road.

We arrived at the farm show and took a nice tour through all the farm machinery to see the newest things out on the market. Then we moseyed through the animal barn. Although everything was under one roof in some areas, there was still a sharp cold tingle in the air. We entered a large, brightly-lit arena where there was a muleteer sitting in the middle of a homemade seat on a hay carriage.

He had a bushy beard and the stump of an unlit cigar in one corner of his mouth. As he spoke to his eight-mule hitch, he would roll that stump of a cigar from one corner of this mouth to the other. This old long-legged fellow wore a floppy hat and blue overalls. He fit right in with his mismatched team of red, black, brown and white mule hitch. Most people would like a well-matched team, but on the other hand, most people would love to have a team that would work like his. He was working those mules with a jerk-line (a single line running through a ring on the hames from each mule to the lead mule).

We all took a seat on some boards that had been placed there for the on-lookers. He backed the wagon between some barrels that weren't any more than far enough apart for the wagon to pass through. Those mules had superior ability and he was really putting them through their paces. After stopping for a late lunch and more tobacco, we started back down the road to school. We actually wasted more tobacco than we smoked while trying to roll it; it was falling out both ends and over the top of our cigarette paper at the same time. We got back to school, and it had let out after a full day of classes.

266

Then my friend Bernie Yox drove me home from school. All was well—Mom didn't have any questions for me, and I didn't have any for her. She thought that I smelled a little rauchy from smoke but didn't say much about it.

The next morning before I arrived at school there was some gossip around that some boys were missing the day before. As soon as I got off the bus, Sox Seabold met me at the door. I noticed that he seemed a bit priggish and that wasn't like him at all. Sox was very opinionated and seldom if ever misunderstood. His first question was, "Where were you and your friends yesterday?" I wasn't going to pretend that I was perfect. Mr. Seabold was the nicest person and a good friend. I said that we thought for sure that school was going to be closed. Sox interrupted saying, "Well, don't that beat all!" I continued, "So we went to Schaeffer's, got some smoking tobacco and smoked until we got sick, sat in the car for the better side of half an hour till we started to feel better and then went to Harrisburg Farm Show." He replied, "What on earth do you think you are doing out racing around the country like that? Jimmy, you boys are getting a little too rambunctious. I'm glad you got sick! Smoking, ha! I got sick worrying about you."

He told me that all the teachers knew we weren't in school. Mr. Seabold said that at the first period, the principal would be calling all of us to his office. He told me that he'd give me a note telling the principal that we had permission from Mr. Seabold in the Agriculture Department to represent the class at the Harrisburg Farm Show. I was feeling pretty sorrowful and guilt-ridden about disappointing Sox Seabold that way. He was the best teacher and friend a fellow could have.

When called, we all went to the principal's office. I knew Mr. Lindley was easily riled and as Dad would say, "A still mouth is a wise mind." That means it's better to stand there and look like a fool, than to open your mouth and remove all doubt. As Mr. Lindley read the note, he just kept looking at me. Then he would look at the note again, and put his hands over his mouth in a praying position, with his elbows on the desk. He said, "I don't know what kind of a concoction this is, but you boys over there in the Agriculture Department are always causing some kind of a ruckus."

He looked at the note again and then he said, "This is fine, but I'm looking for some volunteers to carry coal in to the furnace for the next week. Do you fellows know of anyone?" His look was one that made me think that we should volunteer for it. I looked at my friends and they said, "Whatever you think." I was thinking it over and figured for the betterment of all, let it be. This was better than facing the firing squad. With a smile I said, "Sure, we'd be happy to help out." I don't believe he liked my choice of words, or maybe it was my smile. He said in a grouchy voice, "Well, be here tomorrow morning at 5:30. I don't know about this. Your parents should have given me a note since you were leaving the state. I think I'll call them and see what they know about your trip to the Farm Show." This took the larger part of twenty minutes, which seemed like a week. I was amazed that I could get into so much trouble in so little time. Finally he said, "Okay, get back to class." I told my friends that I didn't know what kind of salary a principal made in 1956, but we were making sure he was earning every penny.

Well Mom didn't know about the trip and wouldn't have approved of it. She drove me to school for one week. Every morning she told me that I should be ashamed of myself for making her drive me to school. After about the second day I was pleading with her to let me walk. "I've got a good mind to let you walk," she said, "but not in this weather. I love you too much." I asked her not to love me so much and let me walk.

For a week Mom told me all the things I had ever done wrong in my life. She told me, "God only knows how hard I've tried to be a good mother. Heaven only knows I tried to bring you up proper. I don't know what will ever become of you, Jimmy. Now, if you think you're going to get off easy, then you have another think coming. I swallowed my thought, "Now ain't that the dying truth." What have I ever done to deserve this?" This is what Mom told me every morning on the way to school. I sure was feeling like the scoundrel of the year. Then on top of that I had to carry the coal to the coal bin for three and a half hours before school started. For a week I was walking around looking all shame-faced, without getting any sympathy. The following week Mom's warm sweet smile returned. I learned a lesson out of class that was just as important as one in class.

Hog Butchering

Dad always handled his pigs with a lot of care. He was constantly watching them, making sure that they were not being overcrowded at the trough. If pigs get too close to each other while eating, they'll push and fight. There'll be a constant battle until they finish eating. This can cause them to be bruised, and a bruised ham can spoil.

Dad liked his pigs to be calm and unruffled. Pigs don't have sweat glands. If the pigs are hot and excited on butchering day, the meat will be in a feverish condition, making it much easier for souring to start before the meat can take the cure. The hogs were killed in their pen. It was important to remember that the hogs should be handled quietly and calmly. If we got excited the hogs could sense it. After they were killed and stuck for bleeding, they were pulled out of the pen, put on a sled, and hauled to the scalder.

It was usually cold weather in the fall when we butchered. With the ground frozen and temperatures at 30? or less, it wasn't so sloppy working around the butchering kettle. Dad liked to see his hogs weigh in at about 190 to 220 pounds. That made them somewhere between eight and 10 months old. This prevented you from butchering a fatty hog.

Butchering was a long, hard process. We started weeks in advance cutting wood and gathering kindling for the kettle and scalder. We used hickory for the smoke house. Any kind of fruitwood is good for smoking. I know some people who prefer apple or pear over hickory; each smoke creates a different flavor. We used five or six kettles that ranged from 30 to 70 gallons. Because they were cast iron, they would rust, but we prevented the rust by greasing them good with lard. So after every use, they were cleaned and put away with a light surface treatment of lard. Then when we wanted to use one of them, we had to wash out the lard that was left in. It took four strong people to carry the hog scalder and put it in place.

A little lye or wood ashes were added to the water to help make scalding easier. The lye in the ashes loosened the hair from the skin of the hog. We placed boards across trusses (sawhorses), making a table, which was attached to the hog scalder. Then we made sure that everything was level and sturdy so the pig could be placed on the table. We rolled the pig from the table into the hot scalding water. By pulling the long fork-type dipper that rests on the bottom of the scalder and is connected to it from the outside, the pig could be pushed in the scalder and dipped up and down. When the handle was straight up, the pig was in under the water. When you pulled the handle down, the pig was out and ready to be rolled onto the table.

It took days of preparation before it was butchering time. We used regular scrapple pans and five-gallon lard cans. When full, the lard cans weigh 50 pounds. I gathered them up, along with fine rags and towels. We always tried to put things together like the lard press. I first experienced the preparation and butchering at Twiford Farm where we butchered 10-12 hogs simultaneously. After we moved to Beaver Brook Farm, we butchered three-four hogs for the Thompsons and two hogs for my family. This was a job I always enjoyed.

I helped build the fire under the butchering scalder. We made sure the water was hot before George Stairs shot the pigs. Dad stuck the pigs and drained the blood before bringing them to the scalder. If a good bleed is not obtained, then blood left in the joints can easily cause souring. After giving the hogs a quick dip in the scalding water, everyone used a round hog scraper to remove the hair. When the hog was placed on the table ready for scraping, everybody found his favorite spot. Mine was the foot. I held the foot and scraped against the curl of the pig hair, which was up the foot towards the leg. Sometimes there were so many men scraping the pig that it was difficult to find a spot to begin. After the hog was scraped, it was shaved with a sharp knife and hung up on a gambrel stick. A gambrel stick is in the shape of a horse's hind leg and is used to hold the pig's rear travelers apart to make cleaning and gutting easier. (My father always said it was called a gambrel stick because it was a gamble as to whether it was going to hold the pig!) After that, the pig was washed with cold water.

Dad took care of sharpening the knives. He did such a fine job that you could shave with them. He said that more people get cut with a dull knife then with a sharp one. Dad had built his own butcher's box that he kept his tools in. He made  a lot of his own knives, meat hooks, forks, etc. He was very handy around a forge with blacksmithing. He had a sticking knife, skinning knife, boning knife, butcher's knife, steel for sharpening, meat cleaver, bell scraper for taking the hair off the pigs, meat saw, pot hooks to remove the kettle from the fire, and a large meat fork.

Butchering knives were all scalded before making any cuts or openings on the carcass. Any that were dropped would be re-scalded. Then the hog was gutted and everything was saved except the squeal: the heart, liver, brains and even the guts (large intestine, sometimes called chitterlings; and small intestines, which were cleaned and used for stuffing the sausage).

I have seen my mother stand over a wash tub for hours, using the back side of a knife cleaning the small intestines, also known as casings, in preparation for stuffing sausage. First she scraped the inside and then turned them so she could do the outside. Just to turn them was a major job. After this long, hard task, the casing was washed in lukewarm water. If they were not used that day, they were packed in dry salt for future use.

The head meat and the hog jowls were used to make pudding and scrapple. In some areas scrapple is known as ponthaus. The belly or hog mauls (sow belly) was cleaned and later used for stuffing with potatoes, carrots, slaw, sausage, etc. The brains were served as a meat. Blood pudding and kidney pie were very popular, but not with my family. The tongue was washed, boiled and scraped and then cooked with the head meat.

A quick and thorough chill is a very important factor in turning out good meat. The weather was used to the full advantage for getting a good chill. A good rule to follow is to kill in the afternoon and have the cool night air for a swift brisk chill. A good job of cutting up cannot be done on warm meat.

Dad always cut the meat up. He started by cutting the carcass down the middle while it was still hanging on the gambrel stick. After the pig was gutted, he took out the tenderloin. This is the small lean muscle, which lies underneath the backbone. It's one of the most popular of all pork cuts to be used fresh. Dad called it the "fish." I guess because it looked like a fish. It didn't taste like fish but it sure was good.

Then he took half of the pig off the gambrel stick and put it on the butcher table. Next he removed the feet. The toenails and dewclaws were a treat for the dogs. Grandmother usually pickled the feet, but Mom mostly made souse. Some people called souse headcheese. Why? I don't know: It's made from the feet! I guess it sounds better than toe cheese.

Next the hind leg was cut out. This is where you get the ham. Dad would lay it aside and trim it up later. The front shoulder and leg were taken off and trimmed up with the hams. Dad left a quarter-inch of fat on the hams as he trimmed them. The fat shrunk after it was cured, giving it a nice smooth appearance, plus protecting the meat. He did a great job making them round. The bacons were squared off. The bottom end of a side of bacon is called gammon. All the meat scraps were thrown in for sausage. Then with the meat saw, he carefully cut out the porkchops from the backbone. Then he used the meat cleaver to chop up the spare ribs.

After all the sausage meat was cut up, the scraps were put through the meat grinder for a coarse ground. Our choice was to grind it twice. We used two-thirds lean meat and one-third fatback. Fatback is the sweetest of the different types of fat. Then the ground meat was seasoned with salt and pepper and mixed together. To pack it in the sausage stuffer, I carefully threaded the casing on the brass spout at the bottom of the press. With one hand I turned the crank on the press and with the other I guided the sausage into the washtub. We would get around a couple hundred pounds of meat this way.

On the last day we cut the sausage into four- or five-inch links and set it in the kettle to fry it down. After it was finished we put it in mason jars and then poured hot lard on it, placed a lid on top and sealed it with a ring. By turning the jars upside down to cool, we caused the lard to turn back to a solid form and rise to the surface. This helped to seal the jar and protect the sausage for long-term storage. The jars were then turned right-side up. That way the lard made it airtight, so all the lard on the bottom was now on the top, leaving the air space on the bottom. This way no air got to the sausage. The jars had to be kept in a cool place. If the lard turned back to liquid, it could turn rancid. Otherwise, it would keep from one year to the next. That last jar tasted just as fresh as the first. My grandmother used stone crocks, and after filling them with the sausage and pouring lard on top, she placed dinner plates on for lids. Grandmother could make do with anything.

After cutting up the head meat, we cooked it, put it through the meat grinder and then put it back in the kettle. We would season it with salt and pepper and cook it some more. Other folks like sage and spices added also, but we never did. In this form it's called pudding. We dipped some pudding out and put it in scrapple pans to cool. After it is cooled, it can be taken out and if not used, put in the freezer. We ate a lot of pudding and hominy. The remainder of the pudding left in the kettle was used to make scrapple. We sifted together one-third flour and two-thirds yellow corn meal. After it was mixed thoroughly, using three parts water to four parts head meat, it was put in the kettle and brought to a boil. The rule of thumb was to stir it for about one hour. You have to stir constantly or it will stick. The longer it cooks the thicker it gets and the harder it is to stir. Scrapple is one of my favorite breakfast foods.

We also made lard. There is a thick layer of fat between the backbone and the skin. This is known as fat back. Sometimes it is cured. Leaf lard is a long strip of lightweight fat that is pulled out from the rib cage. The caul and ruffle fat is the fat found in the stomach. The clear plate is the fat that is the covering on top of the shoulders. It's very hard and clear and sometimes used in curing. The leaf lard could be put aside to be saved for making soap. Mom used it because it didn't have much flavor and was softer.

To know if the lard has cooked long enough, you take a string and dip it into the boiling kettle of lard. Pull it out with your left hand, and with your right hand take a match and try to burn it from the bottom. If it doesn't burn, it needs to have more water cooked out. Once the lard is finished cooking, it's pressed together. The process of running the lard through the lard press is called rendering. The skin, after it is pressed, is called cracklings. Once the fat is strained, it's known as lard and looks like vanilla ice cream and smells like bacon. For whitening, the lard should be stirred occasionally while it is being cooled. Some people peel a potato and stir it in the mixture as it cools. They claim it takes out the impurities. Once it becomes a creamy consistency, it's ready to be poured into 50-pound lard cans. Lard has many uses and is the foundation of lots of good recipes, like pies and cakes. Lard is easily digested and high in nutritional value. Of course it's one of the softer fats.

I carried cracklings in my pocket to school and nibbled on them during the day. Upon request I shared with my friends. The only problem with carrying cracklings in your pocket was that they left a large grease spot on your pants, which was no problem because my mother made her own soap, mixing lye, lard and salt in a dishpan. Her soap was so strong that if it didn't get rid of the grease that was okay, because it left a hole at the spot where the grease stain had been!

The butchering itself took us at least three days at the farm. After the hog was cut up, my father began the long task of curing the hams and bacon. This lasted several weeks. Good meat, of course, depends on many factors: kind of hog butchered, proper fattening, handling and weight. Dad said curing begins with the live pig. The quality of the finished ham on my dinner plate depends a lot on how the pig was handled. From the time they were born until they were slaughtered, he insisted on cleanliness in the pen where they were raised and on the butcher block. His pens were cleaned out daily and fresh bedding was added. About once a week I was told to put one good size shovel full of clean dirt in each pen. This was to keep enough iron in their bodies to make them healthy.

There are basically two methods for the lost art of home-curing meat. One is the sugar cure and the other is the brine. Salt alone will not produce quality-cured meat. Salt will harden the muscle fibers. It tends to make the meat overly salty and dry. To produce quality-cured meat, other ingredients must be blended with the salt, like saltpeter, black and red pepper, brown sugar and borax. After this is done, you have what is known as dry sugar cure. Then the cure is rubbed all over the meat, taking your thumb and pushing it down the hock and knee joints, working the cure all over. The meat pump, which looks like a giant syringe, can be used to add water to the cure. You can pump the cure in next to the bone. This is the safest way for you're curing from the inside as well as from the outside. Joints make an excellent place for bone taint.

The meat can be packed in a box or barrel or on the table. The heaviest pieces should be packed at the bottom and covered with a cloth to keep flies off. While the meat is being cured, it should be broken down and overhauled at least twice. That means to take the pile apart and rub any bare spots and places that resisted the cure.

The brine was made in a wooden barrel, starting with water. The water should always be boiled first and then cooled. Boiling the water removes germs and bacteria, which helps to make the brine pure. Then enough salt is added to float a hen's egg. Other ingredients are added before the meat is placed in the barrel. This process takes two days per pound, so a ham weighing twenty pounds took forty days to cure. This curing time varied with different butchers.

My Grandmother Cartzendafner's brine recipe was quite different. For every one-hundred pounds of meat, she used two pounds of brown sugar, one-quarter pound black pepper and one-quarter pound saltpeter. After the cure time was up, the hams were wrapped in heavy brown paper bags and enclosed in clean feedbags. Red pepper and borax were used to help keep flies and insects out. That is, if they could get through all of those bags.

In the summertime while the meat was curing, you had to look out for skipper flies. Skipper is the larvae of a small black fly. These flies are small enough to go through an ordinary window screen. They lay eggs in crevices of the meat. The skipper hatches out and feeds on the meat. It's a slender white maggot about one-third inch long and in no time can ruin a good piece of meat.

Once the curing process was completed, the meat was taken to the smokehouse. This is where we used the green hickory. We used some small, dry chips to start the fire, topped by green wood. That way it just smoldered along without a blaze. Quite often we had to start the fire more than once a day. That was okay, for we wanted a cold smoke. We used only a very small fire right in the center on the dirt floor. If the fire got too hot, the meat would actually cook.

The smokehouse had one door and no windows. A small hole next to the floor in the back allowed enough air to control the fire. Fall weather was a good time to start the fire because smoke hangs closer to the ground then. In the fall, you could usually count on rain, snow, fog or just heavy hazy weather, so there wasn't a problem. The hams, bacons, and other cuts were hung around on crossbeams six or seven feet above the fire. The pieces couldn't touch each other. Ventilation was needed to keep air circulating, so the meat wouldn't sweat. Sweating could start decay and actual spoilage. Meat absorbs smoke flavor and the smoke helps it to cure. The meat should always be kept away from direct sunlight because it discolors the meat.

Bacon is ready for the table after smoking for 18 hours. Bacon, however, never kept very well; it didn't even keep well in the freezer so we ate a lot of it at one time. We ate it for breakfast, lunch and supper, but we didn't mind for it was such a treat. At the time I didn't appreciate what a good cook my mother was. I never gave her the credit she deserved. She could fix bacon and other dishes in so many different ways that you never got tired of eating the same thing. Sometimes she'd cut a hunk of meat off the slab of bacon before it was sliced and boil it up with cabbage, string beans, etc. I am sure she could teach the top gourmet chef a thing or two. The best hams would take a year and a half (yes, 18 months!) to cure. Mrs. Thompson would only eat Dad's hams when they were at least 18 months old.

Mom often sent me to the smokehouse to get a ham. I washed off the ham with a stiff brush to remove some of the brine, borax, red pepper, and mold. Then Mom soaked it a few hours. Sometimes she baked it whole and other times she sliced and fried it. When she cut one of Dad's hams, it was a delicate pink and delicious in flavor. It made excellent gravy; it was the finest in the country.

I had a good time butchering and continued much of the same process until recent years. I'm pleased that my sons have all experienced some form of butchering hogs with me.

Electricity on the Farm

The farm manager's house had electricity in it. Each room had a single, fifteen-watt bulb hanging down from the center of the ceiling. No shades or chandeliers, just a plain bulb—some with a switch and others with a pull chain. The three downstairs rooms each had an outlet on the washboard that stuck out about six inches.

I asked Dad what an electrical outlet was for. He told me it was for electrical appliances. I asked what was an electrical appliance, and he said that it was something like a toaster or iron—things like that, which run off of electricity. Why would anybody want to use an electric toaster or iron if they have a good cookstove? We made toast by placing a little butter on top of the lid on our cookstove and dropping a slice of bread on it, then using a spatula to flip it over—there you've got your toast! I didn't think that was so much trouble. Dad said, "It's time for you to go to the barn?"

Dad was attracted to the innovative way of having electricity reduced manual labor. Whenever our electrician arrived for something he followed him around asking questions. He started picking up ideas on how to reduce the speed on an electric motor by using larger pulleys, how to increase speed with a smaller one and how to develop more horsepower with an old transmission out of a car. With electricity already in the barns, dairy and shop, he thought about putting motors on different things to save on manual labor. I agreed that that was more important than an electric toaster. My dad used electricity for things like a hacksaw, hay elevator, grain cleaner, meat grinder —he even used heat lamps for hog brooders and the list goes on and on.

The fan mill was a way to clean grain, which was going to be used for reseeding. It had a large wheel with a handle. I was too small to be able to make a complete turn without moving my body forward on each revolution. It was critical to keep the fan on the bottom well greased to keep down as little friction as possible making it a fast smooth easy spin to get a lot of air. We poured the grain in a trough through a screen at the top of the trough and which fell into a basket on the floor. The air blew out chaff along with the unwanted dust and dirt.

Dad got the idea to put a pulley on the fan mill with a quarter horse power motor to turn it. He took off the old hand crank, drilled a pilot hole in the shaft and attached a big pulley. The motor was mounted on the bottom. For a high rate of speed he put on a pulley about the size of a squirrel's ear with a setscrew in it and lined it up with the pilot hole. Then we plugged it in and it worked. Because of the fast steady speed

it was far superior as to anything I could do. Oh boy, I was out of that job. That was one living step into the future that I liked.

The Consolidated Gas Electric Light and Power Company of Baltimore, later known as The Baltimore Gas and Electric Company, learned of the many things that Dad was doing with electricity on the farm and published a newsletter dated July 1950 entitled "Rural Power Pictorial." It was to help promote electricity on the farm showing modern development in time-saving labor. It may be said that Dad had a clear vision of the future.

Dad and Richard are on the front cover of the newsletter. The picture shows them taking hay off a hay wagon, placing the bales on an electric elevator, which carried it up to the top of the barn with the greatest of ease. The caption read, "This electric elevator loads hay and grain twice as fast as the work could be done by hand." To me that seemed real funny for the dude that wrote those words must have never tried throwing a bale of hay over his head into our barn. It saved the work of two or three good men. The old elevator never tired. Twenty minutes later the hundred bales of hay was in the mow. Now only one man was needed to unload the wagon by himself in half the time. It saved many hours of hard labor all within one day alone.

I remember stepping out of a blistering haymow that had reached 120° and seeing our herd of cows. The hay season naturally was in the heat of summer. The sun was so hot the cows spent the day fallowing the shade of a big oak tree as it moved across the pasture near the barn. Their only concern was finding relief as the shade moved. They stood up, stretched, swatted some flies and moved about to find the depth of a darker shadow. Finding their contentment, they lie back down and comminuted chewing their cud (a ball of food that a cow belches up and chews twice before digesting it again.) All the while we worked and sweated throwing bales over our heads into the barn. I wanta tell you that I have the highest regard for that stubborn old man, Mr. Thomas Edison, for his wonderful invention of electricity. Tommy used to say, "I have not failed. I've just found 10,000 ways that won't work." Finally he got the charge he was looking for.

I admire Dad for his invaluable gift of finding easier ways of reducing manual labor and making our existence more cushy. Dad's ingenious ways never wore out. By the 1950's he used electricity to move cables attached to false headgates and tailgates on the wagons, saving on manual labor. With this modern technology and electricity Dad was able to fill silo by himself in three days. In the 40's it took six to eight men and four or five boys over a week to do the same job. Dad moved some priceless "labor-lickin'" accomplishments forward into the future, which was wonderful. The sad thing is that his time-saving labor never put an extra dime in his pocket. He consistently lectured and showed others how to make life easier, not for the money, nor the thank-you's, but for the betterment of future farmers.

Electricity then was cheap even for its time. One day I went with Mom to visit a neighbor and I remember them talking about her electric bill. Our good neighbor was very conservative with her electricity—sitting in the dark and never using her new appliances just so she could save on her electric bill. She told Mom that she never paid more than her standard $7.00 basic charge at the end of the month on her electricity bill. Mom told her, "I'm sure you're paying for a lot more than you are using." Mom was a master at turning things around.

The Milo King

My father was a modern-day kind of farmer who lived on the cutting-edge of farming. Dad was happy to move on to tractors and leave the horses and mules for someone else to tend. He was always thinking of a better and easier way to farm—a true agriculturalist who set a high hook.

During the first part of the last half of the twentieth-century, milo was one of Dad's many new adventures. Milo is an organic grain that comes from the sorghum family. It's an ancient grain that's been used for hundreds of years in Asia and South Africa. It's drought proof and blight resistant and since there are no reasons to presume weather conditions are more favorable one year over the next in Maryland, it seemed like an appropriate crop for the area.

Milo has a large long oval cone-shaped head known as a node. Each node stands stiff and erect on top of a hefty red feathery stalk. At maturity it has hundreds of tightly knit seeds known as berries. These berries are small and round and can vary in color from white, cream and brown to red. Milo will keep well if stored in a cool dry place for over a year without becoming moldy or rancid. If it gets wet and rots, it smells to high heaven. The Midwest started using milo many years ago, Texans love it, but it wasn't popular on the east or west coasts.

When Dad decided to introduce milo to our part of the country, he chose the dwarf-type brownish red berry that grows two- to four-feet high. We tried it and Dad thought the risks were worth the wait. It was easy to harvest as a standing crop much like wheat, barley or other grains that can be cut with a combine when ripened. Milo can be cut at a tender age as a green fodder crop, hauled to the barn, chopped and blown into the silo with an ensilage blower for future use. The sweet heavy aroma of a freshly filled silo is absolutely delightful.

However, during the next six weeks of fermentation in the silo, the sour silage produces a typical rank odor that gets worse before it gets better. After the fermentation period, the ensilage is made ready for wintertime use as cow feed. We set aside a certain number of acres for filling the silo, in addition to saving some to be seasoned for dry seeds. The dry seeds were crimped, doled out and fed on top of the ensilage as a replacement for corn. The rest of the stalk was mowed down and baled up, heaved into wagons, carried to the barn and stacked for the winter. The bales of milo were fed as dry fodder much like hay. Nothing was wasted; it stored well, kept well, harvested easily, and carried about the same amount of protein as corn.

There are approximately sixteen-hundred seeds to the pound. We only needed four pounds to plant one acre. Milo can be planted in early spring as soon as the ground can be worked up. Rows are drilled with a grain drill ten inches apart. A grain drill is a machine used for planting small seeds (kernels) close together in a shallow furrow. Cornrows were planted thirty inches apart. We were able to plant a lot more milo in the same amount of ground compared to the same size field for corn. Milo can be planted and harvested early, leaving enough time before winter to plant another crop, like winter oats, in that same field. With corn you had to wait until all dangers of frost were over before planting and that would be sometime in May. Dad figured, if possible, no later than May 5th for a good full crop to be harvested by late October. Dad was convinced milo was the crop for him.

I don't recollect Dad mentioning that we didn't have corn worms in milo. But I tell you, that was a big advantage for me as one of his corn cutters. Corn worms are large fat ugly green caterpillars with flabby folds circling their chubby bodies from front to back with smooth skin. The crummy has a mouth full of razor-blade teeth and plenty of super jaw pressure. They feed on corn tassels and corn silk. Smut is a nasty gray mass of fungus that forms on the outside of an ear of corn after the corn worm has finished with it. By harvest time, it becomes black, dusty and dirty.

As I gradually moved down the cornrow using a corn knife to cut one stalk at a time for making a corn shock, corn worms would fall gently and lovingly from the top of a six-, seven- and eight-foot tall cornstalk onto my shoulder. They could hardly wait to bite me on the side of the neck so hard

Corn Knife

that it would raise a whelp the size of my little finger; they are fierce lovers. Dad would say, "Did you pull his teeth?"

My only other option was to button up the collar around my neck, wear a long sleeve shirt and wrap my neck with a kerchief. It's not always fun walking down a cornrow with black dust settling about you from head to toe and being bitten by corn worms with your collar turned up on a hot sweaty day. But when Dad said, "Do it," you do it. I say, "Milo is better than good." Probably one of the reasons the Lord made milo.

Being the first in the neighborhood stimulated enthusiasm at the Baltimore County Agent's office about Russell Fox raising milo. They visited the farm often and brought along representatives from the University of Maryland to see what was happening with his venture crop. It wasn't long before the County Agent and his staff also brought interested farmers around to show them what a trouble-free crop milo was and how easy it was to grow.

As they introduced Dad, they'd say, "I would like you to meet the Milo King." The word got passed around and perked the attention of other farmers. They dropped in from time to time unannounced and asked, "Are you Russell Fox, the Milo King?" Dad was one to always remain humble and say, "Yes, I'm Russell Fox. I raise milo, but I don't know about that king part."

Dad was happy to share his secrets on how he reduced the cylinder speed on his combine to half the speed that he used for wheat. Because the stalks of milo are larger than that of wheat, you needed to make the adjustment so you wouldn't lose so much grain. The speed ran between 750 and 1300 rpm's.

I think Dad was seasoned and ripe for the picking when he initially stumbled onto milo as a replacement crop for corn. I failed to mention that when Mrs. Wheelwright offered Dad the Farm Manager position, he was honest and spoke of his limited education, explaining that he couldn't read very well and was barely able to write. He was a wizard at math but only in his head. He knew the answer but was unable to put it on paper. Mrs. Wheelwright said, "Excuse me Fox, you're a strong respected leader among your co-workers and an able farmer. Perhaps Mrs. Fox can keep any written records we need."

I always suspected that Dad was dyslexic, but back then no one knew. His education had been sadly neglected and unfortunately he was bumped up to the third grade when he was encouraged to quit school and help on the farm. So in 1919 at the tender age of nine, Dad started his farming career that lasted for the next 65 years. My mother used to say, "I think your father is going to die in the harness." He never wanted to retire.

He didn't want to be more than himself. Dad was what he was and never considered the bitter fruits of rejection. As Eleanor Roosevelt said, "No one can make you feel inferior without your consent." Maybe he felt a wee little bit on the unbalanced subject of religion or politics, but he was faithful and hinged to his beliefs. My father was a farmer's farmer, respected for his wisdom, and loved for his honesty and kindness.

A Farmer's Farmer

My dad was a person of good reputation and fair dealings. He had a dry sense of humor and a warm personality. He stood straight with good posture and was able to control his quick temper. Dad had nothing to do with a dishonest person. He would always say, "Everybody has to carry their own hide to market." As a young man he had jet-black hair, but by the time he was thirty, it was starting to turn gray. He had piercing hazel eyes that could let me know when I was about to be in big trouble.

When he was 16, he had all his upper teeth pulled in one sitting. He told me he was unable to eat for about a week. I said I was surprised, and he asked me why that was. I replied I would have thought it should have taken at least a month. He laughed and said, "I thought the top of my head was coming off that first day." So he had a set of false teeth installed. He enjoyed teasing his grandchildren by showing them how he could drop his teeth. They tried to get their teeth to come down by pulling on them with their fingers. The harder they pulled, the more he laughed.

Dad hardly ever went to church. Because of his limited education, I suspect he felt people frowned upon him. He helped out with different activities sponsored by the church, attended picnics and other outdoor functions. He was very fond of the pastor, The Reverend William Louis Piehl, and had many long talks about church with him. Upon request, Dad went to church on Christmas Eve. The pastor would say, "Well, Russell, it's nice to see you here even if you can't make it any other time." Dad replied, "It is better to make it once or twice a year than not at all." Then Rev. Piehl and Dad both laughed.

"Pop Pop" as the grandchildren called him, was fondly remembered by all for his "puncher jar." Pop Pop kept thin pretzels in a cookie jar and as soon as one of the grandchildren arrived, he'd ask them if they wanted a "puncher." He enjoyed his pretzels and the kids felt it was a real treat from their Pop Pop.

There wasn't anything Dad wouldn't do for a neighbor. He liked everybody. He enjoyed giving, whether it was things out of his garden or a helping hand. He was there for them. I always knew he was in good standing with the Lord and am sure upon his arrival in heaven, he'd earned a golden plowshare.

As Good as the Almanac

The weather is a farmer's companion. A good farmer instinctively becomes attuned to the changes in the weather, and a smart farmer learns to respect the weather, which can have an enormous impact on the rhythms of farm life. My dad knew the weather and understood its changing nature. He always said if there was plenty of dew on the ground in the morning, there'd be no rain that day, and that the fifth day of the month always predicted the weather for the remainder of that month. Also, he said that when the wind was coming in from the south, there was a storm in the air somewhere. He was generally right.

The worst snowstorms we've had come from the south, just like Pop Pop said! When there was a nice, gentle rain that lasted all night and the sun came out on time for work in the morning, he called it "a poor man's rain." He also used to explain that during a thunder and lightning storm, you could determine how far away the actual storm was by counting the number of seconds between when the lightning hit and the thunder clapped. He said about every five seconds was equal to one mile.

There were times too when Pop Pop said, "I smell a rain coming." He had a rain gauge and for years kept records of the amount of rainfall. A person from the weather bureau stopped by to check Beaver Brook Run. When he learned of Pop Pop's records, he asked to borrow them. Who knows, Pop Pop's records could now be the official records for the Chestnut Ridge area! With all his knowledge and his keen observance of the weather, he was able to mow, rake and get his hay in the barn without getting it wet. That's a real accomplishment for a farmer!

Farming is an Art and a Science

People will never forget many things about my father. We had a shop filled with all kinds of tools and there was a place for every tool and every nail. He had his days planned down to the minute and felt everything should be on schedule. He had to have each piece of farm equipment in tiptop shape. Tractors, after hard use in the field whether from mud or dust, had to be washed off before going into the shed. He loved to build truck beds, hayracks and wagons, and he built them to last. Every fence was hog-tight, horse-high and bull-strong.

Dad was quite the inventor. He built a walk-though gate from the parking lot to the pondfield at the farm. Why? Because persons were forgetting to close the gate and the cows got out. His small gate was incorporated in the fence line with two fenced wings, one on each side so you could step in close to the V part, push the gate in the proper direction, step around the gate and out the other side, without ever unlatching the gate. Even a small animal had trouble getting through this gate because when they pushed on it, the gate was stopped by the wing fence making it a solid fence line once more. I'm not sure when his idea popped up or when he dropped anchor on it, no matter what, he made it work.

My father told me one time how he preferred to combine rather than bale hay because he believed that anybody could sit on a tractor and pull a baler around, but pulling a combine around required a lot more concentration. If you didn't stay focused, you wouldn't have as much grain in the bags. Sometimes he got on his hands and knees and looked to see if any grain was being left in the field.

Back in the forties on my grandmother's farm, Dad cradled around the wheat field to make room for the binder, so the horses pulling the grain binder didn't step on the wheat. A cradle is like a scythe with the exception of having wooden fingers, so that the grain is able to lie evenly as it is cut on the fingers after each swipe and then dropped on the ground. After two or three swipes, Dad dropped it in a little pile, making a windrow. Then I followed to tie the wheat up in little bundles to make a sheath. One man was able to cut an acre a day. If he was good and started at daybreak, he could do two acres. With a 20- or 22-inch cradle, you can make about a six-foot swath. Dad only needed to go around the fields two or three times. The first time around is the hardest because he trimmed around all the fence posts and trees and along the hedgerow. He was good at it though, and was able to shave closely around the post. To have all the wheat stubble evenly cut was quite a talent.

The shaft or handle of a scythe is called a snath. The width of the blade varied by about three inches. The metal was rather thin and tempered to a hardened steel so peening was the best way to sharpen a scythe. Peening is the beveling of the edge. Dad then put the blade on the anvil. The square hole in our anvil was where you placed what we called a dog (also known as a hardie or fuller). Dad dropped the square shaft of the dog in the anvil. A big shoulder on the dog prevented it from falling through the anvil. The main v-shaped body of the dog rested on top. There are many different types of dogs. Dad used a peening dog. By placing the blade backwards and taking a peening hammer, he would strike three times, each time with the same amount of force and each time moving closer to the outside edge. A peening hammer has a round and narrow head. By putting the blade to one of those old-time grindstones, which some people did, they would cause it  to lose its temper. The blade would last a lifetime if it was taken care of. The funniest thing is that in peening the edge, it didn't always come out even, but did get razor sharp and that was all that mattered. Dad referred to his scythe as his armstrong mower.

One time I was using a scythe for mowing. The mowing blade is the thinnest blade. A grain blade and a grubbing (bush) blade are the thickest. Grass will cut better wet with a scythe.

Many of the old timers would scythe around the hayfield in the rain and let the horses rest. If you used a horse mower, the hay drug up. I was using the scythe to go under fences and was doing a good job.

It was late in the evening on a Saturday. I had a honing stone in my hip pocket and had stopped and set my scythe on the snath with the blade in the air. I was getting good at touching it up (to sharpen) and was going at it pretty fast when it slipped and put a big gash in between my thumb and forefinger. Mom took me to the doctor. He washed it out and stitched it up. I don't think I even got a tetanus shot and all was okay.

The grain binder was used in the field to cut the wheat. The size of the binder determined the number of horses required to pull it. One man drove the team and another rode the binder. The wheat was cut and went up a moving canvas with little wooden strips across it and was tied up in sheaths. At a certain place in the field, the rider on the binder pulled or pushed a lever or treadle (called a trip) to drop all the sheaths that it had bundled into the field.

A ground crew followed after the grain binder. Once they went through and made small stacks called shocks, the sheaths coming out of the binder would be tapered on one side. The short side was placed inward when making a shock. There were about twelve to fourteen sheaths to the shock and sometimes a cap in case of rain. In July it was usually pretty hot and dry and didn't take the grain long to dry out before the thresher came.

It was a spectacular sight to see a tractor pulling this massive thresher down the road. The thresher was so big that it took up most of the road. When the driver of a car saw the threshing machine coming down a narrow dirt road, he'd find a good spot to pull over to give the right of way.

Threshers came and set up their machines wherever you wanted them. My Grandmother Cartzendafner liked them to set up in the upper part of the barn. That way they could shoot the straw out into the barnyard, which created a great big straw stack. One time my grandmother called our house and asked for help because the cows had been rubbing up against the straw stack and it fell over. Some of the cows were buried under it. My father took all the men from the farm up to my grandmother's and dug the cows out. Several of them died, and that was a big loss at that time.

The neighbors all got together and helped each other out at threshing time. They liked to have as many wagons as possible to haul wheat to the thresher so it didn't have to shut down any more than necessary. It took a well-experienced person to run the thresher because if it was not set up properly and the belt was too loose, it got to flopping and jumped off; and if it was too tight it got hot and broke. You wanted to feed it fast but not choke it down.

In the field it was important to know how to load the wagons. There was one, sometimes two, people on each side of the wagon with long two-prong forks throwing sheaths on the wagon. One or two boys on the wagon placed the sheaths in the proper places. The wagons were loaded with the heads of grain inward on the wagon.

I recall staying with my Aunt Grendaline, who rode the grain binder, and my Uncle Russell, who drove the tractor. They gave me one of the two-pronged forks with a long handle that seemed six-feet long. The fun part was trying to throw a sheath of wheat up when a black snake came rolling out. I dropped the fork and ran. Uncle Russell really teased me about that. He laughed at me, saying, "You thought that snake had you, didn't ya?"

The Frick threshing machine, one of the more popular ones, was capable of handling two sheaths at one time. The wagon was pulled alongside the machine and two men worked the wagon. One man unloaded from the front and the other unloaded from the back. Each one took his turn to fork a sheath on the conveyor that carried it to the thresher. The wheat came out of a pipe and went into a grain wagon on the side; the straw or chaff came out the back. The number of acres of wheat planted was based on the size of the farm. Wheat was a crop that was depended on to pay that year's taxes, with a little left over to give the chickens their scratch.

Threshing was an exciting time on the farm and in the kitchen. My grandmother started days in advance. I helped her pick raspberries along the hedgerow (a dense row of shrubs between two fields) going back to the woods so she could make raspberry custard pie. I also pulled rhubarb for pie if it hadn't gone to seed by then. If she could find any ripe peaches in the neighborhood, we had peach pie, too. The day before she made the pies, she also killed some spring chickens that had gotten to be a good frying size. She got a ham out of the smokehouse, washed it up and got it ready for braising. She put a long bench outside by the pump. The wash basins were lined up so when the threshers came to dinner, they could each grab a basin, pump some water in and wash their face and hands. She pulled the table out and put extra leaves in it.

Grandmother had a summerhouse right next to the main house. That's where she cooked the meals in the summer time. If she cooked in the main house with a wood burning stove, it got too hot to stay in there to eat. A lot of neighbor ladies came to help her out in the kitchen. You could see them hurrying back and forth from the main house to the summer kitchen. My grandma was pigeon-toed, and as she walked, she kinda rocked from one side to the other. After the men ate, the women did the dishes and reset the table, and then they ate. Kids from weaning size to ten or twelve years ate with the women. The older boys filled in with the men at the table.

Uncle Manuel (Grandmother's brother) stopped at the garden gate and took out his wad of tobacco and placed it on the gatepost to save it until after dinner. As he walked in he'd call out in his high-pitched squeaky voice, "Lizzy, what's in the oven?" She always said the same thing, "I've got turkey in the oven. Come on in." And then she laughed. I don't think my grandmother ever fixed a turkey in her life.

Grandma didn't want anybody to be a stranger at the table. She kept sending the main platters around the table. If she thought that you didn't eat enough, she'd said, "What's wrong with ya?" Grandma was only about 16 hands high (5 feet, 2 inches) and weighed about 180 pounds with a good appetite. When dinner was over, Uncle Manuel stopped to pick up his wad of tobacco and start chewing. Then he kinda rolled that chaw of tobacco around into one corner of his mouth. After he spit, he was ready for some after-dinner conversation. They sat around outside and visited, laughed and told jokes. Uncle Manual liked to tease my father. He saw a calico cat sitting alongside the summerhouse and it took its right hind foot and started to scratch behind his ear. Uncle Manuel said, "Bud, (He always called Dad, "Bud") I bet you can't do that." My father replied, "I don't think I even want to." They all laughed on their way back to work.

One time Dick Gartlin, our neighbor who lived on a farm on Ivy Hill Road in Baltimore County, told me that his father was getting ready to combine. He asked a neighbor of his if he could borrow a horse. The neighbor offered not only to lend him the horse, but to bring the horse over the next morning after the dew was off the wheat, and give them an extra hand.

Dick said that they got there about 10:30 ready to go to work. They got their grain binder out and hooked their horses to the binder, one on each side of the tongue. Mr. Gartlin hooked the neighbor's big gray horse in the front of the tongue. Dick's older brother, Dan, was going to ride the grain binder and the neighbor man was going to drive the team. He climbed on the off-side horse (the horse on the right-hand side of the tongue) and went to the field. They got lined up and Dan threw the binder in gear. Right after he threw it in gear, the binder started to shake, rattle, squeak and make a lot of other moving binder noises. That big gray horse rared up, snorted and ran off with the other horses and the binder.

The neighbor man slipped off the horse he was riding and fell in between the two horses on the tongue. He held on for a while but soon slipped off. He went down under the tongue with his left hand in the air under the binder. The knives and mower guards cut his arm down to the bone close to the shoulder. Dan jumped off to see what he could do to help him. Dick and Mr. Gartlin were in the barn and heard all the commotion. They ran out and heard Dan yelling, "Call the doctor!" Dick ran through the woods to George Harr's house to call a doctor in Cockeysville. That was about a mile and half through the woods. Mr. Harr was the only person with a phone for miles around.

The rest of the Gartlins went to the rescue. They put a tourniquet on him the best they could. Then they brought him to the house. By this time he was weaker and still bleeding. He passed out so they put a rope around his wrist, put him on one side of the kitchen door and stood him up. They put the rope over the door and fastened it to the doorknob on the other side.

The doctor got there and stitched him up and put his arm in a sling. He told them he'd be back in a few days. The doctor said if they hadn't tied him up the way they did, he would have bled to death. He said they'd saved his life. The doctor came back in eight days. He took the stitches out and took the sling off. The neighbor man couldn't move his arm. Dick said that his arm never moved again, but that he was able to do as much with one good arm as he had with two.

Dick told me he had eleven brothers and sisters. They all lived in a two-story log cabin that his father had built. There was one room downstairs and two up. They only had a fireplace to cook on, so in the summertime they ate outside and slept outside under a tree near the springhouse where it was nice and cool.

It was late in the wintertime when Dick and his family heard their dog barking at something. They all knew it wasn't just a wild animal. His father took the shotgun and went outside. It was a pleasantly cool evening with a nice moonlight. He saw a man coming out of their smokehouse with a ham. Mr. Gartlin yelled, "Stop right there!" The man stopped, dropped the ham, and put his hands up. Mr. Gartlin asked who he was and what he was doing in his smokehouse. Well he was a pitiful-looking colored man from Cockeysville. He said that his wife and kids were hungry. Mr. Gartlin said, "Okay, but don't come pokin' around back here again." The man thanked Mr. Gartlin for not shooting him and started to leave. Mr. Gartlin said, "Don't forget your ham!"

I used to go by the Gartlin Farm and see Dan out working with his horses. He had one white horse and one brown. The white horse was always walking about two heads in front of the brown one. I couldn't understand why. I finally stopped to ask, "Why is that white horse walking so far in front of your brown horse?" He looked at me for a long time and said with a smile, "I guess he likes pulling more than the other one." Well, I didn't understand why he didn't tie the white horse back, but it wouldn't be proper for a young boy to tell a full-grown man how to hitch a team of horses. So I said, "Oh, I see."

Plant a Garden and Be Happy for a Lifetime

Dad always had a big and rewarding garden. When I say big, I mean big. We had a couple acres behind our house. Then another two- to three-acre plot up from there, and yet another piece of land in the back of the farm where we raised sweet corn, or roasting ears, as it was called then. We planted Country Gentleman and Shoepeg. These two types of corn couldn't be planted close to each other because they'd cross-pollinate. Later years brought along hybrid seed like Silver Queen and replaced a lot of the standard open pollinated seeds. Dad grew everything. He could grow more on five acres than most people could grow on ten. He had a nice-sized workable row but used every bit of space. So this was like a truck garden. Anything smaller than a quarter of an acre was a kitchen garden. Back by the corn, we raised enough pumpkins for one dumpcart load for pies and jack-o-lanterns.

My father could take a mule, a tractor, or a hand garden plow and lay off a row for planting. He was known for his straight rows and square fields. He had an early garden and a late garden. When we were out visiting someone and saw their garden, they apologized to Dad for their winding rows, even if there were the slightest curves in one of the rows. He told them, "Oh, that's okay. You can get more in a crooked furrow than if it was a straight one."

In early spring he used 200 pounds of Cobbler potatoes for seed. Later he changed to Kennebecs. He liked to try to have them in by St. Patrick's Day. After the potatoes were purchased, the first rainy day we all sat around the stove in the shop and cut potatoes. We had to make sure there was only one eye to each potato seed. After all the potatoes were cut, we sprinkled lime on them. This kept them from starting to sprout in case it took a while before we were able to plant them.

If we didn't have enough new potatoes to finish out the patch, we got some potatoes that were left over in our root cellar from the previous year. We had to sprout them before we could use them. Potatoes go into a dormant stage over the winter. Then when it gets warmer the potatoes start to grow in the bin. I have seen potato sprouts a foot and half long coming out of the bin.

After the garden was plowed and the ground worked up, Dad laid the rows off and then plowed out the furrows. These furrows were three-feet apart and ten-twelve inches deep. Then we walked along with a bucket of fertilizer, taking one hand and throwing fertilizer up and down the row. After that was done, one of us took a long chain, put a couple of knots in it, and pulled it up and down the row until the fertilizer was mixed up in the soil. I volunteered for that job. I remember putting the pulling end of the chain over my shoulder, then putting my entire weight into it and digging my toes in the fresh dirt. I was able to get enough traction to be able to move the heavy log chain.

Then we each got a bucket full of the potato seeds and started up the row. When I first started planting potatoes, I wasn't much higher than a gatepost so I got the smallest bucket. You made one step in the row and then dropped a potato in front

of your toe. Then you made another step and dropped a potato in front of your toe by placing your heel up against the last potato you dropped (about twelve inches) so you were making tiny little steps in the middle of the row. If I tried to hurry too much in this deep row, I'd fall down. After all the potatoes were planted, one of the men used a horse and springtooth harrow to pull the rows shut.

The potatoes had to be hilled up after they were about half grown. That is to pull the ground up around each plant, known as a hill of potatoes. Some people did this by hand with a hoe. We did most of this with a horse and a three-legged cultivator with wide shovels attached on the bottom. Louis Long, our neighbor, did this with his horse named Donald. He told the story that if Donald was in a bad mood, he'd step on every other plant. If he missed one, he'd get it on the way back.

After the potatoes came into blossom, we had to be careful not to knock the blooms off while working around them. Beetles and potato bugs were always a problem. Before the days of dusters or sprayers, we took a granary sack made of burlap, put lime in it and tied the top shut; and by holding the bag over each potato hill, with a couple jerks, the lime came out the bottom and gently fell over the vine. It also fell on my legs and bare feet. Dad had beetle traps that hung from a metal stake. Once the beetle entered the trap it was stuck. About once a week we emptied the trap—the goldfish in the pond loved them.

One year when the potatoes were up four to six inches, just getting through the ground good, we had a hard black frost and all the potatoes turned black. I thought for sure all the potatoes had died. After a long time the only thing living in the potato patch that I could see, were weeds. Dad took a spike tooth harrow and worked the ground up. I thought, "Oh no, we have to do this again." Dad said, "I think they'll come up." They came up all right. The vines were small but we still had too many potatoes for me to be picking up by myself!

We started our garden as soon as possible so we could get the early crop in and out in time to have a fall garden. After the potatoes were dug, we picked them up and bagged them. Then we used the horse and dumpcart to haul them to the root cellar to be kept for the winter.

Grandfather Cartzendafner dug a potato pit in the middle of the patch. He lined it with straw and put the potatoes in. Then he added more straw and hilled the dirt on top so the rain and snow couldn't trickle in. As soon as the potatoes were put away, the ground was worked up and string beans were planted in the potato patch as the late crop.

I remember going to the woods to help cut lima bean poles. We cut only hard wood like hickory, oak, or dogwood. Something like pine or poplar would rot out before the summer was up. We had to keep all the poles the same size, and the large end had to be sharpened. Then the poles were chucked in the cart and hauled to the garden.

Our favorite pole bean was King of the Garden. Pole beans are hard to germinate, so we soaked them overnight. Then we planted them three to the pole, one pound to one-hundred poles and four feet between each pole. It took between ten and fourteen weeks before maturity. Sometimes there'd still be a lot of beans left on the pole after the first frost got them. We used those as dried beans for soup.

Asparagus gardening was an early morning back-breaking job. The asparagus was given a good coat of manure in the fall by using a horse and dung sled. In the spring the ground was worked up and rock salt was applied. This helped to keep the weeds out. I don't remember how big the bed was, but it didn't take long to fill a five-gallon bucket full of asparagus. Dad's beds would last for forty years. Most beds lasted maybe twenty to twenty-five years. I was told that it had to do with the way it was cut. Never cut the bed on top of the ground. Cut it down under the ground so it doesn't die off from the sunlight. If you like white asparagus, put a Mason jar over the new shoots and wait a day or two before cutting the asparagus. We used the canning jars with a chip or crack since they could no longer be used for canning. The jar keeps the air out and the asparagus turns white.

There was always a pickle patch. In other words, we grew a lot of cucumbers so Mom could make pickles. This patch was mulched with straw for cucumbers. It took a lot of water to keep the sun from baking the ground. We all liked pickles, and Mom made many different kinds: bread and butter pickles, dill, sweet, and kosher. She made gallons and gallons. The sweet pickles were called seven-day pickles, because she had to do something to them every day for seven days.

There was a fall crop of cabbage for sauerkraut. Fall was good because there weren't as many bugs or worms in the cooler weather. My grandmother made sauerkraut in five- and ten-gallon crocks and kept them in the cellar. Her cellar had a dirt floor and stayed nice and cool with an even temperature. Using about 120 heads of cabbage, depending on the size, some of the local farmers made 55-gallon barrels of sauerkraut and sold them later in the winter. To cut the cabbage, the farmers pushed the head through a knife, which fit in the middle of the long board on top of the barrel. You'd keep turning the head until it was down to the heart, which is the hard part in the center called the core. The cut cabbage fell into the barrel.

My good friend Roger Howard was telling me about a time when he was preparing to help his mother make up a barrel of sauerkraut. Roger and his brother Sam were cutting the cabbage and handing it to their mother. She was loading it in the dumpcart. After it was loaded, their mother said she wanted to ride on top of the cabbage to the house. Roger and Sam rode on the front of the cart, and their mother on top near the back. Sam was driving the horse and nearing the tree in front of the house by the porch where they wanted to dump the cabbage, when his mother started hollering to him, "Stop, Sam stop! Let me out of here." Sam liked to tease his mother, so he quickly stopped and pulled the locking stick out in front of the dumpcart to dump the cabbage. Roger said Mom was on top and then all of a sudden, Mom was on the ground crawling from under the pile of cabbage. Sam was ornery and just laughed. Roger told me Sam got a good tongue-lashing that day.

Turnips were a fall crop and stayed in the ground most of the winter unless it got cold early on. Usually if there was a little straw around them, you could find some up until January, depending on the weather.

Carrots were planted after the ground was nice and warm and no longer in danger of frost. Sometimes carrots got worms or ground bugs that would eat on them if the weather turned hot. After maturing, they were pulled up and tied in small bunches. The carrots were carried to the root cellar in a wooden wheelbarrow. In one corner of the dirt floor we dug a hole, put the carrots in and covered them up. They kept until the following year.

Onions were a valued crop that we planted in early spring. I don't think there were many evening meals that Mom didn't have onions one way or another. The onion sets were planted one at a time with the root down, then pressed hard in a shallow furrow and set about four or five inches apart. With a garden rake, they were covered up. Sometimes these little bulbs were used as scallions before the onion was formed. If not pulled as a scallion, it matured into a full-grown onion. The best scallions were planted in the spring from the leftover onions of the previous season. Sometimes if there were late onions planted in the fall and covered up, they kept over the winter. In the spring they sprouted and came up in bunches of five or six to the onion. These mild and crispy onions were known as bunching onions.

Once onions matured, we stepped on the tops, knocking them down flat to the ground. After we left them alone for a week, we pulled them up and laid them out alongside the row to cure for a few days. Then we gathered them up in baskets and stored them in the granary. Dad made a special crib to hold the onions. It had a half-inch mesh ratwire on the bottom and a little wooden side so the onions couldn't roll out, and it hung from the rafters by wire so air circulated all around them. They were laid on the wire without touching each other. This allowed us to keep the onions over the winter.

My mother was a good canner. I had to help in the garden, and I remember Marvin and I both had to help in the kitchen with the canning and freezing, especially the peas and corn. Corn was the biggest crop. Early in the morning we would pull 25-50 dozen ears, put them in the trailer pulled by a tractor and haul them to a large shade tree by the side door to the kitchen. First thing, we husked and silked them. While all of this was happening, Mom was getting the water hot so she could boil the corn for three minutes to blanch it. This seemed like a lot of work for only three minutes. After blanching it, we took the corn back to the shade tree for cutting it off the cob. We then bagged it and popped it into the freezer.

I remember my grandmothers going into the field and pulling what some people call horse corn. It wasn't just for horses; it was field corn for all the animals. If you got the old open pollinated field corn when it was young and put some sugar in the pot, it wasn't bad.

Oyster plant or salsify was something we planted early. It was a root like a parsnip but much whiter and smoother. Mom grated it, cooked it with milk, salt and pepper, and it had a flavor like oyster stew. Actually it was kinda tasty until you learned that there weren't any oysters in it!

Peas were harder to do; it took a long time to work them. Just to pick a bushel of peas seemed to take forever. To hull a bushel of peas took ten times forever! I remember one time Grandma Fox came down to stay during pea-picking time. She hulled almost all the peas single-handedly—that was eight-ten bushels of peas. Grandma sat under the shade tree hulling peas. She sat on the side porch hulling peas. You could see her sitting in the kitchen hulling peas. Everywhere you looked, you saw Grandma hulling peas!

Mrs. Wheelwright and all the farmers and their families were dependent on my father to make the judgment calls for successful crops. He determined when to plow the garden, how to work the ground, when to plant, when to harvest, and how to preserve. With his wealth of knowledge and know-how, he could supply food for the pantries and cupboards of the families to last over the winter.

Grandma Fox, Dad and Mom

In 1951 we got a television set. That was a big deal at our house. Not long after we got it, NBC had a special advertisement about how to cut your family grocery bill in half. If you had a family of six, you could save up to $100.00 a month. Mom and Dad got so excited about this show coming. They expected they'd learn how to save money at the store.

The day finally came. We were hoeing in the garden, and Dad kept pulling out his gold pocket watch to check the time. With just minutes to go, Dad yelled out, "Okay, let's go to the house!" We hurried out of the garden to the end nearer to the house where we rested our hoes against a post and rail fence holding up a grape arbor, and headed to the house.

Mom had the television turned on and up full blast. As we walked in, the show was starting. Everybody took their seats, pulled straw hats off and wiped their brow with a kerchief. The show was moderated by a handsome young man, who leisurely walked downstairs to a nice large-sized cupboard in one corner of the basement of a well-manicured house. He slowly opened the door and told everyone the secret to saving money on your grocery bill each and every month throughout the year. He said the only thing you have to do is learn how to plant a garden and plant enough to last you for one year. "Look here," he said, as he picked up first one jar of this and then another jar of that on and on.

306

Dad and Mom were extremely disappointed. We had already saved at the grocery store. They both thought they were going to learn something new. Dad said, "Well, let's go back to work and start saving some more money." We'd been saving money on groceries all our lives. Along the path to the shop, Dad asked me how I liked saving money. I said, "It's mighty blistering work, isn't it? I guess whoever has the most blisters saves the most money."

Dad had a day-hand helping out in the garden. He was a big jolly man and although he was invited, he didn't want to come into the house with us. He said he would take a break and rest in the shop for a while out of the hot sun. We were in the house about fifteen minutes and then went back to the shop to see if our helper was ready for more work.

When we got to the shop, we were kinda surprised. Mr. Gardener-Man had picked up a full quart can of Dad's "Happy Motoring Esso Oil" and had it stuck in his overall pocket. He must have heard us coming and, purely as an afterthought, tried to hide it. He couldn't get it in and couldn't get it out. With a big pull, he lost a few stitches and it came out. With a harsh look, Dad told him to be careful so he wouldn't tear his pants. I think he could have been knocked off his feet with the gentlest touch of a feather duster. Nothing more was said about the oil.

Along about 4:30 we stopped to do our evening chores. Dad was in the shop shaping a scythe; I was coming up from the barn after milking the cows with two milk buckets, one in each hand. The day-hand said, "Mr. Fox, I would like to talk to you before I go." Dad asked, "What is it?" "I would like to say I'm sorry about that oil this afternoon. My car is almost out of oil and I don't have any money to buy more."

307

Dad told him, "Next time, try asking." Dad walked over to the oil shelf and handed him the same can and said, "Here." The old man said, "I certainly thank you." Dad said, "Don't let it happen again."

The Lord said, "So long as the earth endures, seedtime, and harvest, cold and heat, summer and winter, day and night shall not cease." Dad's saying was, "If we can't do it right, we're not going to do it at all." Working a garden is a big responsibility but a favorable one.

He Who Takes His Hand to the Plow

"He who tills his land will have plenty of bread."
Proverbs 12:11

Farming fills the senses—the smell of damp earth and the sight of rich topsoil being turned over was a pleasure for my dad as he plowed the fields. When my father grew older, he

decided to rent out most of the farmland, and the new "modern" farmer didn't plow the soil as Dad had. He would say, "Look at that no-till plowing. Isn't that a dirty way to farm?" No-till plowing is a method of cultivating crops where the soil is not turned over by a plow; instead, the new crop seeds are drilled directly into the debris of the plant residue from the previous year.

With no-till plowing, weeds are controlled with repeated and heavy applications of herbicides. My father felt this was a big mistake and couldn't believe that poisons were better than plows. All the poison ran off the fields and down into Beaver Brook Run. He said that proper plowing is still the best way to do it. The only things you really have to worry about with plowing are not to plow when it is too wet or too dry, or to plow the plow pan. The plow pan is a layer of compact soil at plow depth.

On a farm where the crop rotation is corn, oats, wheat and hay, and then back to corn, any particular field needs to be plowed only once every four years. I believe he is right: no-till farming is a dirty way of farming. My favorite way of plowing is with my horses, but then, I don't plow for a living.

Mowing

Mowing was another favorite of Pop Pop's. Ninety-percent of the field should be in blossom before starting to mow down hay. Remember to always keep an eye out for hornets' nests when mowing hayfields. Pop Pop loved to hear the chatter of the mower. By listening to it, he could tell what was happening even without looking at the mower. If the wind was blowing, the cut grass fell over like waves to the ground. Perhaps you have to enjoy this like Pop Pop did to understand and visualize it. I liked mowing then and still like it now.

The owner of the farm down Greenspring Avenue, known as Valley Hi, called me every four or five weeks during the growing season to take care of his field. He liked his thirty-five acre meadow to look manicured at all times throughout the summer. His field was lined with yellow, red, black, and white cherry trees. These trees were the exception for the area.

The limbs were hanging so low over the fence that without ever getting off my tractor seat or standing up, I could pick a  hat full of cherries in no time flat. This was a pleasant field to mow while cherries were ripe and that was most of the summer. The aroma was mouth-watering. I rode around the field mowing with my hat stuck in between the gearshifts, eating and spitting cherry seeds. I called Mr. Howard Miller's pasture my 'sit and spit field."

The Art of Making Hay

My father liked to rake up the hay in the evening whenever possible, when the dew was just starting to soften the hay. He didn't like to hear that rattling sound of hay that was too dry. His second choice was raking in the morning with some dew still on the hay. He didn't like to put a lot of moisture under the windrow, but some was okay. The book says that hay shouldn't have more than 16-20% moisture content to avoid spoiling in the barn over the winter months.

We never had a moisture meter; instead, Dad would go by feel. Many a farmer has been fooled by hay that seemed dry to the touch when picked up in the middle of a hot day; and it wouldn't cure out in the barn. The obvious cause: dead dry hay contained internal moisture, hidden from the touch. The old standby tests of twisting a handful hard or scraping the thickest part of the stem with your thumbnail are certainly worth the efforts.

If the hay still had too much moisture to store in the barn, we had to "ted" it. To ted is to use a side-delivery rake (or you can use a hay tedder), which has a lever on it that you can move forward and backward. While in the backward position, the  tines ran backwards and you were able to fluff the hay up. Hay, while in the barn, goes through a sweat. That's called curing. The smell of fresh cut hay and a barn full of it is absolutely wonderful!

The Woods, My Dad and Me

When I went to the woods after Pop Pop passed, I felt comforted knowing that Dad and I had shared many wonderful times working together there. The woods have always been special for me, and I attribute much of that to having fond memories of my Dad working in the woods.

The clear, cold chops of the axe hitting on the wood could be heard echoing through the hollow: 20° and no wind, a light snow falling and spitting in my face. Cutting firewood can make a body feel humble. There is something in the quietness and the sparkle that makes me feel the presence of an angel. It's as if I can feel the power of heaven, and it's all falling around me.

I've never experienced loneliness in the woods. To me it feels more like spiritual ground. It seems to me that I have an understanding with the Lord that this is my place of worship. The Lord and I have been talking together in woods from the time I was old enough to walk. He has brought the light down and helped me in the worst of times.

I really enjoyed working with my father in the woods. I wish I knew all the different types and kinds of trees and shrubs that my father knew. And he could sharpen a chainsaw with such ease and have a perfect job. I've sharpened lots of chainsaws and could never do such a fine job. Before we arrived in the woods, Dad made sure the chainsaws, axes and wedges were in tiptop shape. Not only did this save time and energy, it provided for safe labor. That was my first lesson.

Then you looked for the right tree. You never cut a nice straight tree. For firewood, you use only the ones with broken tops, or leaning trees, or deadwood. When you found a leaning tree, you had to know how to cut it down. It had to be cut so it fell to the ground without hanging up on other nearby trees. This takes real skill. For Dad, it was second-nature and took only minutes for him to determine where to notch it and how to cut it. If he had to use a wedge, he knew what size to use. If I went to cut a tree down and asked, "Do you think I should notch it here?" He would say, "Do you want it to fall on you?" I'd ask about another area, "Do you think I should notch it here?" He simply replied saying, "What about that tree over there? Do you feel like pulling it out of that tree?" Working with my father in the woods was a special treat, and I learned a lot over the years.

Before he left the farm, Dad and I worked together back in the woods and had a lot of fun doing it. He trained me well. This is one thing I really miss about my father. Every time I go back in the woods, I always think of him.

Hog Heaven

When we moved to Beaver Brook Farm, Dad built the hog house that he he'd always wanted. It was placed down over a little hill facing the morning side. It had inside and outside pens, a small door between pens, and a small door at the entry of each pen so hogs could be moved as necessary from place to place with very little trouble. He made cement troughs, one for feed and one for water, and there was a slanted board from the entry to the trough so you never had to reach over the top of the pen. This provided safety from hog bites for the farmer or visitor. In a corner a brooder board was placed, held up off the floor by two sliding gate bolts. This allowed the baby pigs to run under the board to a space where a heat bulb was hanging from the ceiling, and gave the little pigs heat as well as safety from the danger of their mother inadvertently lying on them.

My father reduced the number of hogs accommodated in this house to six or eight because pig production was of a higher quality and thus he could reduce his herd size. Dad still wasn't completely satisfied as he was looking for a butchering pig that wasn't fat or overly large. He wanted his pigs, weighing 190-220 pounds, born in February and butchered around the last of November or early December.

The American Chester County White is a large heavy breed of

pig that was famous for rapid growth and reported in Types and Breeds of Farm Animals by Professor Charles S. Plumb, to dress out as much as 365 pounds at nine months of age. Now that's a lot of lard. We didn't have use for that much lard.

Dad wanted something small-  er and leaner. The Yorkshire pig is all white with a cute curly tail, a short turned up nose and a sweet deep-dished face. They're smaller than the Chester Whites. Although a Yorkshire is small and short, it's a good, firm meat pig. They have many fine qualities, are even-tempered and good mothers. They throw healthy piglets with an easy birth, but don't grow as fast as the Chester Whites.

Dad's quick mind jumped fast when he learned of the Chester White. He purchased a Chester White boar hog from Blakeford Farm on Eastern Shore and crossed it with his Yorkshire sow. He kept a special focus on his Yorkshires until he bred them with just the right Chester White boar hog to meet his needs.

The gestation period for a sow is three months, three weeks and three days. If more piglets are born than the mother has nipples for, the others will die. When they are born, each piglet is assigned to its very own dinner plate "teat" and no others will touch it. It's rather comical to see a sow lie down to feed her brood with a lot of little pigs jumping over each other to get to his or her dinner plate. Some are jumping up from the bottom, others are diving down rooting under the ones on top to get to the bottom. The sow doesn't always lie on the same side, sometimes on her right and sometimes on her left. The eager little pigs never know where their plate is being set.

Rambunctiously they just keep jumping, pushing, prying and poking with their little noses as fast they can to find their dinner plate.

The average litter size is eight, although one time my dad had a sow that had 21. It can vary; she only raised 18. Yep that old girl had 18 nice dinner plates hanging from her table. She was Dad's prize Chester White/Yorkshire cross.

Dad's crossbred pigs turned out to be successful: one of the best for good meat and the measured growth without so much lard and sowbelly. Just what he was looking for. These crossbred butchering hogs stirred the attention as a market hog. They are easy to brood, easy to fatten and easy to raise. Dad had an interest in hogs and enjoyed working with them. He had a biological gift for animal husbandry and there was a dash and keenness to his passion.

The sows that were back in hog hollow at Twiford Farm produced only one to three pigs per litter. This was a significant difference. Now with these upgraded, healthy pigs and with better feed, the sows' production was increasing tremendously.

Somehow the Purina Feed Company found out what my father had been doing to raise pigs so successfully. Probably the County Agent told the Purina Feed Company representatives. They came out, talked with my father and asked him if he would keep records for them if they provided the feed. Dad's sows had two litters of pigs per year. One litter furrowed in February and the other in August—the hottest and coldest months of the year. I remember the paths we shoveled through the snow to get to the barns, chicken houses and pigpens and how warm and comfortable the animals' living quarters felt after shoveling in the cold winter air.

Poor Ole Frank—Morgan's Mornin' Coke

Mr. Frank Price was a well-known bachelor in our neighborhood. When he was a young man, he'd worked on the streetcar as a conductor for United Railway. That was in the days before it became the Baltimore Transit Company. He said that while he was working on the streetcar, he was saving up his money to buy a farm.

Frank sold all kinds of things off his farm, like eggs, vegetables and fruits. He had an orchard and people came from all around to buy fresh produce from him. Frank used a one-pound sugar sack where he stored his money. Once a month he went to the bank. Often people gave him a check and it was rolled up with the rest of his savings. This sugar sack stayed in his right front pocket. After walking behind his horses, plowing and harrowing for a month, he delivered his sugar sack of money to the bank. The teller at the bank complained that the dates and amounts on the checks were rubbed off from sweat and being wet off and on for a month. The teller was constantly complaining to Frank, "I can't read these checks!" (I can only imagine what that sugar sack smelled like, too.) He always promised to do better.

Mr. Roger Howard told me lots of funny stories about Frank. Roger worked for Frank part-time for many years. Roger said, "Frank was a brute of a man." One winter day while they were working in the woods, Frank told Roger that tomorrow morning after he dropped off the milk, he was going to stop at the blacksmith shop and have them make him an axe, something that would really sink into the wood. Roger said, "I didn't even like carrying that ten-pound axe to the woods, much less using it." But Frank was well pleased with it.

Every once in a while on Saturday afternoon, Frank stopped at the Colonial Inn to get a fifth of whiskey and a case of beer. He brought it home, sat on the dairy step and took a gallop of whiskey and then drank a beer. Roger hung around and did some cuttin'-up, had a few beers and then he'd tell Frank that he was going to start on the evening milking. Frank would say, "Help yourself." Roger finished up the milking and told Frank that he'd be over in the morning to help out. Frank's nod of his head meant okay. Roger reported for work in the morning. He'd open the door to the stable, where Frank had spent the night. Frank jumped up ready for work. Roger's recollection was, "I don't know how he did it, for he'd sure had a snoot-full the night before."

Frank never got married, so Mrs. Howard decided it would be nice if she fixed him a Thanksgiving dinner. Roger said that Mrs. Howard fixed up this nice dinner in a roasting pan with a turkey, stuffing, potatoes, carrots and what have-you. Roger carted it over at exactly noon in time for his dinner. Frank was coming in from the field, stopped at the barn, turned his horses in the stable and met Roger at the house. Roger said, "I told him that the old woman sent this over for him." Frank said, "Well now." Then he picked up a dirty fork off the table, wiped it off on the sleeve of his shirt, sat down and started eating right out of the pot.

Roger said that he was helping Frank get corn in every evening after his steady job at Sagamore Farm. That pot of turkey stuff stayed there on the table and whenever Frank got hungry, he picked up the fork, wiped it off on something and started eating until it was finally gone. Roger said, "Jimmy, his belly must have been like a cast iron pot the way that guy ate."

The floor at Frank's place never got washed. He set out newspaper on the floor and when that got dirty, he just put more on top. Roger said it must have been a foot deep. He told Frank he ought to be careful and not let it get too deep or his head would hit the ceiling.

One time Roger was cleaning out the cow stables and Frank was mowing down hay, when Roger heard this God-awful noise and hollering. Roger ran to the stable door. Here came Frank down through the orchard with the five-foot sickle bar mower. It was bouncing off first one tree, then another.

While Frank was mowing, he'd run into a hornets' nest and cut it. The bees were after Frank and the horses. Roger ran out, grabbed the horses and checked Frank. Frank was okay, but that mower was busted up so bad it couldn't be fixed. The bar was broken off and one wheel was still lodged in an apple tree. Most of the tongue had hit a dip in the ground and was still standing there.

Frank told Roger, "Well, let's be gettin' these horses unhooked and put them to that four-foot mower. I got hay to cut." Roger checked the horses over, replaced some torn harness, and Frank was ready to go back to mowing. That guy was one toughy.

Frank had a Holstein bull that was getting a little age on him. Roger had been telling Frank that he shouldn't be trusting that bull so much. When he was standing in a box stall, that bull gave out a low, mean bawl. Frank entered the pen with the bull walking around loose. He fed, watered and cleaned the stall with the bull inside. Roger told him, "Frank, watch that bull. He'll hurt you." Frank's reply was, "I don't think he's going to hurt anybody."

Well, one morning it was better than daylight when Roger got over to Frank's to go to work. The bull was out in the wagon-yard, pawin' and throwing dirt up over his back, bawlin' and running around snortin'. Roger looked over and the bull charged the wagon and moved it back about four feet. Roger's recollection was that Frank was under the wagon on his hands and knees running along with the wagon as it moved. Roger said something to the effect of, "What in the world are you doing under the wagon?" Roger had a natural way with profanity that I am reluctant to use here. Frank said, "That d--- bull has gone crazy this morning. I think he's trying to kill me." After a while the bull moved back to one corner of the barnyard. Roger was able to help old Frank get out.

Frank told Roger that he thought he was going to call Bob Teedermann to come and haul the bull to the stockyards. Mr. Bob lived right down the road and was the local butcher for the community. He had just purchased a brand new Ford truck so he could pick up pigs, steers, sheep, and other stock to butcher for his customers. Mr. Bob said he could come over in a few hours and haul this big bad Holstein bull to the Baltimore stockyards. Bob didn't think the bull was as bad as Frank said.

Roger and Frank finished up the milking and were hanging around waiting for Bob. The bull's attitude didn't improve much. Before long Bob came in his truck where they were going to load the bull. Frank let the bull out. He immediately ran up to the truck, started sniffing, and then quietly boarded. Frank and Bob slammed the door shut. That bull got startled and began running around inside the truck. Finally, he got one horn hooked under one of the sideboards. That made him mad. Then he raised his head up and with his horn, broke the sideboard in two, which freed him to jump out of the truck.

He was running around all wild. It was every man for himself. Frank dove under the truck and the bull followed right after him. Bob went behind the truck and Roger went over the fence into the barnyard. It wasn't long 'till the bull was smacking the truck all over. He didn't like that new Ford truck. After a while, he poked a hole in the front fender and lifted it up. The whole fender came off. It looked like the truck was going to upset. Frank said, "I think we'll stop this." He made his way to the house, got the shotgun and came out, stood in front of that charging bull, fired a shot, and stopped him dead in his tracks.

Frank had a German Shepherd "police dog." He'd get a 50-pound bag of dog food, open the top and let ole Prince eat right out of the bag. As he ate down in the bag, Frank just rolled the bag down until it got to the bottom.

Roger said that when Frank's mother died, he asked Roger and Beulah if they'd pick him up to go to the funeral. That was fine with Roger, so he stopped over Frank's house to get him. He was still upstairs putting on his suit when Roger took a seat in the kitchen waiting for Frank. After a while, Frank entered the room and ole Prince caught a glimpse of Frank all dressed up. Prince didn't recognize him. He ran over, grabbed a hold of Frank's leg, and tore a hole in his new pants.

Roger said, "Well, I had to take him over so the old woman could sew it up before going to the funeral." Roger was telling Mrs. Howard about what had happened and she sent Frank into the bedroom to take off his britches. He came out wrapped in a bedspread, sat in the living room talking to Roger and cussing the dog, while Mrs. Howard sewed up his pants.

Frank had a nephew, Calvin Price. Frank told Mrs. Howard that Calvin was getting married and that he really liked that boy. He wanted Mrs. Howard to select a wedding present for him to give to Calvin. Mrs. Howard asked what he would like and Frank replied, "I don't care, just get him something nice. I don't care what it is or how much it costs." Roger said that he carried the old woman over to Hutzler's Department Store in Towson, and she picked out the best brass floor lamp they had. She told Frank it was $35.00 and Frank said, "Good, as long as you think he will like it." ($35.00 was big bucks in those days.)

Frank shipped milk, along with other general farming things. When it came time to take the milk to the station, he hooked his gray horse, Morgan, to his two-wheeled cart, loaded it up with his cans of milk and headed down Gwynnbrook Avenue toward the train station.

Later he left the cans for the milk truck to pick up. All the farmers placed their milk cans at a stand at the corner of Gwynnbrook Avenue and Bonita Road. Each farmer had his name and a number written on a brace plate and welded to the can for identification. Most farmers had their milk shipped to the Western Maryland Dairy.

Our school bus passed Frank's farm on our morning route to school. I'd see poor ole Frank and Morgan on the road to the milk stand, which was built up off the ground at the same height as most trucks, so then the truck driver could slide the milk cans from the stand to his truck without too much lifting. Once in a great while old Morgan was in a trot and I'd say, "I guess poor ole Frank's late today."

Morgan knew right where to go. He walked in the same exact spot every day. There was a small rut along the edge of the road where the wheel had made its path, and every day Frank made the trek to the station. After unloading the milk, the next stop was Wisner's Store on the opposite side of Reisterstown Road. Frank pulled up to the front of the store, dropped the lead line for Morgan. Frank walked in straight to the pop

321

cooler and got a Coke. Then he stopped to give his "good mornings" to Mr. Wisner as he paid for his purchase. He'd stand around drinking half of his Coke. Then Frank walked out to Morgan who would whinny and stick out his lower lip. Then Frank poured the other half of the Coke into Morgan's mouth.

Frank told everybody that Morgan could make the trip by himself and that he just came along to unload the milk and get a Coke. In the wintertime our school bus passed Frank and Morgan going down the road with poor ole Frank sitting in his cart holding his hands between his legs, hunched over and half asleep, bumping around as they jogged along. He was wrapped up in a big black full-length overcoat out of the cold.

As often as needed after his milk run, Frank went to Groff's Mill, the local feed store, to pick up supplies for the farm. The milk had to go in all kinds of weather. In Baltimore, the weather can become brutal, pouring down rain at the drop of a hat. Roger said that Frank wore his black wool full-length overcoat like a raincoat. In the cold and rain of winter, cow manure would stick to his overcoat. After hauling cow manure for several days, he'd ride down to the milk station in the freezing rain. After that he headed on over to Groff's Mill and warmed up by their potbelly stove. That overcoat was full of cow manure, horsehair and everything else that comes from the farm. You can just imagine how it smelled.

Mr. Billy Groff, Jr. said, "Frank sure knows how to clear out a room." It didn't take long for people to leave. The longer he stood there rubbing his hands together to get warm, the worse it got. After you could see the steam coming from his coat, you knew it was top-notch stuff straight off the farm. Anybody in a reasonable distance from the Mill knew Frank was there.

Frank's two-story house caught fire and half of it burned down. Frank didn't care. Roger said he spent as many nights in the barn as he did in the house. He didn't bother to repair the house and just lived in a couple rooms upstairs and down. One of the upstairs doors that probably had led to another bedroom was now an outside door. So he just kept the door closed. I used to say that I hoped poor ole Frank don't get drunk and try to walk through that door to go to bed. That first step would be a "lily."

One day Frank crossed over Reisterstown Road to go to Wisner's Store. A tractor-trailer came down Reisterstown Road, ran off the road, hit a telephone pole, and then ran into Frank and his cart. The cart was busted up and Frank was hurt badly. He was laid up in traction for a long time in Maryland General Hospital.

Roger described it, saying, "You wouldn't have believed it. Ole Morgan was unhurt and just stood there. I reckon that convinced anybody that Morgan was a good horse. Wire was dangling all over him with sparks flying and he didn't move. After the current was shut off, they started taking him out of all that mess of wires." I bet Morgan was plenty glad to get back to the stable. Luther Larkins, a local farmer, and Raymond Price (Frank's brother) did the milking twice daily and took good care of Frank's farm until he was back on his feet.

Frank didn't live long after that—a few years maybe. I think he was 83 or 84 years old when he died. All those years I was thinking poor ole Frank. He doesn't have enough money to hardly get by on. All that time he was a man of independent means. Frank died a wealthy man and left the nearby four churches and two volunteer fire companies each a big pile of money.

The Mind Boggler

Through a friend, I bought a nice three-year-old Percheron horse with good lines and a deep chest and strong legs. My friend didn't know anything about this mare because he bought her through a West Virginia horse and mule dealer, who let on like she was "broke the best."

My friend was told that she was broke to ride, drive, and work single or anywhere in a team. In early afternoon I tried to ride her and she bucked and tried to throw me. I learned real quick that she was not broke to ride. A few days later we had a skiff of snow that lay on the grass in the hay field. I hooked her up to a sleigh and she ran away. It wasn't too bad. It was in the open and she ran herself out, but I came back to the barn with some concern. Then later she ran away hooked to a wagon, and again I let her run it out.

I was still believing I had a horse that was safe, so I invited a friend's wife to bring her children over for a sleigh ride. Thinking that would be an experience that these young children would never forget, we ventured through the hay field, down over the hill, up to the next knoll and then Byrd, my mare, got spooked when a bird flew out along the hedgerow. She took off like a stick of dynamite, and these children had the experience of a 30-mile per hour sleigh ride with everyone holding on tight! I didn't predict this hair-raising incident for my little friends, although it's something they'll never forget!

I liked this beautiful dapple-gray mare, but realized she was a runaway. Trading a donkey for a bunch of work harness, I thought if I hooked her to something harder to pull, with patience I could re-train her. It wasn't long after when I was pulling some logs around that she tore up her harness trying to get away. I was able to hold her from getting away. This did it for me: I didn't know what I was going to do with a horse with that kind of a rebel attitude.

I started calling horse people and telling them about the incidents and asking them if they'd heard of anything like the way my mare was acting. They all claimed to know all about horses but said, "Sell that mare and try another."

It kinda occurred to me that if you knew horses, you didn't just get rid of them, but that you knew of a way to stop them from running off. I thought I'd take the time to visit some of my Amish friends to see if they had any better advice. In making many trips to Lancaster, Pennsylvania, I spoke to several for their advice.

Finally, a horse friend of mine, Martin Kemper, told me about an Amish friend of his who worked with horses and knew a fair amount about them. Martin and I decided to make a trip to see Martin's Amish friend. I left the house the next day when it was still dark. By the time I got to Martin's farm, it was just starting to break daylight. As I stepped up on the porch I could smell the country ham coming from the kitchen. I hollered hello through the screen door. Mrs. Kemper yelled to come on in, that the dog wouldn't bite.

Martin was sitting at the end of a long table. He didn't bother to get up. Just took the back of his hand, holdin' on to his fork, and wiped the egg off the corner of his mouth. He continued chewing, and with the fork he pointed to a chair and said, "Sit down and have something to eat." I said, "Coffee will do me just fine." He replied, "Suit yourself." He reached over to the piping hot woodburning stove and picked up the coffee pot without getting up, dropped the pot on the table and said, "Help yourself."

For a dog that didn't bite, Martin's dog sure liked to curl up his nose and show his teeth. He kept one eye on me all the time. Every once in a while, Mrs. Kemper would walk past him and poke the dog with her toe to let him know to behave himself.

Martin's son came in from finishing up the barn chores. He took a seat at the table, looked at me and nodded his head hello. Mrs. Kemper brought a plate of scrambled eggs pitched high in the middle—looked like at least half a dozen—and set them in front of him. Without any complaints, he looked around, took his fork and stuck it deep in another plate that was full of pancakes. He came up with four or five hanging on and let them slide off the fork on the top of the eggs. Martin said, "That boy knows how to eat, don't he?"

On the way out I thanked Mrs. Kemper for the hot brew. After I danced around the dog, we lit out for Harney. We pulled up in front of the barn and stopped. Jonas walked out of the barn with a big smile, surrounded by a bunch of little mismatched lightweight kids with their black hats sitting squarely on top their heads and cute as could be. Jonas took his hat off and pulled out a dark brown handkerchief, wiped off his brow, told Kemper to get out of my truck, and asked who his friend was. Kemper said, "This is my friend, Jimmy Fox." Jonas stuck out his hand and we said our howdies and stepped back. I could tell they were thrilled to have some visitors.

I have found that the Amish people are generally polite and don't ask too many questions. If you want to tell them something, they listen, but if you don't, they don't ask. At first we talked about the weather and how nice it was and carried on a conversation that was of no particular importance. I could see that Jonas was puzzled with our presence.

Then Jonas changed the subject by asking what we were doing in his part of the country. I told him right off that we had planned a special trip to meet with him. He asked what the trouble was. I explained about the runaway horse and filled him in on her dangerous habit. He said if it had happened a lot maybe there wasn't any hope for her to stop running off, that once a horse got it in their head that they can run away, they'll continue to do so.

Jonas said that with wintertime coming on, he'd have the time to work with her. He had a lot of manure to haul and he'd hook her up with three other horses that didn't run off. This would take a month or so; "Bring her up, I'll work her and take some of the shine out. Stop back in a month."

I stopped back. Jonas said, "I didn't have any trouble with her until yesterday. We went out through a gate going into the field and the manure spreader hit the gatepost. It moved the spreader over to one side a little and startled your mare. She ripped up the harness so bad that it can't be repaired." I told him how sorry I was about that. He said that was okay, that it happened a lot with the old harness they used. I guess it did. Most of his harness was repaired with baling twine. Sometimes it was hard to see the leather, for all the baling twine dangling every which way.

He asked me if he could keep her for another month and I agreed. I stopped back about three weeks later and he said the same thing happened again. I suggested to Jonas that it might be a good idea to move that gatepost back a bit. He thought that was pretty funny, and we all got a good enough laugh out of it.

I was starting to get more concerned and continued to call around about my runaway horse. People continued to tell me to get rid of that horse. I even stopped by the racetrack to ask what to do. This continued to boggle my mind. I went back to see Jonas and there was no more trouble with my horse. He thought I could bring her home but to watch her. I got her home and never had any more trouble with her. But my question hadn't been answered.

I continued to ask how to stop horses from running away. I went to Lancaster to several harness shops to see if there was some harness that would keep a horse from running away. The answer was always the same, "No." I continued to work my horses without a problem. They weren't the best-matched pair but I didn't have any more trouble. Then one day I decided to ride up and visit Mr. Frank Stitely, a neighbor of Grandpap Cartzendafner's. I knew Frank had worked with horses and he knew Grandpap well.

I walked up and knocked on the front door and Frank hollered, "Come on in, the door's not locked." He was sitting in a rocking chair in what I thought of as a rocking chair room. The whole room was full of rocking chairs. He started to get up to shake hands and I told him to keep his seat. I walked over to him and we shook hands. You could tell by his swollen knuckles and shifted fingers that his hands had seen a lot of hard work and much abuse from the many farm chores. I told him it was a good thing there wasn't a bunch of cats in here. He laughed and said, "By golly, Jimmy, I think you might be right. There sure would be some sore tails."

Frank had lost most of his hair except a little around his ears. Frank hadn't been one to shirk his responsibility of hard work. He was getting along in years. His face was pale and his eyes were starting to lose their sight. He was showing the many signs of old age. Frank continued to wear his work uniform, green pants and work shirt to match. With the aid of his wide suspenders, he wouldn't have to worry about losing his pants. He was sitting there rocking and looking laundered and all done up.

We talked and reminisced for a while. Then I asked him if he remembered working with horses before the days of tractors. He said yes, he remembered it well. I asked him if he'd ever had any runaways. And, yes he did. He said that if anybody ever worked horses or mules, they had runaways one time or another.

I asked what he did about them. He said, "I had a contrary old mare that didn't have any scruples and was bound not to do anything right. I put her in the center of a larger hitch and adjusted the double-tree so she'd be pulling more than her fair share." That was a good enough answer but didn't help me with my horse. I told Frank about my horse. He said I'd done the right thing by taking her to Jonas.

Frank started to sorta gaze out the window, and casually said, "One time a young man brought your granddaddy a runaway road horse. I don't remember his name." Frank frowned like he was getting a dim view of the past and said, "This young man had a horse that was barn sour. The man tried everything to stop his horse from running back to the barn. The horse only went a mile from the barn. Then he'd spin around in the middle of the road, rare up and run for the barn. I recall your granddaddy walked around the horse and made some adjustments on the way the horse was hitched. After it all met his approval, he walked in front of the horse, stuck his finger under the throat latch (that's the strap that goes under the horse's neck on the bridle), unbuckled it, pulled it up to where the skin starts to wrinkle, and tightened it enough that he had to push pretty hard to get his forefinger under it."

Your granddaddy told the young man, "Hook this horse up just like I did, but don't trot him." He said, "This throatlatch pulled up like this will give him enough wind to walk, but he won't be able to run with the throatlatch that tight. On a runaway horse, the nostril becomes enlarged and the windpipe expands so a horse can't run very far before he'll choke himself."

Then he told him, "If your horse goes down after running fifty feet or so, just let him stay there until he gets his breath and he'll get up. Most of the time after running, he'll just stop and stand there all spraddle-legged, wobble around until he gets his wind, and then he'll walk off."

I thanked Frank for sharing this with me. He laughed and said that Grandpap had a trick for any horse that had any improper misdoing. It was Grandpap who had the answer to my question. I never even met my grandfather; it must have been a spiritual destiny.

Gertrude and Other Geese of My Life

I raised five white Emblem geese and six African geese. I got them when they were only one day old. The baby goslings were kept in the hen house. Geese become very tame if you're around them and talk to them in a soothing voice. I took excellent care of the goslings and they grew up in a happy environment. In about six weeks, I took them to the horse barn so they could have more room to play. I let them out, and they found their way to the pond where they spent most of their time. They came to the barn to get fed and enjoyed pecking around under the horse trough.

After eating they always headed for the pond. The geese got all excited and would start running for the pond, which was down over the steep hill from the barn. When the geese reached the crest of the hill, they were running so fast that they became air-borne. I didn't know domestic geese could fly so well. While they're young, they can do a fairly good job of it. After they were in the air, they could fly by flapping their wings sloppily and then by gliding several hundred feet to the pond. Their landing gear didn't work as gracefully as that of the Canadians; they sometimes landed with a nosedive or a big splash. But the geese were happy to be there, no matter how they arrived.

One goose, Gertrude, made friends with my oldest Percheron mare. Byrd was a beautiful gray mare that weighed about 1600 pounds at the time. She had strong legs, a straight back and an attractive chiseled head. Byrd had the nicest personality. Draft horses are known to be gentle giants.

This old goose followed Byrd around the field. One day I noticed that the goose was sitting on her back while she was lying down. It wasn't long before this became a habit. When the horse lay down, the goose jumped on. Then I noticed that the goose was picking flies and bugs off Byrd.

Byrd and this goose got to be best friends. It wasn't long before I started seeing that when Byrd was grazing, the goose flew onto her back. When Byrd came into the barn to get fed, the goose rode along. Byrd started eating and the goose jumped down and started eating, too. Anything that Byrd dropped was fair game for the goose. After dinner, the goose flew back up on Byrd. When Byrd was finished, I turned her back out, and she ran down to the meadow in a graceful swinging foxtrot. The goose put her wings out, flopping like she was flying to keep her balance.

One day the flock of geese decided to leave the pond and follow the stream out to Beaver Brook Run. When they got there, they turned left and swam upstream to Ridge Road toward the bridge. They were swimming and playing and having a grand ole time in a wide place in the stream, where lots of people driving by could stop to see them. One of the by-passers came into the farm and said, "There are some geese down on the stream." He said, "I have driven this road many times and have never seen them there before." I told him that the geese belonged to me, and I'd get them before dark.

That evening after taking care of my chores, I got a stick and started for the bridge. I had this bright Sunday afternoon idea to wait for feeding time and I could take a stick and drive them home. I arrived at the bridge to see that the geese were having a fine time paddling around. I walked over the bridge and down to the water where the geese were. As soon as I got there, they moved to the other side. So I went back to the first side. They moved again.

I knew if I really wanted to get wet, the only thing I had to do was walk in the stream up to my waist and they'd come out. That thought was turning around in my mind with a faint view. But that water was cold so it occurred to me that I wouldn't mind the cold water so much if I sent Smoke, my black Labrador Retriever, in instead. If I could sic Smoke on them, that would be better for me. I whistled and old Smoke dove straight in. That did it. Those geese came right out. I met them on the other side and we headed toward the barn.

332

I had a nice long stick. You can drive geese pretty well this way. We were along the side of the road and a car came along. The driver stopped and said, "What are you doing?" I said, "I'm driving my geese home." He replied that he'd "never seen anything like that before." I didn't think it was so unusual. Before I reached the driveway, three more cars stopped me. Folks were amazed to see somebody driving geese up the road. I had to ask where they lived. Did you know that city people don't drive their geese with a stick? Actually they don't even have geese. After they told me where they lived, I understood why they'd never seen geese being driven before.

This was during the fall when the weather started to get colder. It was getting pretty nippy that night. I thought maybe I should be thinking about penning my geese up at night. But they were happy at the pond, and I hadn't seen any foxes or coons around. I thought I'd wait until the weather got cold, but I wanted to get them in before the pond froze over.

I waited one night too long. The temperature dropped, and the pond froze over. The ice was so solid that if you dropped a stone on it, you could hear the 'zing' in all directions. The Indians call this "singing ice," for they knew that if they heard that sound, it was plenty safe for walking on. The fox knew it too. He walked out on the pond that night and caught Gertrude. After that, I knew it was best to sell the geese. I didn't have a place to pen them up for the rest of the winter and I wasn't able to keep them or the fox off the pond.

I got my remaining geese up to the barn, put them in a horse stall, caught them one at a time and put them in a wooden orange crate. We arrived at the stockyards safe and sound. The following year I got more geese, but never had another one like Gertrude.

Button

On the 4th of July 1950, my father suggested that we go to the Reisterstown Volunteer Fire Department Carnival. Complete with fireworks, this carnival was a social event for neighbors, family and friends to congregate. As we were walking and visiting through the carnival grounds, Dad ran into Dave Martin who said, "Oh, Mr. Fox, I would like you to meet my wife." He pointed to where his wife, Elizabeth Mae Raver Martin, was sitting on a bench under a big oak tree. For only 21 years old, the poor soul looked so miserable and hot. It took her awhile to travel from her seat to her feet to say hello. It didn't take us long to see what the problem was. Libby was about to have a baby and it looked soon to me. I was wrong. Her baby wasn't due for almost three months, but I was sure she wasn't going to make it.

We knew Dave from working at the farm where he was one of the many carpenters who'd been employed to remodel the barn. We were happy to meet Libby. She was a delightful young lady, good-natured with love for everybody. Dave and his charming wife soon became great friends of the Fox family.

Dave and Dad built a fine-looking brick BBQ with a nice tall chimney. Throughout the hot summer months, Mom and Dad along with Libby and Dave planned and enjoyed picnics and cookouts on an almost regular basis. The old folks sat around playing cards, pitching horseshoes, telling jokes, eating and laughing.

Toward the middle of October, Dave asked me if I'd help him out on a job the next Saturday instead of working on the farm. He had contracted to screen-in a porch over in Jacksonville, some 15 miles east of the farm. We were working along and by the middle of the afternoon came a hard downpour. We gathered our tools and started for home. On the way home the rain turned into hail, and we had to stop under a tree in fear of the hail cracking the windshield. As we sat there, Dave started talking about his baby daughter. We were closer to his house than mine, so Dave said, "Let's stop by my house and I will show you Button." He called Mary "Button" because she was a little night owl and whenever he went to her bedroom in the middle of the night, she was awake. The lonely little thing was lying there looking at the toys hanging on her crib, and all he could see were two little eyes shining through the darkness. It reminded him of two brightly glazed buttons. So her nickname became Button.

Baby Mary was born October 2, 1950, hollering and screaming with almost no hair. Libby placed the dumbest looking big old bow on top of her head to tie up only a few strings of hair. My grandmother had a saying: ugly in the cradle, pretty at the table. I could hardly wait for her to get to the table.

Dave picked her up and walked about patting and bouncing her up and down, proud of his brand new baby girl. He asked if I would like to hold her. Being polite as possible, I told him, "No that's okay, I don't need to hold her."

Dave and I hit it off with each other like ducks to water. He enjoyed hunting and fishing. Neither my father nor my brothers enjoyed hunting, but Dave and I were a match for each other. We both loved to hunt. We found plenty of sport on the large track of woods on the farm. I didn't own a shotgun or rifle. At the time Dave let me use his Stevens-Over-and-Under. It was a 22 long rifle on the top and a 410 on the bottom. In other words, it had two barrels made together, one over the top of the other and just the right thing for me. I fell in love with his gun. I was able to shoot a squirrel on the run with the 410 or pop a squirrel sitting in a tree with the 22.

My heart longed to own a gun like his. By and by I asked Dave if he would ever consider selling it. With a grin he said, "It all depends on who wanted to buy it." "Well, if it would be somebody like me?" "Maybe so," was his reply. "Well, would you?" "Would I what?" "Would you sell it?" "To who?" "To me!?!" "Are you saying it is you that would like to buy this old gun that you can't hit anything with?" "Yea it's me, the one who shot that big gray out of the top of that hickory over there yesterday." "All right, I'll sell it to you only if you promise to be careful and not shoot yourself in the foot or anybody else." "It's a deal."

We continued walking when I asked how much? "How much for what?" "This old gun that I couldn't hit anything with." "Make me an offer like it was a good gun and we'll talk." I was thinking on it and thought I had saved up roughly $35.00, and it might be worth that much to me. I wanted to leave a little room for some bartering so I said, "How about $31.50? You already know it's no good." Dave said, "Give me twenty bucks, and you can have it today if your daddy says its okay. It's a done deal."

Mary got cuter, but at the same time she got "bad-er!" The friendship with my parents and the Martins grew. By the time Mary was two years old, she was very much in charge wherever she went (as she is today)—at her house, at our house or anybody else's house. My mother and father dearly loved Mary. This little kid could do no wrong in their eyes. She called my mother Granny, and my dad Pop Pop. They had no grandchildren of their own at the time. They only had Mary.

When the Martins came to visit, Mary ran in the door to her

336

Pop Pop. Dad picked her up lovingly and hugged her, and kissing her little face while she pulled his glasses off and threw them down. While playing cards, he put her on the table. She walked all over everybody's cards, kicking them on the floor. Dad thought she was so funny, "Oh, look at her now!" I thought they were playing a little loose with the rules. Believe me, I never had the privilege of walking on the table. For me it was, "Be seen and not heard." I presume modern ways changed from previous generations. As we grow into grandfather-hood, I realize this from my own experience.

As she grew, so did her rosy desires. She ran though the house with one broad sweep, clearing everything off the coffee table. A flashing trip to the linen closet, down with the towels; then she sped off with a stumble and fall into the cookie jar, followed by a dashing dive down under the sink and out with all the pots and pans; and a rush back to the bathroom to run out with the toilet paper. As grandmother would say: that girl is loose out of the woods. The little dickens was into everything.

After awhile the card players would say, "Jimmy, please take Mary outside for a walk. Walk her down to see the chickens." Well I did, much against my will! Believe me, she didn't get the pampered treatment with me. But when she got outside, she calmed down and was always better outside than in. Mary did love those chickens. Every time she came over, I had to take her to see the chickens. When Mary got old enough she would come to me saying, "I wanna go see the chickens."

After high school, I'd gone to work for Guy Waddel as a house painter. I didn't care for that very much, but he was a great boss. He started a spring water company and asked me if I'd rather drive a delivery truck, and I enjoyed that more. Unfortunately, his new company failed. I then took a job at Troy's, Inc. (an International Harvester dealer) as the manager of the Parts Department. I liked that job a lot but found it hard to work indoors all the time.

My mother told me that she loved me no matter what, but didn't understand why I couldn't be more like my brothers and join the fire department. "That's what all the young men are doing nowadays. You're always running off hunting and fishing and learning how the Indians lived, that's not important." For Mom's satisfaction, I joined the Reisterstown Volunteer Fire Department and also once Chestnut Ridge started a fire company, I joined that too. Then I became a member of the Junior Chamber of Commerce and this made Mom very happy, but I wasn't.

I have an enormous amount of respect for my brothers and their chosen profession. Unable to trans-form, I realized that I'm me and very much my own person. I prefer to follow the footpaths of nature, study Indians, early American history and stay on track with the good ol' ways of country living. I've never gotten any applause for being me. This is who I am and I find myself marvelously rewarded with a soothing ego.

Jimmy Fox, 1957

The years passed and I got married in 1960. Mary's parents were divorced by then, but Mary and her mom came to my wedding. I rented the upstairs apartment in John and Edith Raver's home. That was one of the most pleasant experiences

338

in that marriage. The Ravers, Mary's grandparents, were delightful people, happy and willing to share whatever they had with others. I would look out the window and see Mary and her friend Carol Boone doing cartwheels and standing on their heads. I used to tell them that I believed they spent more time on their heads than they did on their feet.

Six years later, a failed marriage had ended. It wasn't the life I'd planned, but it was what I got. The storm left me with an empty house, a fistful of bills and my two wonderful sons. I lived in the basement and rented out the upstairs until I got on my feet. An unplanned path lie ahead.

For me in 1967, good luck was hard to find. Being down and out with nothing left but my name, I was barely able to get a small loan to start a landscaping business. I called it my shoestring business because I had no place to go except up. Having always enjoyed the challenges and freedom of working for myself, Jimmy Fox, the "depression-ridden landscaper," grew into F. James Fox, Inc. on its own dime. Farming of course was my true love, and there was plenty of work, but no money in it.

Edwin and Libby Tunis were favorite customers of mine, and I took care of the landscaping on their property for over 20 years. Edwin was the author of many books on 17th and 18th Century American history. We had loads of long talks about Indians and frontier living. He died in the mid-'70's, and my relationship with Libby continued until she passed in the late '80's. Each year he gave me one of his books for Christmas until I got his full collected works. I remember Libby telling me that the book Ed wrote on Indians was used in the fifth-grade and had been translated into several different languages.

Now a seed had been planted. I wondered if I could possibly write a book with my limited education, along with my problems in reading and writing. I thought I could tell my story in my own country lingo. Good literature need not always be difficult and hard to read, nor does it have to be long and boring. The Tunis books are well-written and easy to read for any age group. My book could be simple, downhome country writing and could be knowledgeable, exciting and fun. With hope and perseverance after being diagnosed with cancer in 1993, I started writing, <u>The Legacy of a Country Boy</u>.

Mary Grows Up

The friendship between my family and Mary's family flourished through the years. I thought of Mary's family as my woodpile relatives. They weren't related but always there if you needed them. In 1969 Mary invited the Fox family to her wedding. My mother even held a surprise bridal shower for Mary. Mom thought as much of Mary as if she was her very own granddaughter. Amazingly, Mary had grown into a model young woman, and the love for her Granny and Pop Pop had never changed. Mary had moved off the Ridge; now my parents only saw her on special occasions. Two years later, I asked my parents how Mary was making out as she went through her divorce.

Mary's grandfather John Raver and I were great friends. John became deathly ill and was weighted down with years and not much hope. I'd stop by often to visit him. The day came when he passed on, and naturally I went to the funeral home to pay my respects. Mary was there. She looked so cute in her blue and white polka-dot suit. She was a real beauty. When the pretty little thing smiled at me, she made my heart go pitter-patter, putting my thoughts in a churn. Yep, Grandmother was right once again: ugly in the cradle, pretty at the table.

The next day after the funeral services, everyone was invited back to the Raver house for a luncheon. Mary's father had died the year before. There were lots of flowers, so she asked if she could take an arrangement to put on her father's grave. Mary knew I thought highly of her father and asked me if I would like to ride along to the gravesite.

We struck out for a delightful trip and enjoyed it to the limit. We had lots to talk about on our ride. The trip seemed short for the miles. On the way back, I asked her if she would like to stop for a cup of coffee. Once again time flew by. I expect we were wedded to our country roots. She never caught on to the fashionable ways of city living.

The era of our childhood days on Chestnut Ridge was disappearing. Old ladies were no longer walking around with their nylon stockings rolled down below their ankles. Cows weren't being driven across the state highway at milking time. Roads were becoming wider with overwhelming traffic; there were more people and fewer farms, the old folks were dying off. The few lingering farmers left were forced to post 'no trespassing signs' pleading with the public not to tear their fences down. A new time was on the rise. For many the past was becoming a faded picture. But for us, all of this was of little concern. It was family, friends and neighbors that attracted us two together.

Our mothers were instrumental in attempting to predict the future. Through love, they each continuously dropped hints to us as to what the other one was doing. We could hear the unspoken words loud and clear. After our trip from the gravesite later that night, Mary returned to spend the night at

341

her mother's house on the Ridge. Her mom asked, "Well, did he kiss you?" Mary's reply, "Yes he did." Her mom continued to question, "Did you like it?" And Mary said, "It tasted like more."

I'm a well-guarded person, storing my inner feelings within myself. The thirteen-years' difference in our ages no longer seemed important. We began dating almost immediately. Chuck and Mark, my sons, loved Mary from the very first minute they met her. When Mary came up from Gaithersburg to visit, she spent time in the kitchen making cookies. Chuck and Mark huddled around her like a pair of little kittens. When she was outside cooking on an open campfire in the backyard, they were always under foot. And when Mary tossed a football to them, they were surprised and pleased. The echo of so long ago was ringing and the timing was perfect. I proposed marriage. I knew she was going to be a great mom. You only make one trip through this world, and we decided to do it together.

Mary's mom and stepfather, Joe Crehan, decided to take Mary's grandmother, Edith Raver, on a vacation to Florida and invited Mary to go with them. I was raising some homing pigeons at the time and asked Mary if she would be willing to release one every time they came to a new state line. She put the box of pigeons between her feet on the floorboard in an already overcrowded car. That certainly tested her stamina. She released all the pigeons and everyone came back except one.

On January 17, 1975 we were married. Mary is the light of my eye and the joy of my heart. My beautiful bride and I went to Mystic Harbor, Connecticut for our honeymoon. Getting caught in a blizzard made it even more romantic. As a landscaper/farmer, who took care of snow plowing and feeding animals, I usually had lots of responsibilities during such harsh weather, but not this time, for I was in a comfortable hotel room with my beautiful bride.

Unbridled with excitement, our imaginations ran wild planning the beauty for our simple life. When we returned to the Ridge, Mary moved her things into our little aged cottage, ready for a new beginning of old ways. Our life together on the Ridge and at the farm was wonderful. Mary visited the chicken house that she remembered from her childhood. Instead of a little girl, I saw a lovely young woman standing in my chicken house.

On November 7, 1977, our son David Martin Fox was born. Dave loves his older brothers. He grew up respecting them and looking up to them. Dave said having two older brothers was like having two extra fathers. They taught him about dirt bikes, fishing, hunting and camping, even girls; and he taught them about video games!

After Mr. Thompson's death around 1983, Beaver Brook Farm went into trust for the grandchildren. It was only a short time after that that my mother and father moved off the farm into a small apartment in town. Mr. Wayne Townsend, Vice President of Mercantile Bank & Trust, came to the farm and asked if I would be willing to take over my father's position as Farm Manager. It was no longer operating as a farm per se, but they needed an overseer—someone who could maintain the property and watch over it until they decided what was to be done with Beaver Brook Farm.

Their requirement was someone to take care of the manor house and the rented tenant houses, as well as doing lawn and field mowing and trimming. He knew I had started renting some of the farm buildings, the pastureland and the front hayfield from Mr. Thompson as far back as 1971. We agreed on a yearly contract for my use of the farm buildings, pond field, orchard field, and the front hayfield along Ridge Road. It was a very workable arrangement: I paid them and they paid me.

In 1988 Pappy, Mary's stepfather, died unexpectedly. Her mom needed us, and we immediately moved in with her until we could get our new house built on the adjacent acre of land which Mary's parents had given us. Mary designed the layout of the house, and I acted as the general contractor. We moved into the house by Labor Day and were now only a mile from the farm.

We used a path through our neighbors' woods to get to the farm. The winter of 1996 was a bad one with 38 inches of snow during one blizzard. My four-wheel drive was of no value. I needed to get over to the farm to take care of eight head of horses, steers and goats, guineas, geese, turkeys, and chickens. Dave had an Arctic Cat and a John Deere snowmobile. He said to me, "I'll take you to the farm. Are you in a hurry or do you have plenty of time?" I asked him why, and he explained, "The Cat will get there in a heartbeat if it doesn't stop on us. But if you have the time, I'll have you there in about twenty minutes with old slow dependable Johnny." Old slow Johnny was fine with me.

The snowmobile was so heavy that it sank down in the snow, just like riding in a tunnel. Dave drove by standing with one knee on the seat so he could see. We passed a few foundations, which had been dug for new houses in the part of the woods that had been sold. Dave was driving and I was holding on to the bottom of the seat behind him. Rather than go around the giant hole in the ground, Dave yelled out, "Hold on Dad, here we go." Like a ski jump, we went straight out, then down and hit the bottom; a cloud of snow went up and faster than it could settle, we were gone.

I told Dave that was a bad one. Dave said, "Oh no Dad, that's not the bad one—this is the bad one!" Down we went and up over the top with a jump. A large mound of dirt from a foundation stood high up on the far side, and we went straight up and over it. As we were coming down, my heart was still going up in the air. On the way back, I told Dave, "Take old slow Johnny around all the holes and dirt piles." Dave drove me back and forth for three days, and I was mighty happy for the ride, but I was awful glad when the county roads were cleared.

The Cattle Drive

Chestnut Ridge is a beautiful area that sits high above two lush valleys in Maryland. Things on Chestnut Ridge are a little laid back; it's a country of father's fathers. Only a few outsiders could be called new. Country boys are fresh and alive on Chestnut Ridge and look after one another.

One day Mr. Thompson asked me if I'd like to lease his pasture field. He assured me that I could make some extra money, so after checking on the price of cattle and turning it over in my mind—and he persuaded me that I could afford it—I told him I'd give it a shot.

After going to several livestock auctions and speaking with various "high-class" cattle dealers, I perched myself on top of the fence where I could see what type of stock was for sale. I felt I was getting pretty well posted on the price of cattle. After shopping around at some of the nearby farms and making some inquiries on their small stock, I picked up one here and another one or two there until I had most of what there was for sale at the time. With only seven, I knew that wouldn't yield enough profit to meet my rent, so I went to the Western Maryland Stockyards and picked up five more.

A local farmer happened to call, asking if I was available to put up some fence for him. I told him I would be happy to do it if the price was right. He told me to come up early Sunday morning so he could show me the job, and we could talk about it. I got there when it was just starting to break daylight. He was coming out of the barn with a dog following him. We drove back through a large pasture field and looked the job over. I gave him a rough price.

He hadn't thought that it would cost that much and told me he didn't have that kind of money. I said, "Well, how about if you buy the fencing and I trade my labor for those sixteen scrawny little bulls?" He said, "Tell you what I'll do. I'll give you half of them." I said, "Okay, I'll do it, but when you're ready for the other half of the fence to be put up, give me call." My farmer friend was really bragging on those scrawny little bulls, and I wasn't grieving too much for that fencing job. He looked at me for a while, then looked at the ground and kicked his toe in the dirt. At that point, I knew he was thinking good and hard about it. So I thought I better help him along with his decision. I said, "Taking all that fence through the woods is going to be a lot of work. Maybe you'd like to get a price from a fencing company."

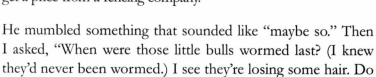

He mumbled something that sounded like "maybe so." Then I asked, "When were those little bulls wormed last? (I knew they'd never been wormed.) I see they're losing some hair. Do you think they're shedding this early in the year?" I knew they were lousy and full of cockleburs. I took the attitude that if he thought he was pulling one over on me, I'd get them at a better price.

He looked up and said, "Okay, that's a deal." I didn't want to look overly pleased and said, "Okay, but I hope you'll deliver them." He jerked his head up and said, "Oh no!" Then I said, "Okay, well, you can have the fencing materials put in the middle of the woods first thing Monday morning, and then I'll be up ready to go to work." I knew he wanted the fence up right away. He walked around in a circle and reset his hat a couple times and said, "Okay, where do I take the cattle?"

After he got those little fellers home for me, I put them in a lot to themselves. I made a trip to the local feed store to pick up some lice powder, de-wormer, vitamin shots and a mineral block. I doctored them a little.

A few weeks later they were looking dandy and on the mend. I went to the barn one morning and there stood one of my little bulls. This booger was acting like he was mad at the world. He had this low, deep-sounding bawl and stood there shaking his head, pawing up dirt and throwing it over his back. Although this little bull wasn't more than 500 pounds, he could hurry you over the fence if he had a mind to do so. I thought it would be time to calm him down, and figured I might as well do all the bulls at once.

One at a time I ran them through the cattle chute, castrated them and turned them into my best pasture—the pond field. With the rest of my cattle, now I had twenty-eight in all. Mr. Thompson thought that I was going to do just fine with this set of cattle.

I thought, "Well, this isn't the best-looking herd of cattle," but I didn't have any more trouble. Some were smaller than others; some were steers; others were heifers and most were miscellaneous dairy breeds, and beef types. But I had one thing in my favor: they were all paid for. I didn't have to take any on consignment.

Things went well, I had good grass all summer and an

excellent hay crop. I was set for the winter. I bought these cattle in early spring and pastured them all summer. Winter came and I gave them a little feed and all the hay they could eat. In the spring my hay mound was going down and I was trying to decide if I should sell them to pay for the rent or keep them through the summer in the pasture and sell them in the fall. The pasture field looked worthy of being able to hold them over until fall.

It was April and a good time to sell. One Saturday night, a hard old thunder-buster rolled across the farm. My friend, Eddie McCracken, had been out at a party and was coming home at four o'clock in the morning. He gave me a call and said that he thought he saw a large herd of cattle about two miles down on Greenspring Avenue. He didn't know who to call, or if they were mine, but thought he would check it out with me.

It'd not surprise me if these were my cattle because the fences at the farm were in bad shape. I jumped out of bed, grabbed my rain slicker and gumboots, got in the truck, and drove down Greenspring Avenue.

I knew at a glance these were my cattle. During the night the lightning and the thunder had caused them to stampede. They ran through the fence, into the woods and kept going until they got to Greenspring Avenue, where they were milling around in the middle of the road. It was pitch dark out, and cattle can't see well at night. Cattle have poor eyesight and when they charge, their eyes are closed. This wasn't a problem for me. They were still huffin', puffin', and blowin' from running such a long way. I knew that the slightest thing could spook them and start the stampede again. I stepped out of the truck real easy and started to talk to them so they'd know it was me. Then they started feeling more content and at ease.

I walked around them and counted to make sure that they were all there. After I was satisfied they were there, I got them turned around and started up both sides of the public road. I was hoping that I wouldn't have to deal with an oncoming car. If I did, I was sure I'd lose them. By now I figured Eddie was in bed and no one else in the neighborhood was out at that hour, so it was possible to get them back to the farm without seeing anybody. I was sorry I hadn't brought my dog Smoke. He was a reliable dog with a lot of cow sense, and with a good amount of patience.

I don't know if you've ever tried to run out on the side of a herd of cattle in a pair of gumboots that were too big for you. I can tell you that that sends the perfect plan into a nosedive.

Up the road we went. I knew I had to turn them in on Ridge Road, a hidden entrance off Greenspring Avenue. I was concerned that if a car popped over the hill, they wouldn't see us coming in time to stop. The problem for me was getting to the front of the herd to turn them. They were all strung out with no intention of doing the right thing. I was taking a pretty big chance because they weren't staying together.

A new road had 15 or 20 houses that led off of Greenspring and cut into Ridge Road. I wasn't going to take that road but when we got there, a bolt of lightning hit on the road in front of them. Some of the cattle dropped to their knees, jumped up with their tails wrung over their backs, and they all took off in a dead run on that new road. This didn't bother me too much. I kept walking in hopes that they were heading towards the farm. I walked about half a mile and then another lightning flash. Now I could see the cattle at a distance behind the new houses.

It had already rained for three days and nights. The ground was juicy and had thawed out from the winter. I could see these eight hundred-pound steers sinking into the lawns in back of those new houses. When I caught up with them, they were just standing there shaking from fright and panting, with steam rising off them.

I thought I might be able to get them into the woods without doing any more damage. Some people had put up small fences next to the woods and the only thing I could do was let them follow along the edge. Twenty-eight head of cattle bunched up makes a good-size circle. As they walked along, they were wading through people's flowerbeds and last year's vegetable gardens, sinking in up to their knees.

I finally reached Ridge Road. It was a little easier to make the turn because they liked following the woods. We were on the road, taking up both sides and then some. By now it was just starting to break daylight. One of the old-time neighbors was coming out of his house to feed a pack of dogs around the porch. He had on a nightshirt, trousers and his house shoes. He saw me with a road full of cattle and said, "Good morning, Jimmy, you're up early." I said, "Yes, I like getting up early and taking my cattle for a morning walk." He laughed and asked if I needed any help. I said, "No, they're no trouble at all. Looks like you haven't decided if you're getting up or going to bed." He smiled, waved good-day, went inside and closed the door.

The cattle stayed on the road and trailed pretty well until we got to the driveway, and then in almost single file, walked in the driveway. I thought, "Why couldn't you have done that before now?" They knew where they were and walked straight to the barn. I breathed a big sigh of relief.

I fed them good and put out plenty of hay, made sure the gate was locked. I thought it was best I check the fence line before going home. There was an aged red oak that stood alongside the fence close to the woods. That's where the herd gathered during a storm for protection. Yep, the lightning had struck the tree, and with a mighty blow tore it open about eight inches wide. It hit 15 feet from the top and followed straight down, blowing a hole in the ground two feet deep. I guess these cows got a good tickle out of that. I'd traded my work for this herd. They could have been gone in a split second. That's how the stampede had started.

I was cold, wet, and hungry. By now it was getting along mid-morning. I had another truck at the farm I could use, so I decided to stop at the local country store and pick up a hot cup of coffee. I stepped inside the door and shook myself off, said my hellos to the owner and his staff.

351

While pouring my cup of coffee, I was within earshot of some people talking loud and excitedly about some giant animal that passed through the back of their new houses. They said the giant animal left footprints the size of the largest bear you'd ever seen. I started pouring a little faster and went to pay for the coffee. More conversations about "Big Foot" that lived out here continued.

As I was opening the door to leave the store, I heard one of the guys—a friendly fellow whom everybody liked—hollering from one car to another waving his arms about how the lightning poked holes in his garden. I knew that these fellows who were talking about Big Foot were new to the area and a long way from their home range. They sure weren't from around this neck of the woods.

Many a good old country boy grew up on these lofty "spreads" of father's fathers. The ancient customs of life's long stretch has steadily inherited its age. But some of that treasured spirit will always live. Farm life will give you every kind of reward you would ever want, except money. The good ole country life that I was accustomed to around here was gone.

Horse Scents

While many of my friends were busy attaining their wealth, I was content working my horses, plowing, planting, or making hay. In the winter on Sunday afternoons, I enjoyed going for a sleigh ride through the woods and in the snow-covered fields.

There's something about the smell of a horse that makes a country boy become alive. That is, until you pick up a hoof-pick and start picking manure out from around the frog (the center of the hoof). Then it gets a little intense.

In the midst of winter on a deep-freeze day, walking up to the stable-door and hearing my horses nickering for their morning feed was something special to me. I'd step inside out of the cold, into the warmth, for a friendly good morning greeting. The smell of hay and the aroma from the horses gives me the sense of ease and comfort.

I like to hear the horses as they crunch on their corn, and to rub their ears and touch them on the temple as it goes in and out when they're chewing. If you've never taken the time to watch a horse take a drink, well you are in for a wonderful treat. They take in a great big gulp of water. Then there's a knot you can see from under their jowl bone that runs down their long slick neck into their deep muscular chest, one knot after another until they've had their fill.

There's a lovely old Indian legend that says water sleeps. When a horse takes a drink, he must wake it up first. That's why a horse blows on the water, then takes the tip of his nose and jerks it back and forth until it makes ripples or little waves before starting to drink, making sure the water is awake.

My generous and lovely wife Mary wanted to give me a draft horse for my birthday to match the one I had in the barn. Mary had seen an ad in the local newspaper for a horse that was for sale and thought we should see about it.

Harley was a three-year old runaway Belgian gelding, not a Percheron; he was brown, not a dapple-gray. But Harley was unquestionably gentle with lots of personality. In fact, he was like an overgrown kid who weighed about a ton. He was a "chunk" type of draft horse, slick and well kept. Obviously, he wouldn't match his stable mate.

I don't recall the young lady's name who owned Harley; I'll call her Sam, which is a name that I always admired for a young

353

lady who liked horses and the out-of-doors ways. While working around on the farm, I called my wife Mary "Sam."

Mary and I arrived at Sam's stable. She was a very nice young gal, dressed in riding britches. As we pulled up in front of the stable, she came strolling out with a German Shepherd hanging close to her heels and keeping an eye locked on us.

Mary and her Harley

She knew we were coming and had Harley cross-tied in the entryway. He'd been brushed off, looking shiny and slick, like a brand new silver dollar. Hanging from the ceiling were several rolls of Tanglefoot (a thick clear paper with a sticky substance for catching flies). Sam was walking around waving her arms and pointing to Harley without getting caught up in the Tanglefoot. She was showing us Harley's finest qualities, telling us that he was an outstanding horse of his breed. I could see he was exceptional for his type, a nicely-made gelding.

Sam had an awful lot of complimentary things to say. It's my belief that the best of us might have a speck of larceny in us; for others I suspect it might be a tad more. As Grandpap would say, "Burned once, a lesson learned." Being a chip off the old block, I wasn't planning on letting that happen. I had a notion he might be on the "skittish" side. Sam pointed out how well he carried his head to denote the quality of a good horse.

She said, "I'm asking $1,500 for Harley." I just kept running my hands over him and up and down his legs, picking his feet up and checking his fetlock for scratches. In less time than half a bit, she told me firmly that she'd take $1,200, saying it in a tone like that was as low as she wanted to go. I thought that was a mighty big drop.

After becoming better acquainted, Sam was telling us that she and her husband were getting a divorce and that was the reason she had to get rid of Harley. (I could tell all of this was going rather hard on her.) I told her how sorry I was about that. She said, "I really only paid a $1,000 for Harley and would be satisfied to just break even on him." Once again she was trying to convince me he was a "heavyweight," without any defects.

One more time she made it clear that this was her last offer. Up to this point, I hadn't tried to barter with her. I made a few hmms and ahs. Sam was becoming very friendly. I had a feeling that today was the last day for her ad to run in the paper. I asked if anyone had previously looked at Harley. She replied, "No, but he's entered in the Draft Horse and Mule Sale next month in Harrisburg, Pennsylvania where I'll try to sell him." I knew that at the Harrisburg Sale, she'd pay a large commission and couldn't be sure of a set price.

She was telling us all the things she did with Harley and where they'd gone. And she kinda let it slip that one time Harley had run off with her and some friends in a surrey; they went down an embankment and upset. She didn't mean to say that, but it was too late; now the cat was out of the bag.

It wasn't exactly clear who was going to get hooked: me, Sam or Harley. If Harley couldn't rid his bad habit, it was going to be me; if he turned out promising, it was Sam. But Harley was getting hooked in any event. After a while she asked me if I would make an offer on him and I said, "Sure, $500." I was expecting to see some dissatisfaction in her eye. Instead, she said, "Could you make it six?" I said, "Well, if you deliver him." She stuck out her hand and said, "Done deal."

We got loaded up and then struck out for the farm. Sam brought Harley early that evening, safe and sound. I turned him loose in the paddock and he flirted around my Percheron mare. Byrd laid back her ears, spoiling for a fight, and full of it. After a little bickering and still looking perturbed, she realized Harley was harmless. Harley was pretending he didn't know what her fuss was all about.

I had a passel of goats—I think fifteen in all. Each time I added a new one to my little herd, I put a bell around its neck. Fifteen bells created a fair amount of jingling. A few of my goats had kids over the winter. One nanny was standing under the over-jet in the loafin' shed. She was teetering timidly on three legs while nursing her newborn. She had her fourth leg pulled up so high it looked like she was going to upset. I could tell that really tickled Sam. She was leaning up against the gatepost with a broad smile.

Harley was a bit standoffish. He didn't know what to think about all these goats running up to him like that, and rightly so. But it was strictly between Harley and the goats. Harley stood there all spraddle-legged and wide-eyed, afraid to move with the goats scurrying circuitously under his belly. Sam was watching and said, "Harley won't hurt them." I said, "I hope they don't hurt Harley!" We all laughed. Harley wasn't too sure about this new life, but we all knew he'd be just fine. It was getting dark fast and Sam said, "I think it's time I start up the road before it gets too late." We bid our goodbye, got her trailer turned around, and she headed for home.

It wasn't more than a week or two before we had a light snow. I hooked Harley to our sleigh in mid-morning for a sleigh ride in the hayfield. After a few rounds, I thought it would be nice to let my friend Wayne Kelly and Mary continue to drive Harley. Wayne got in the driver's seat. Harley bolted forward and took off like a shot. I thought, for a horse that was presumably broke, he's as rough as a corncob.

I was standing in the hayfield about a hundred feet in front of the fence which was between me and the barn when Harley took off in a dead run toward the stable. Waving my arms up and down and flapping my jacket around in Harley's sight, I managed to turn him back out into the field. With Wayne and Mary both pulling the lines to turn Harley, he didn't know it, but he was just running as fast as he could in a big circle. Finally Harley stopped on his own. I got into the driver's seat. Mary stayed in—she was having a grand old time. I kept tapping him up until lunchtime. Then after lunch and an hour's rest, I hooked him up and drove him until feeding time that evening.

To break, train, and school a horse, all you need is a fair amount of patience and a general knowledge with horses. Draft horses are far too large to even think about trying to manhandle. They can be outsmarted or with a simple adjustment of harness, a teamster can likely take care of the majority of problems. God gave us two ends: one to sit on and one to think with. Your success depends on which end you use. "Heads you win, tails you lose."

I do believe you have to be kind, gentle and caring, but consistent and firm. Only if you are heedful and stay in control, will you earn their respect. When I reflect on it, it takes a strong desire, a heap of dedication and a bunch of determination.

The next day this three-year old gelding was so stiff, he looked at me as if to say, "Oh no, not you again!" We went for a short ride that morning. Harley learned a good lesson, and never ran away after that.

I had a billy goat that looked a lot like a Holstein cow with big black and white spots. For those who had the honor of getting a good whiff of Bill, they would swear he was the first cousin of a polecat. Bill and Harley had quite a shine for each other; wherever one was, that was where the other one wanted to be.

Harley was suitably saddle broke. Mary, with her two black labs, Bill, and five or six nanny goats running along behind, would go for an early morning ride in the woods. One day there was a poacher in the woods. He saw Mary on her big brown horse with her two dogs and a billy goat running out of the woods. I learned later it was John Burke, a fellow who soon became my friend. He told me about the incident. "Mr. Jim, when I saw that great big horse, those two dogs, a billy goat and a bunch of nanny goats running along the edge of the woods with cowbells ringing, I just knew it was time for me to get goin'."

It was a flaming hot August day, blistering and sultry. It had been a dismal forecast for a full week and according to the way the sky looked, it wasn't going to get any better. I was fixing fence along the road in the front field of the farm in the middle of the afternoon. A car stopped and an old man with gray hair, long past his working years, got out. He moseyed up to me, took his broad-brimmed summer hat off, reset it a couple times and said, "Mister, I've been around this part of the country for a long time. I've just seen the darnedest thing!"

I asked the old man what that was. He looked at me, raised up his hat, scratched his head and then said, "I think I just saw a lady riding a big brown horse. She had two black dogs and, and, and then . . ." I interrupted and said, ". . .with a big billy goat and a herd of nannies all around under her horse?" "Why yes, did you see her?" I said, "Oh yes, many times." He said, "Well, who in the heck is that?" I said, "Oh, that's my wife.

358

Sometimes she has a big white rooster that runs along behind her, too." The old rooster generally stops before they get to the woods. Mary didn't know it at the time, but she had really lightened up his day.

So far we hadn't found any foibles with Harley—only that he was a little breechy (hard to keep in the field). This early in the fall, grass in the pasture was still in good condition. Harley was quite a grass-hog. Grass was always looking better on the other side of the fence.

Our good neighbors for many years, the Weldons, had a few horses. Their farm was adjacent to Beaver Brook Farm. Sharon Weldon called me and said, "Jimmy, your big brown horse is over here in our field with my horses. He's not hurting anything, but I thought you'd like to know where he is." Her voice was expressing concern. Mary and I took a walk down to where Harley was. That part of the meadow was low and flat with a small stream. Several meadowlarks were running around. They're the nicest little birds: their little legs were just moving with their heads up and backs straight—they were running so fast and were as cute as could be. Yes, Harley was there, standing under a shade tree on three legs looking all comfortable and pleased with himself, enjoying his new friends. He was stomping flies and swishing his little bobbed tail.

The block-wire fencing had been in service for 45 years and had seen better days. It wasn't able to hold up to Harley. He had stuck his head through a little hole in the middle of the wire and just kept pushing and eating, eating and pushing until it stretched and broke enough for him to walk through. Such behavior was natural for Harley.

Affectionately, Mary walked up to Harley. He lowered his head so she could reach up and slip the halter on, then she snapped up her lead rope. In the meanwhile, I found a forked stick, and I stepped on the bottom part of the broken fence. With the stick I pushed up on the top part of the wire to hold it open. Mary walked through the hole, but with all my pushing and tugging, it still wasn't high enough for Harley. Poor old Harley, without half trying, he got down on his knees to get through the fence. Mary said, "Look at that big old horse trying to look small, doesn't that beat all!"

In Baltimore County there are lots of hard, heavy rains in the fall of the year. One fall evening during a running rain, Harley got out of his stall and walked around most of the night on the lawn at the manor house. The next morning Mary and I found Harley down on the tennis court. There was a small walk-through gate on the open side of the tennis court, bath-house and pool area, which was barely large enough for a medium-sized person to walk through.

I told Mary that we would try to take Harley through the gate. It was still raining and I didn't want to walk him over the lawn any more than required. Harley's pie plate feet made very big holes in the wet lawn, and I knew it was up to me to do all the necessary repairs to it. Mary put the halter on, then snapped on her pull-in strap, and walked him to the gate. I was waiting there patiently while Mary walked through the gate. Harley didn't jib. He followed right along behind, but about halfway through he got stuck. We couldn't get him to back up or to come forward. He was grass-bloated and looked like a barrel. I was on one side and Mary was on the other; I told her to push his stomach in as much as she could and I would do the same on my side.

We pushed, than we pulled. Harley, acting with little concern, would take a mini-step forward. Once his stomach passed the gatepost, in less than no time he walked free. Harley was so

360

good-natured and easygoing, I could have turned him around and done it all over again. He wouldn't have minded a bit. In Mary's usual forthright way, she grabbed a handful of Harley's mane, shimmied up his leg, climbed hand over hand up his side, swung herself sideways onto his back and then turned around, sat up straight and said, "I'm ready, you can lead him back to the stable now."

Byrd was my lead horse. After harnessing her up in the stable, I'd open the door and turn her loose. She walked out, stood in front of the hitching rail and waited alone. Next I'd harness up Harley, and he'd walk out and stand right by Byrd. They both knew where to stand and did it exactly the same each time they were tethered. They both understood their job and did it well. Then I'd put on the check lines, two straight lines, each having a second line running off it called a check.

If I was plowing, the billy goat, Bill, walked along next to Harley, round after round on the landside. The unplowed part is called the "landside"; the plowed part is called the "moldboard side" or the "furrow bank." If I was mowing or raking up hay, Bill would stop and eat a little, then run to catch up. After catching up, Bill had this habit of acting like he was mad at Harley for not waiting for him. He reared up on his hind legs, arched his neck, turned his head sideways and butted Harley on the side of his front leg. Harley never paid any mind to him and just kept walking. For Harley it wasn't anymore than a love tap.

By late fall cockleburs were a big problem at the farm. As a horse gets to eating closer to the edge of the woods or along the hedgerow to get a more tender grass, he'll get cockleburs stuck on his fetlocks, mane and tail. This is a rough job for lots of grooms, but there's a sure remedy: diesel fuel. Take a brush, dip a little on, brush out the mane, tail, and fetlock, and it makes the hair shiny and slippery. Any burrs that are hanging will pull out easily. Diesel fuel is also handy for the split hoof. Just take a can and squirt it on. Mary would tell people that Jimmy couldn't raise horses if he didn't have diesel fuel.

Harley was a sorrel with flaxen mane and tail to match. It had been a hot sticky day—one of those gloomy days that was too hot to do almost anything. The horses' manes were looking a might jute. I got the clippers and roached Byrd and Harley's manes. As I was doing it, I was wondering if this was going to meet with Mary's approval. I knew I was getting a little iffy for she loved that long mane hair. But it was fine with Mary and considerably cooler for the horses.

The horses had three days of rest, from the day I clipped their manes until Saturday. As soon as the dew was off the hay, I started raking it up. This was the fourth cutting of hay out of this field for the year. (A fourth cutting is rare for me.) It looked like I'd be spending the weekend "buckin" hay (old hay-stacker's term), if it didn't rain. I finished up raking all the hay by late afternoon and the baler finished shortly after I did. On Sunday a crew was coming to carry the hay to the barn and stack it in the mow.

On Saturday evening after feeding time, I turned the horses in what we called the orchard field. Actually it was an ex-orchard, left with less than half a dozen trees. As the apples ripened and dropped to the ground with a thump, the horses would chase after them at a lively gait. Harley had his favorite tree. Under it was a nice-size sapling. Harley bit off the top. It was just the right height from the ground so he could stand mesmerized, with the sapling under his belly and without moving his feet, sway back and forth to scratch his tummy. With his rump to the road, from a distance, it looked like he was doing the Hoochie-Koochie dance.

Each year I generally raised a hundred chickens for the table, fifty in the spring and fifty in the fall. The brooder house was in the orchard field. Because the weather was hot, I took the window out to get a little cross-breeze. The window was quite large and only two feet off the ground. I left Harley and Byrd in the orchard overnight. The next morning I couldn't find Harley anywhere. I thought I'd do my feeding and then take off looking for my horse. The little peeps were the last thing to do. I opened the door, and there stood Harley in the brooder house with the peeps all running around pecking on his feet. His head was lowered with his withers up against the roof.

At first sight, how he'd gotten in was a mystery. Then I figured he'd pawed out the screen in the window and just walked in. I wondered, "How will I ever get him out of here? Oh well, he came in through the window, so I'll try to take him back out the same way."

I thought I should go home and get the camera, for nobody would believe this. (In my judgment, sometimes we shouldn't be in such a trot.) But with a bunch of hay in the field and helpers coming, I figured there wasn't enough time. Harley hopped out through the window as nice as you please, then hurried to the barn for breakfast.

After we got the hay in, the next thing on my list was to plow out the potatoes. I usually planted 100 pounds of taters, making twelve rows three-hundred feet long across the garden. I harnessed Harley up, then put a wagon saddle on him. Mary rode Harley, guiding him up and down the rows, while I worked the potato digger.

We'd plow out a few rows, then let Harley rest a while. We picked up the potatoes in the plowed-out rows, put them in buckets, and emptied the buckets into 100-pound feedbags.

Every once in a while Harley would get a "bull-on." Showing contumacious attitude, he'd balk, walk on top of a row, turn too sharp, or do any number of ornery things. We had just gotten to the far end, and he turned ready for the next row, stopped and wouldn't move. Mary kicked him in the sides, but Harley did nothing.

I was getting tired and short-tempered. Without telling Mary, I stepped into the horse barn and picked up my whip. I came back out and yelled to Harley to come-up, but he didn't move. After I snapped that whip around on his right hind hock and released it with a big crack, Harley jumped to attention. Unharmed, he started down the row like he was supposed to. Mary was not too happy about this and said, "What if he decided to run off with me up here? Next time, you ought to give a little warning. Let me know what you're planning to do!" I told her he wasn't going to run off pulling a potato plow. That was his last balk. A little "giddy-up" got him going like it ought to.

When the grass got shorter, I started putting out feed twice a day. Arriving at the barn in the morning while the horses were still in the meadow, I let out a whistle. In the early morning I could taste the freshness of the air as the breeze came out of the woods. It was so pleasant that I wanted to chew the aroma. I could almost hear the stillness as the fog was lifting above the pond. If the horses were too far away and couldn't hear my whistle, I called them by taking the backside of my metal feed scoop and hitting it up against the outside of the barn.

From the calm and quiet, the horses could detect the pounding of the scoop, echoing out through the little valley by the pond. You-bet-chum, they'd come a-runnin' on the double. The horses ran up the hill in a full gallop. With flared nostrils, breathing hard and blowin', they waited with patience and good manners for their turn to be let in the stable for their morning feeding. Each knew its own stall. I seldom ever tied them. They each had a 14' x 14' free roaming stall, until we got five more horses. Then, I started tying two to a stall, to cut down on the snorting.

In the six-foot-wide entryway I could stack up bales of hay two wide and four or five high. I still had plenty of room to walk around to do my feeding without any problems. The boards in front of the stalls were only four-feet high. Harley had to stretch, but he could nibble on a few long straws sticking out of a hay bale, and that gave him enough leverage to pull that bale over closer to him so he could get a good bite out of it. Then he picked up the whole bale and pulled it over the fence. Like a rat terrier, he shook it until it fell apart. The same was true if a bag of feed was left too close. He picked up a 100 pound of feed, lifted it over to his side and made sure every grain was out of the bag, tossing it aside and beginning to eat.

A faucet on the entry side between the two stalls had an up-and-down straight six-inch-handle. One morning I went to the barn and the spigot was on, water flowing out from under the barn door. I couldn't understand how that could have happened. A few days later the same thing happened, and again I couldn't understand it. Mary said, "You don't think Harley could turn it on do you?" I replied, "Maybe so." I was thinking he couldn't do that! A week later after I had done the feeding, I was working on some harness, and heard a noise. I looked around and saw Harley. He took his nose, pushed the handle down and got his fresh drink of spring water, then turned around and started eating more hay. Well, I nailed some boards in front of the faucet and that stopped that.

In the evenings or during the weekends, Mary and I went horseback riding. I rode Byrd and Mary rode Harley. Wherever

Byrd went, Harley was sure to follow. One day I took Mary down past the front field into Beaver Brook Run. The horses liked to stop in the middle of the creek to paw and splash with their left front foot and then their right. We had to be careful they didn't lie down and roll; you wouldn't want to be under Harley if that happened.

There were several beaver dams along the trail we took. It was quite exciting to stop and watch them as they worked on their dam. They were constantly pulling logs up and down the stream, packing mud higher and higher. What engineers they are!

Then we headed back out to the public road, where we had to cross over a metal bridge. Byrd gingerly walked over. Mary bellowed out, "Wait up!" I looked back and saw Harley had come to a full stand-still, and was acting a little snorty at the metal bridge. I yelled, "Take your crop and whack him on the caboose." I rode back across the bridge, dismounted and approached Harley in a friendly kind of a way.

I pulled the reins together under his chin to check him up a bit. Then I patted him on the neck, rubbed him on the nose. No, he was not going to move; he had become rooted to his spot. Finally, I urged him enough to where he made one step, but he didn't like that empty sound and clanking that you get from walking on a metal bridge. Next I pulled with the reins while Mary kicked him in the slats. I got behind him, pushed and squalled at him. No matter what we did, he wasn't going to budge; he acted like he was frozen. I cut a good-size hickory switch off a nearby tree and stung him on the hocks a little, but he wouldn't stir a hair. Mary said, "Don't be doing that while I'm up here."

I was contemplating what to do next. If somehow I didn't get this beast across the bridge, I was going to be in a heap of trouble, for he'd never do anything I asked of him again. A while later I got this bright idea that if he couldn't see the bridge, all would be okay.

Harley was easily bamboozled, so I took off my jacket, threw it over his head and covered his eyes. He trembled for the first few steps and then walked cautiously to the other side in his gentle-giant manner. I hoofed him back and forth several times, thinking we might as well do this until he gets it right! He didn't exactly cotton up to the idea, but his jim-jams were better, and he learned that bridges didn't bite. Harley got an education that day on how to cross bridges.

In 1996, we found we were moving to Colorado. Mary's mother had her annual Palm Sunday dinner. One of Mary's cousins asked me about Harley and what was going to happen to him. He said that he'd passed the farm many times while I had my horses out working in the front field. He said, "I love that big sorrel Belgian with the flaxen mane and tail. (Harley was a romancer and everybody loved him.) What kind of price do you have set for him?" We agreed on a price.

The next morning it was pouring down rain so I was working in the shop. The phone rang and it was Mary's cousin Johnny. He asked me to bring that big horse to his farm. I said, "Johnny, it's really raining here." Johnny said, "I don't care. I want that horse now." I hooked my trailer to the truck, walked down to the meadow, brought my horse up, drove him to Johnny's, and said my good-byes.

They Called It Progress

The people of the Chestnut Ridge Community Association put up a bulky fight against the farm being sold for development. The farm had been there longer than any of the residents, and they didn't want to see it sold. They held community meetings at the firehouse explaining that the 317-3/4 acre farm would bring too many houses and people to the community. It involved expensive legal battles over rights, permits and so forth, but the land developers got their way.

Then in 1996 Mary had a job offer in Denver. We had always loved Colorado and often dreamed of living there. She asked me how I felt about moving. I told her my dream is being in your dream; that I might as well die in Colorado as in Maryland. I had just gotten the word that the farm was sold, and it would only be a short time before new homes would be built there. Without any advertisement except word of mouth, we sold our house, livestock, machinery, and business.

Everything fell into place. Our life in Maryland ended and a new life in Colorado began.

Epilogue: My Paha-Sapa

I grew up alongside two brothers and a sister but felt I had different convictions from my siblings. I was my mother's one and only anachronistic son, belonging more in the past than in the present. Not once did I ever feel lonesome. Being alone is good if it's a matter of choice, especially if you enjoy your own company. I'm a slow, reluctant talker among strangers, I think a lot but don't talk much, which fed a need to discover who I am.

At the age of 13, I joined Pleasant Hill Methodist Church. My mother took Marvin and me to church. Marvin sat on one side of her and I on the other, probably to keep us from harassing each other. Mom enjoyed singing hymns and was not bashful about it. When she hit those high notes, I thought she'd crack the stained-glass windows. I felt the traditional worship in church was okay, but I needed something else to gird up the spirit.

At church, I made sure that I didn't sit behind Mrs. Jones. She always wore a big hat mixed with lots of ostrich and peacock feathers. Nobody in back of her could see around either side of her. As she moved her head the feathers were constantly flopping about, looking as though they were ready to fly off her head. On the back of each pew was a hymnal and Bible rack where hand-held fans were also kept. During hot weather, it was fun to use a fan and get those nice, fluffy feathers, which decorated the ladies' big hats, moving around. Mom would poke me and say, "Stop that and sit up straight!"

At home, after my chores were finished, I spent most of my time in the woods, exploring and hunting, or fishing in a stream. People who knew me well realized that changes in life were not as easy for me as they were for many others. On the "out-post" of my mind, it became harder for me to accept and respect the newer ways. This tendency must have come from a self-generated feeling of kinship with the land. Many people desire, and few achieve, life without a spin; nevertheless, they won't submit to the value of just being ordinary. Our forefathers never had the objective of one man being better than another. At birth one person is not placed above the other. We mold ourselves and become who we are.

While an adolescent, I had what the Indians called a Paha-Sapa, a sacred place in the Black Hills. My sacred ground was a little valley in the heart of the cheery woodland right in the middle of Beaver Brook Farm. When the flow of my spirit had been broken, my Paha-Sapa provided me a place of solitude and to review hidden thoughts. The stick and tangle brush, called "Brush-Harbor," is the place where wishes, dreams and praises were made.

The frequent trips to the woods counseled me through nature, and brought satisfaction. My religion was not the typical church-going type. Religion ultimately settles down to a contact and sometimes conflict between man and his Maker. Jesus didn't preach from a pulpit; I didn't feel the need to sit in a pew.

Mother Earth and Father Sky are for the use of all and belong to none: a theological structure that many Indians believe. Religion is one of the most intense things men have fought over from the dawn of time. Differences of opinion are com-

372

mon and shape the guidelines for moral conduct, helping us express ourselves as individuals. We've been given different religions according to our understanding. The Great Spirit and God must be brothers—one in the same—for they've both been doing battle with the devil from the beginning of time.

I'm not a Bible thumper, and was plain raised, but I sure do believe strongly in The Almighty. Less traditional than some, more conservative than a few, my convictions are strong. I'm about two-thirds environmentalist, almost a full page from out of nature's book. Country space breeds its own kind of people, not necessarily better or worse than those who grew up in cities and towns but the result is freer, more open and friendlier. In the country we call that "earthy." In the country, I crafted my own spiritual ways. That's where I learned who I am. The power of prayer is a weapon of peace, a good way to untangle the mind. To face the call in hard times is the best test of all; it can make you drop to your knees like an anvil. Once on the relief plan, a soul is enlightened and restored. No great secret; it's as easy as falling off a log.

So whether we're surrounded by the well-dressed in church or sitting on the ground, our Father and the devil do battle over our souls. In the distance of heaven, no one has the right to stomp the other.

Many people figure they've been given a tough row to hoe. When difficult times came, I knew it and headed for the woods. I found a stump and rested my thoughts. I searched every nook and cranny of my mind. Death, beauty, madness all lie within the lines. No hidden grip, mostly wordless, my conversation was usually direct and uncomplicated; words spoken aloud were sparse. There were plenty of seeds sown from this ole stump, and today I can reap a crop of memories that's a pleasure to harvest and a joy to tote. The slower gait like mine is not for the "hyper-excitable" if you like living on the quick.

In my Paha-Sapa, in the valley of the soaring oaks, treetops reach wayward to the sky. High aloft on the open tips, songbirds sail in and out. Beneath the canopy, a frisky little stream swerves clear sweet water ticklishly along the contour of the floor. Plowed smooth with age, the threaded course was  no wider than a crow-hop. It forged itself into a waterspout with an abrupt dive and spilled over into a falls. Trees with sprawling limbs and deep roots stood mighty here, forming a strong conviction.

Days grow short in cool crisp weather. Squirrels scamper about grabbing nuts. Battles are fought and lost as they jump from limb to branch. They're fat and ready for the hard charge of winter. There's charm and excitement in this isolated part of the woods. Actions unfold on schedule every day. "No new noise here!" It's been like this for generations.

Much of the old ways are like ours; we work hard to survive in lean times. Days grow cold and short and without the helping hand of our Maker, we won't endure. Too often we forget when the fruit hangs low and heavy over our heads. We have a tendency to take things for granted.

It's all essential to the Master's plan. Nature puts an extra thump in my day. We need that extra stir in faith if we are going to persevere. Nature provides that special blend for me;

odd as it might seem, it's extremely private for me living among all the noises of nature.

One thing I remember clearly is thanking Him for all the good things in life but not asking Him for special favors or gifts. I felt that communications with my Maker were helpful in my understanding and accepting myself and my ways of life. I recall my mother and father asking me where I'd been, and I'd simply say that I went for a horseback-ride, without telling them how I'd stopped off to pray.

One day, Mom happened to mention that she was feeling very unsettled. Her exact words were "I am feeling tipsy-turvy." I told Mom that there was this special spot back in the woods that helped me feel better, that after being there, I felt unbelievably good inside. She started walking in the woods—I don't know if she ever found my spot, but she must have gotten close. She told me about her stroll and how wonderful it was just to be there in the quiet. It was so pleasant that surely the devil must have been in bed.

With a steady eye I learned from my parents the "whys" and "what-fors," without ever asking. Near neighbors were far, and friendliness sometimes derives from loneliness. Many times folks passing by knocked on our door during a storm: their car had slipped off the road. Mom and Dad invited the trembling unfortunate strangers inside to make them feel beyond welcome, shoving them up to the table for hot coffee. I could tell our hospitality made them feel pretty comfortable, like they were almost delighted to have had the accident. Even with their worldly wisdom, the rub of politeness and candor of openness often met strangers with great surprise. Much has been written on the subject of etiquette, and many rely blindly on these books and formal training. I was never tutored or read much on the formal rules, but saw how it was supposed to be: help your neighbors for it's not a free bounty to heaven.

As the years passed, a nagging knowledge of genuineness thrived and I continued to go to my Paha-Sapa. That is, until I moved away. Changes in life come to stay. Despite all the "drum-beats" from the neighbors, the thrash ended without conflict. Matter-of-factly, the hatchet got politely buried, and with great sadness, the farm was graciously sold. Beaver Brook Farm held out longer than most. Actually it was one of the last to go, if not the last farm in the area. It wasn't necessarily an offer of peace, but a matter of course for its time. There's an old saying, "It takes three bankruptcies to make a farm die hard." That certainly wasn't the case here.

Dragging its heels over the matter for some time, the unspoiled paradise made its turn. The old homestead passed into history, the end of the age of farming had been sealed. The woods were raped by a crowd of builders watching for the day of lustier homes. Building them from the bottom up, they are setting them on the land of yesteryear. There was a change of life with shifting shadows. New strangers are charmed by this fine example of country living left for them. Country beliefs and manners haven't entirely been shunned; politeness still exists there.

The last time I saw my Paha-Sapa, I took a long, hard blink. Many houses now scarf up the water right from out of the winding spring. The last few dribbles from the little falls fell one by one. The droopy little brook gave up her falls. It lost its flow. The waterspout turned to sand, and now it's become bone-dry. My ear lost the rumble of the falls, but my heart still holds the sound. We never miss the water until the stream runs dry, as they say. Father Time sired the years.

My Grandmother Fox never went to church much, but she did get religion in her final years and I'm mighty glad she did. She told me that it's harder for a rich man to enter the kingdom of heaven than it is for a camel to get through the eye of a needle. That relieved me emotionally of any doubt concerning my Godly treasures. To be rich or poor is the assurance of what you are. It's not the pot of gold you hold or the monetary rainbow you desire. On my mother's side, it was a rarity for anyone to miss church, from horse-and-buggy days to the grave.

As complex as death might seemingly be to understand, we consume a blissful contentment knowing there is a better place. If you follow the path of the four seasons, it's basically pretty simple: a seed is planted, it sprouts, it grows, it matures, it turns to seed and falls to the ground. It bears the same similarities to our circle of life. The loss of a loved one is terribly sad, but don't take dying too seriously. There is a lesser amount of need to grieve if you believe. If you don't, I expect it might be a bit more difficult. Birth and death are the keys that lock the axis of life. From the beginning to the end of life, there will be a reckoning of wrongful doings. The settlement of accounts on the register of heaven will be finalized with a careful mothering of the flock. That everlasting truth will hold the value for each and every one of us: kings, queens, sinners and saints alike. Therefore, keep you scale balanced and bubble plumb, live within the lines and weigh the differences of right and wrong.

Some never get far from the cushion; for me I never attained much formal church like perhaps I should have. The little stump of worship in the woods cultivated a tight cinch for my throne of faith. It's been passed on with little notice and unknown ties. I've long since given up most of my primitive ways; I do enjoy sitting in church with my family. With

377

considerable respect to the "modern Eden," I finally reached the omega of my rebellion and individual expression and am mighty glad to be there.

My intimacy with nature—the woods, streams, the natural resources—is something to be cherished and guarded every step of the way. We have to protect and preserve this beautiful land, which He created for our use. Umpteen years ago an Amish farmer, or husbandman, as they are properly

called, told me, "We grow too soon old and too late smart."

The Lord passes out all kinds of gifts that aren't measured out in dollars or coins. I think cancer was a gift for me, I didn't know it at the time, but I was better off for it. I sure hope that when I cross over that Great Divide, there's a team of horses waiting there for me to drive.

Looking Through The Kitchen Door

Taste the 1940's
Foods from the Cupboard

Perishable fruits and vegetable were stored in the cupboard in a cool area of the basement for wintertime use. At that time, canning was the main source of preserving food. Mom had a variety of canning jars: sizes from half-pints to gallons; colors in green, clear, blue, amber and yellow; and brands including Kerr, Mason and Ball. I thought the Mason Jar was real cool because it had a raised design of a ship's anchor on the front of it. Mom ran a tight ship. Her kitchen orders were to first sterilize the jars and clean the counters thoroughly before preparing to do any canning.

When it came to canning corn, Mom's rule of thumb was that by no means were we to pull more corn than she could put up from the field to the jar within an hour. It was important to quickly get the fresh corn through the canning process so that during the heat of summer it did not sour. From the house, she governed the rules of the field also. Never pull corn that is too old or too young. And no matter how young I was, Mom always claimed I was old enough to know better. The day I was born, I was knowing how to pull corn. You go by the feel. Don't press too hard on the outer leaves or you can bruise it. Bruised kernels on tender ears will cause it to spoil. It only takes a little to start fermenting and taint the whole jar. Press hard enough to know if it is too tough. If you have to take a peep pull only a little husk down around the silk to see what it looks like.

For years I teased Mom telling people that the very day I was born she sent me to the spud (potato) patch. I crawled down the row to pick potatoes of supper, but in reality, it was the cornfield where I was sent. Corn that was allowed to lounge around on a hot day in a heated kitchen would surely sour. Mom's theory was that the faster the work was done, the better the food was for her table.

Corn was the rush crop as most others were allowed two hours from the garden to the jar. It was very important to use a good sharp knife for cutting up vegetables. A sharp knife cuts the quickest and hurts the least, where a dull knife bruises and that harms the vitamins and causes unnecessary bleeding. For years Mom had a cooking canner that was no more than a rounded oblong copper steamer with two wooden handles that held 10 to 12 quart jars at a time and covered two burners on the stove at once. This method was known as a boiling bath to preserve vegetables. The required time in the bath depended on what vegetable she was canning. In later years, we upgraded to a blue enamel steamer.

When you removed the jars from the bath, it was time to screw the tops down tight. The modern self-sealing vacuum disk and brass rings was the way to go; as they cooled, you could hear the medal tops pop when they sealed and that was good. You knew you had a good seal if you pushed down on the center of the lid and it did not bounce back up. If the lid bounced up in the center, that was not a good seal, which could have been due to a bad rubber or a crack or chip on the top of the jar. That meant the contents of that jar would be served for supper that night. In no way would Mom ever gamble with our food. She no longer used those old large zinc tops with the big rubber or the old glass top wire clip with the rubber seal.

Down in the Root Cellar or Cave

A root cellar or cave is nature's way to store food for the winter—something I'm sure we must have learned from the squirrels. It is nothing more than a large hole dug in the ground and the size depended on the number of families using it. Sometimes it was dug into the side of a steep hill and called a cave: these are the best because being ten feet under ground, it would maintain a 40° temperature and proper humidity for the fruits and vegetables.

Caves did not need to be vented; however, root cellars with steps leading down into them required ventilation. This kept them from being musty and prevented spoilage. Many types of siding and roofing were used, such as wooden or stone walls with a dirt floor. Shelving was kept a couple inches away from the walls for air circulation. Many root cellars were dug out under a building like in the back corner of a barn. At Twiford Farm, ours was under the chicken house and at Beaver Brook Farm, it was dug out on the north side of a bank.

Nonperishable fruits and vegetables were stored there. Potatoes usually had a storage bin up off the ground. To keep potatoes from sprouting, they were kept in the dark and we threw a hot bed blanket over ours. Red beets, carrots, parsnips, radishes, turnips, any type of rooted vegetables were stored here with the tops on. By re-burying them in the dirt floor and leaving the tops stick out, they would last will into the winter. After the last black frost, we gathered up all remaining fruits and vegetables that were good for winter storage, such as horseradish, broccoli, brussel sprouts, salsify, apples, cabbage, anything like green tomatoes, which were protected under heavy foliage. Dad said that lots of people bought bananas on a long stalk and stored them in the root cellar by hanging them upside down from the ceiling and wrapping a sheet around them. He said they would last quite awhile, but he wasn't willing to commit as to how long quite awhile was.

Out in the Smokehouse

Smokehouses were generally stand-alone buildings located for convenience near the kitchen entrance of the home. They were built of round or square logs sitting on a raised stone foundation. Rafters were about one-two feet apart on top of the logs. Hooks for the meat were hung from the rafters. In the center of the dirt floor was a fire ring where we used green hickory or green fruitwood for smoking our meats. We were able to control the fire by adjusting a small door, about one-foot square, built into the back of the foundation. It was important to build only small fires because you did not want to actually cook your meat. Small fires for a cold smoke would often go out and needed to be re-started maybe several times a day. Smoking meats was generally done during the fall of the year when it was damp, cold and misty outside and that caused the smoke to hang close to the ground and to penetrate the meat. I can clearly recall the flavorsome aroma of smoking our own meats.

Although when you think of a smokehouse, you generally think of pork, many folks used their smokehouse to preserve beef, game, chickens, turkeys, ducks and geese—and in some parts of the country—fish. Beef specifically was dried for jerky, chipped beef, summer bologna and the beef bladder was used as a casing for ground beef to create a tasty summer sausage. Of course hog butchering was what our family mostly used our smokehouse for and that is explained in detail in an earlier chapter.

When it comes to hog butchering, families and different areas of the country have preferences. Bacon and gammon both come from pork belly, sugar cured and smoked. Bacon is cut square, while gammon is oblong, three-four inches in width and six-seven inches in length, and is a great deal leaner than bacon. Gammon is sliced substantially thicker than the thickest bacon. Gammon is from the lower part of the pig's belly down close to the leg. My family used the gammon in their sausage, but nowadays our grandchildren prefer gammon over bacon.

Old Tyme Family Recipes

Fifty years ago these foods were mostly fried in lard. Before you get upset, remember vegetable oil was unheard of—at least in Mom's cupboard. Lard is rendered hog fat that we got at butchering time. The taste was delightful and the smell, much like that of bacon. Farm families worked hard, some 14 to 16 hours a day and burned up the calories. It was important to maintain a high protein diet, keeping you cooler in hot weather and warmer in cold. By no means would I recommend trying to use lard in this day and age.

In the 1940's, city folks were being rationed with wartime meals. While my family had little money, we lived in the land of milk and honey. For some during the rugged time hunger was the best appetizer.

Here on the home front, Americans were taking it without a whimper. Some of these recipes will help remind us who we are. Welcome your taste buds to an old country dish. I can say that I was healthy, happy and well-fed during the lean times. Mom's theory was 'fresh from the garden and sink-clean.' Many times, leftovers—or should we call them madeovers—

often turned up on our table in a new dish. Mom was a crack-erjack at using everything up at feeding time. Pot-lickers often reserved liquid after cooking vegetables for soup broth.

These recipes will give you a taste of my heritage that has all but disappeared. Many of these treasures have different names according to different folks. You can change the name, but you can't change the taste.

Farmer's Butter

First, milk the cow and let the milk set overnight. The next day, pour milk into a milk separator, which has two spouts—one for the cream and one for the skim milk. We gave the skim milk to the hogs. Save the cream to make the butter. Let the cream set until room temperature. Pour cream into butter churn and churn. The butterfat will become solid and stick to the sides of the churn. The excess liquid from this process is known as buttermilk and it will have a few small lumps. Take butter out from the sides of the churn and mix in desirable amount of salt. Salt gives taste and preserves the butter.

Oyster Stew for Christmas Morning

1 pint of oysters, cooked in liquid until oysters curl up on sides
1 quart of fresh whole milk
salt and pepper to taste
¼ or ½ stick of farmer's butter
saffron-optional, pinch
Mix all ingredients, heat slowly and serve.
On the Eastern Shore in Maryland, they call the above recipe "She Stew."
If you use the same recipe, but add onion, celery and bacon, it is called "He Stew."

Panhas, mistakenly called scrapple (pronounced ponhoss)
Heat broth from pig headmeat
Add sufficient amount of cornmeal to form a thick paste without any meat.
Add salt and pepper or any type of seasoning you like.
Cook 30 to 40 minutes, stirring frequently to prevent scorching.
Do a taste-test
Pour in scrapple pans to cool and harden. Slice and fry long and slow.

Scrapple

Authentic scrapple recipe can be found under Hog Butchering in an earlier chapter.

Hog Brains

Soak hog brains in milk over night
Pat brains dry and dust with flour
Add salt and pepper
Fry lightly until brown on both sides.

Mom's Mouth-Watering Apple Dumpling—Count Me Twice!

To Make Dough: 2 cups sifted flour
1 teaspoon salt
½ cup lard, chilled
3 tablespoons butter, chilled
Mix ingredients together with a fork
Add (¼-1/3 cup) ice water
Mix dough until smooth and shape into a ball
Roll ball out into ¼-1/2" thick rectangle
Cut into 6" squares

Prepare Syrup for the Apples: *1-1/2 cup sugar*

2 cups water
3 tablespoons butter
¼ teaspoon cinnamon
Add pinch of nutmeg, if desired
6 apples (1 for each dumpling), peeled, cored and sliced
Prepare the dough, set an apple in center of each dough square, pour over small portion of syrup, pull dough corners up to seal, then pour over remaining syrup and bake 45 minutes in large shallow pan.

Tomato Gravy—Mom and Dad survived on this when they were first married.
Scorch flour in butter in a frying pan
Add chopped onion, salt, pepper, a little sugar and vinegar
Stir and remove all lumps
Add cooked tomatoes (chopped and in small pieces)
Stir until thick and serve on bread, crackers, potatoes—whatever you have

Soups: bisque, bouillabaisse, consommé, chowder, potage, gumbo, broth—call it what you like, but its still soup. You don't need recipes for soups. Soup itself is a creation as old as the hills. You use the tags of vegetables to make a garden pulp or any size desired, most types of meat stubs, ground up or left in large chunks, fish heads and tails or any kind of grain, dairy products, bones, herbs, even quahogs (a thick shell edible clam that is tough.) Use them and invent something wonderful no matter what part of the world you live in. Cook slowly and watch the pot smile.

Marrow Butter is the femur bone of a beef or buffalo. It's 10% fat and 90% protein. Before you turn up your nose. The Fort Restaurant is one of the top ten restaurants in this country and they serve over two tons of bone marrow a year. Mom mostly used bone marrow in soups. Personally, I pick up the bone, take a small table knife or butter knife and slowly pull it out in one piece, then spread it on a slice of bread like butter. Or you can crack the bone and broil the marrow ten minutes or so. It tastes like the dripping used to make Yorkshire Pudding.

Leather Bean Soup: Mom told me that Grandpa picked sacks of dried lima beans after the first black or killing frost and stored them in the attic for winter use. He made dried lima bean soup with ham and called it Leather Bean Soup. Vegetables are a farmer's friend all year long. He plants them, raises them and cares for them the best he can, and they keep his family happy to the end.

Potato with Rivels Soup: Here's one you must try —it's home-y heart warming soup that sticks to the backbone —perfect for while you are out in the cold sledding or splitting wood. My mother often said that if ever she had to choose just one thing to eat, it would be potato soup because it is so nourishing. During the Civil War era, people packed potatoes in barrels of brine and sent them to the prison camps to help keep their loved ones healthy.

Rivels are made by beating one nice hen or duck egg with a fork; then add enough flour to make it crumbly and add a pinch of salt. Once you have dropped them into the soup, cook on low for 20 minutes. Do not boil. The same great taste every time

Soup: Peel and boil some potatoes—as my mother said, *"Maybe 6 or 8, more if you like."*
Drain and smash them up coarsely
Add a little butter
Add a good quart of milk (If too thick after cooking, add a little more.)

Add finely chopped celery
Add salt and pepper to taste
Bring to a slow boil
Drop rivels in soup by rubbing rivels back and forth between both hands to crumble

Salsify a.k.a. Oyster Plant and a.k.a. Johnny-go-to-Bed because at high noon, the blooms closed: It looks like a parsnip except smaller but taste like an oyster. Mom made fake oyster stew salsify and it was not too bad. I made it not long ago, but today it is very expensive to buy in the store. Just add milk and Old Bay seasoning.

Oxtail Soup: Use the tail of one beef. Chop in between each joint, cook long and slow in water—tease out the flavor —maybe 3 or 4 hours. Chop vegetables and add along with barley, if you like, to the broth.

Supper Dishes: Friday evening supper was fish night. I asked Mom if it was because Catholics ate fish on Fridays. She told me no that it's because that's the time the stores get a fresh supply of fish in. Mom added that fish is a healthy part of a good diet and we can thank the Catholics for the fresh fish on Fridays. Mom first chose what meat or fish she was going to have for supper; then, the vegetables she served were based on how well they went with the meat or fish she was going to serve. Meal planning was an art that my mother developed long before my time—it was neither complicated nor tricky. She mapped out and planned her meals ahead of time. It only takes 60 minutes and you have saved an hour. Back then with a wood-burning cookstove, it took a long time to fix a meal and you might want to start tomorrow's supper the evening before. An example is if you were to plan on company for Sunday dinner, it would be wise to get the ham out of the smokehouse on Monday or Tuesday so it could soak in water for a few days to extract the salt by Sunday.

Mom loved to entertain. Sunday dinners were special for her. She loved to have family or friends over for a nice dinner. She put flowers on the table and set the table with her best dishes and linen napkins, which were discarded from the Wheelwright family. In later years on special occasions, Mom would provide placecards for her guests at each plate. Mom believed in feasting the eye as well as the appetite. It should be just as good to see as to eat. Her table was set pretty and each dish was colorful with a garnish. She got lots of complements on her cooking, and her reply was always the same, "It was made with loving hands."

Oyster Dressing for Christmas Day
¼ cup of butter
2 tablespoons onion, chopped
1 cup celery, chopped
¼ cup parsley chopped
2 teaspoons poultry seasoning
4 cups bread, cubed
Water or chicken broth or oyster liquid
1 to 2 cans oysters, drained and chopped large
Mix ingredients gently and stuff the turkey.

Sweet and Sour Hot Slaw, a.k.a.
Sweet and Sour Cabbage
1 tablespoon sugar
1 head of cabbage
1 egg
1 teaspoon salt
¼ cup of vinegar
Shred cabbage rather finely, put in saucepan and sprinkle with

salt. Cover pan and place over low heat, steaming until tender. Beat the egg with a fork, add vinegar, sugar and salt. Pour over steamed cabbage. Heat 5 minutes and serve hot at once.

Fresh Peas and New Potatoes

3 cups of fresh peas
12 small new potatoes
1½ teaspoons salt
1½ cups milk
1½ teaspoons flour
2 tablespoons butter

Cook potatoes and peas in separate pans in salted water until soft and almost free of water. Mix the peas and potatoes and add the milk. Bring to the boiling point, then add butter and flour, which have been blended smooth and cook until thickened.

Succotash: Fast, easy and good. The word succotash came from the Narragansett Indian Tribe of Rhode Island and was pronounced "misquatash."

Boil 6 large ears of corn for 15 minutes, cut off kernels
2 cups fresh hulled lima pole beans
2 tablespoons butter rolled in flour
Salt and pepper to taste

Cook lima beans in water until tender. Pour water off limas, add corn, whole milk or cream and remaining ingredients. Bring just to point of boil and serve.

Hog Maw

1 pig stomach
1 pound sausage meat, diced
3 cups boiled potatoes
3 cups sliced and peeled apples
2½ cups bread crumbs

1 medium onion
2 cups chopped celery
chopped parsley, salt and pepper
Clean pig belly well and soak in salt water. Combine all
ingredients and mix. Stuff the belly with the mixture and sew
up the opening. Simmer for 2 hours in a large kettle with water
to cover. Remove from kettle and place in baking pan with hot
fat. Bake in 400° oven to brown, basting frequently. Slice with
sharp knife.

Souse

Scrape, wash and thoroughly clean three pounds of pig's feet.
Place in stew pan with 1 chopped onion, ½ cup chopped celery and cover with cold water. Let it come to the boiling point,
reduce heat and simmer until meat is tender and comes off
bone easily. Pick meat off bone and strain liquid, which should
measure a scant 3 cups (if less than that, add water). Put meat
with liquid into a bowl. Add 3 tablespoons strong cider vinegar, ¾ teaspoon salt, black pepper and several thin slices of
lemon. Chill overnight, remove surplus fat from the top, turn
out on a platter, slice and serve with lemon slices and parsley.

Pickled Honeycomb Tripe: Beef tripe is usually

made from the first three of the cow's four stomachs. First cut
off excess fat and thoroughly wash and clean the tripe. To prepare 2 pounds of tripe, cut it into 2"-3" squares. Place tripe in
pot, add 1 cup of vinegar and cover with water. Bring to a boil.
Drain and repeat the process two more times. Drain, cover
with water and add a bay leaf and bring to a boil; then simmer
for two hours. Drain and place in refrigerator until tomorrow
night's supper. Roll tripe in flour and pan fry in hot fat with
onions. Dad liked his tripe strong with vinegar; he even ate it
cold after it was pickled. He kept the vinegar cruet beside his
plate and poured it on as he ate.

Stuffed Beef Heart

Clean heart, removing arteries and veins and create a pocket for stuffing. Lightly brown finely chopped onion and celery in hot fat. Add bread crumbs, salt, pepper, celery seed and parsley along with a hand-beaten egg. Add a little water if necessary and mix well. Put the mixture in the heart pocket, close up and roll in flour. Then place on a rack with water in the bottom of a roasting pan. Cover and roast slowly at 300° or 325° for 1½ - 2 hours or until done. Uncover and roast for a few minutes to brown heart.

Beef Tongue

Wash and scrub tongue; cover with hot water and add salt, bay leaves, chopped onion and celery. Add chopped carrot if you'd like. Cook slowly for about 3 hours. Cool in liquid and trim any excess tissue and remove skin. Some folks like to slice it and eat it with hot mustard. Our family preferred to then roast the tongue in the oven at 350° for about 30 minutes so the delicious meat was firm. Nobody likes a mushy tongue!

Beef Brains

Remove any loose membranes. Cover with cold water, add 2 tablespoons vinegar and soak for 30 minutes. Drain. Then cook slowly in salted water for 20-30 minutes. Drain. Then chill in cold water. Dip in hand-beaten egg, roll in flour with salt and pepper and fry in hot fat and/or butter.

Liver 'n Onions

Baby beef liver is the best. Cut in 1-2" strips. Roll in flour and fry in hot fat. Go easy on the heat and fry slowly. Liver can get tough quick. Remove liver from pan and keep warm. Add thinly sliced onions to the hot frying pan and cook until tender. Add the liver back in the pan and cover. Fry slowly for a few minutes to bring the flavors together. Blanket the liver with onions and serve.

Crab Cakes

Soak 2 slices of bread in small amount of milk. Add 2 tablespoons of mayonnaise, 1 hand-beaten egg and plenty of Old Bay seasoning. Stir in the lump crab meat (if you can afford it, otherwise, any crab meat will do). Pat into cakes and fry in hot fat, brown on both sides. Serve with cocktail sauce made with catsup and horseradish.

Roast Squab: Dad was a "squabber!" That's one who raised squabs (baby pigeons) for table consumption. Squabs are harvested just before leaving the nest. The meat is young and tender and considered a true delicacy. Mrs. Thompson only served it to her finest guests. We served it to anybody who liked squab and was hungry.

Rinse squab, salt and pepper inside and out. Brown the giblets with finely chopped celery and onion, add bread crumbs and a hand-beaten egg along with salt and pepper. Stuff the little bird and roast in 350° for 35-40 minutes uncovered.

Roast Pheasant: Use young birds if you can. If you're uncertain of their age, boil the bird in water with a tight-fitting top until tender. Keep in mind that the wing feathers on a young bird are more square on the tips; and on an older bird, the feathers are worn from flight. To roast a pheasant and other fowl is much like that of squab – just cook long and slow; the bigger the bird, the longer you cook. Goose, turkey or duck are all about the same. Wild ducks and geese may have a fishy flavor. Like any other bird, it picks up the flavor it feeds on. I can eat most anything and enjoy wild fowl if it's not too fishy, but prefer domestic duck and geese over the marshy wild.

Mom's Fried Chicken: Mom used lard in a cast iron frying pan. She made the fat hot and after rolling the chicken pieces in flour, salt and pepper, she slow cooked it until done. Generally she cooked the first side of the chicken with the lid on; then turned the chicken pieces over, removed the lid and raised the fire a bit. Everybody loved Mom's chicken, but we all knew that the real secret was the farm fresh young birds that Dad raised made the difference. Our little grandson Nick was a big chicken eater like the rest of the Fox boys. In his short life he had experienced chicken tenderloins or chicken fingers without a bone. When he was around three years old, he requested a chicken leg when he was with his family at a restaurant. Much to his mom's surprise, after taking a few bites of his chicken leg, he said, "Hey, Mom, this chicken has a stick in it!" His mom responded, "No, Nick, that's not a stick—that's a chicken bone." Well last year Nick, at age 11, helped me dress live chickens on Friday for Sunday dinner. He learned about chickens from the inside and out, and into the pot. I'm happy to report that the method of picking chickens through the Fox family generations hasn't changed.

Mom's Chicken Slippery Pot Pie: This recipe is a family favorite wintertime dish, especially good on a snowy day. It comes from the Pennsylvania Dutch and Mennonite side of the family. Get a plump hen that has stopped laying for life. Disjoint it and cut up as you would a frying hen. Cover with water and cook with onion and celery. Boil for an hour or so until firm, not tender. Add 2 peeled and coarsely chopped carrots long with 6-8 peels and chopped potatoes. Boil for another 15-20 minutes. Add egg noodles.
Egg Noodles
1 cup flour
1 large hen or duck egg

2 one-half egg shells of water
1 one-half egg shell soft lard
Small pinch of salt
Mix thoroughly and knead dough. If too wet, add a little flour; if too dry, add water. After kneading, let dough rest in a ball for 10-15 minutes. Roll out on table like a piecrust. Use a sharp knife to cut a long strip first length-wise and then cross-wise creating 1½ " squares. Add noodles a few at a time to the pot pie, stirring to make sure they don't stick together. After the whole lot is in a boil, add salt and pepper. Place pot in 250° over until thick and done. This was named slippery because the noodles will slip off your spoon pretty quick. This is a great noonday meal, but in this day and age, be sure you exercise good after eating it!

Yankee Pot Pie a.k.a Yankee Doodle: Put
soda crackers in a bowl, pour chicken, turkey or beef gravy over the crackers. Cover and allow to steam 4-8 minutes and serve.

Dried Fried Corn or Dried Stew Corn:
You could have a taste of summer in the winter with dried corn—it's a summer flavor on a winter table. Both of my grandmothers dried corn. Grandmother Cartzendafner had a corn drier. Mom said it was like a small table with legs, a pan under it to hold hot water and a tray on top for the corn. It toasted the corn, which caused it to caramelize to its natural sweet flavor. She said they also used the back porch medal roof as a drier for corn by using a large sheet pan and setting it on the hot medal roof with cheese cloth over it to keep the flies out. The only problem with that was there were a lot of ups and downs to the job because you had to keep running up and down the stairs to the second floor stirring the corn through the window in her parents' bedroom. She had to run upstairs every little while depending on how hot that tin roof got in the sun that day to stir it.

Using the dried corn, just melt a little butter in an iron skillet, add the corn and the sweet aroma would fill the room. It's a nice crunchy, crispy, squeaky, melodious chew with a mouthful of sweet flavor. My mother never made dried corn in my time that I remember, but lots of other family members that lived in Pennsylvania did and it was great.

Fried Cabbage: Grandmother Fox fried everything— even cabbage. Slice it up as you would for slaw, put fat in a cast iron frying pan and push it on to the back of the wood cookstove. Add the cabbage and let it cook. Add a little salt and vinegar—real good.

Corn Fritters: As my good friend Martin Kemper would say in his slow southern drawl, "It's carwn-frittah time." Corn fritters were a real treat. As the kernels started to lose their milk, it takes on a more gummy, almost solid sugary flavor. Pull large heavy ears of "corn" with tight husks. Pull husk back, roll down and break it off from the cob and "de-silk" it. Using a good sharp knife, slit each row of kernel on top of the ear. Using the backside of the knife, scrap out the thick sticky milk. My advice would be to do this outside under a shade tree for it flies everywhere—to the ceiling, on the windows. doors walls and all.

1 cup sifted flour
¾ teaspoon of salt
1 teaspoon baking powder
2 fresh hen eggs
¼ cup milk, depending on how dry and starchy the corn is
6 ears corn
2 teaspoons melted butter

Combine the ingredients and mix until smooth. Drop by the spoonful into hot fat like pancakes. Serve with maple or King "sirup." Yumm—it's good.

398

Dollies/Rolly Polly/Rolyoly/Sweet Dough/Shortbread

2 cups of flour
2 teaspoons baking powder
1 teaspoon salt
2/3 cup shortening
½ cup cold milk

Mix all ingredients together. Roll out as thin as a piecrust. Spread fruit/berries onto dough. Roll dough and fruit up tightly in oblong shape, like a jellyroll, folding in the ends. Dip a small coarse salt bag into hot water and coat the inside with flour. Place the rolled dough inside the cloth bag, allowing room for dough to swell. Tie the end of the bag closed securely with a string. Using the string, place the bag in a pot of boiling water for 45 minutes. Remove dough, slice into 2" servings. Serve warm with a sweet sauce or milk and sugar over the slices.

Pies: Martha Washington made "pyes" by using a long dish called a "coffin." Later pie pans were designed to be shallow and made round to cut corners. The old term, "as easy as pie" is now true.

Pie Crust

Ingredients include lard, flour and a pinch of salt. Mix ingredients well for the proper consistency to be able to roll out the dough. Occasionally you may need to add a bit of cold water to the dough mixture. This recipe can be used for fruit and custard pies. See earlier chapter called Pies and Fun.

Funeral Pie (One of my father's favorite pies, a.k.a. Raisin' Pie!)

1 cup of seeded raisins, washed
2 cups of water
1½ cups of sugar

4 tablespoons flour
1 egg, well-beaten
Juice of a lemon
2 teaspoon grated lemon rind
Pinch of salt

Soak raisins for 3 hours, mix sugar, flour and egg. Then add seasonings, raisins and liquid. Cook over hot water for 15 minutes, stirring occasionally. When the mixture is cool, empty into pie dough. Cover with narrow strips of dough, criss-crossed and bake until brown.

About the Author

J immy Fox was born October 9th, 1937. He grew up on a thriving farm in Green Spring Valley, Baltimore County, Maryland, where he gained an inheritable amount of knowledge on the subject of agriculture as well as his attraction to nature.

Jimmy attended Franklin High School but never brought home a degree. This didn't stop him from learning about what he loved most—history. He has a well-stocked library of American as well as Native American history books. Not only does he enjoy studying the past, he takes great pleasure in other interests, including raising guineas, ducks, geese, chickens and rabbits along with breeding and training horses with the help of his beloved wife Mary Martin.

Jimmy and Mary married in 1975 and started their life together with a two-month long camping trip around the U.S., Mexico, and Canada. Travel and camping have always been family delights. The first time Jimmy and Mary visited Colorado, it felt like home to them. They believed they were destined to live there someday. God determined the timing in 1996.

Because dyslexia prevented Jimmy from reading to his three sons, he continually and repeatedly told them stories of life on the farm. Later he had a vision to preserve his heritage for the grandchildren. Now his past becomes our future. Writing in a relaxed manner with precious little formal schooling and with an open mind of true wisdom, Jimmy started to draft The Legacy of a Country Boy.

Even through cancer and dyslexia, Jimmy was determined to finish the book. Faithfully believing that the cancer was cured, they decided to move to Colorado for fresh opportunities where he soon became a successful published freelance writer and cowboy poet. His writings come at a time when our country values the nostalgia of a slower pace of living.

Although the cancer returned, Jimmy continued to work on the book and thank God that he healed a second time. Now Jimmy is healthy and blessed saying, "I have had the chance to taste life twice." Thirteen years later he shares his stories with everyone else. In the making of the book becomes yet another legend and the book becomes far more than just a story, it becomes the truth and a meaning of a life—a legacy, The Legacy of a Country Boy.

Jennifer Lynne Fox—Granddaughter

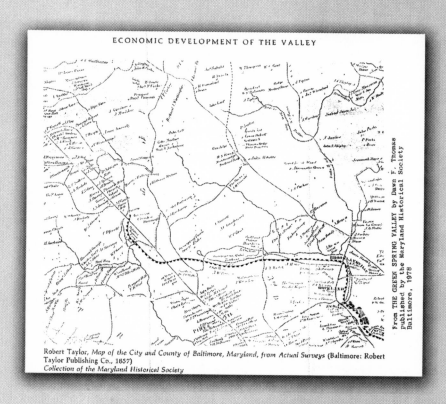

ECONOMIC DEVELOPMENT OF THE VALLEY

Robert Taylor, *Map of the City and County of Baltimore, Maryland, from Actual Surveys* (Baltimore: Robert Taylor Publishing Co., 1857)
Collection of the Maryland Historical Society

From THE GREEN SPRING VALLEY by Dawn F. Thomas published by the Maryland Historical Society Baltimore, 1978

Courtesy of David L. Wilson - Albuquerque, NM

Printed in the United States
76042LV00003B/1-69